ETHICS, ECONOMICS & BUSINESS MANAGEMENT

Richard Robinson

NorthAmerican
Business Press
Atlanta – Seattle – South Florida – Toronto

North American Business Press, Inc
Atlanta, Georgia
Seattle, Washington
South Florida
Toronto, Canada

Ethics, Economics, and Business Management
ISBN: 9780958394950
© 2012 All Rights Reserved.

Along with trade books for various business disciplines, the North American Business Press also publishes a variety of academic-peer reviewed journals.

Library of Congress Control Number: 2012955280
Library of Congress
Cataloging in Publication Division
101 Independence Ave., SE
Washington, DC 20540-4320
Printed in theUnited States of America
First Edition

Preface

The fundamental problem in business ethics concerns the answers to three similar and interrelated questions:

(1) Is the profit motive inherently contradictory with ethical motivation?

(2) Can the profit motive only stem from greed that serves an egotistical result?

(3) Can the profit motive, as constrained by society's sense of ethics, be salvaged as a primary motive for action in an ethical society?

These three essential questions require similar analyses of the role of individual moral motivation in economic agency, analyses provided by this text. Ever since the 18th century moral philosopher Adam Smith published *An Inquiry Into The Nature and Causes of the Wealth of Nations* (1776), the foundational text of classical economics, the profit motive and its associated free-market mechanism for resource allocation through the price system has been recognized as an essential engine-of-growth for economies, an engine that has lifted countless people out from poverty, and given them the freedom and dignity to live fulfilling lives. Smith also wrote, however, about certain immoral practices of business, i.e. the tendency for business to form price conspiracies against the public, and to generate negative externalities. Ever since Smith's contributions, philosophers have examined the interactions of ethics with the free-market system, but this examination has largely been within the school of *utilitarianism*, with its egotistical-consequentialist moral weakness[1].

---

[1] This text explores *utilitarianism* in Chapter IV. It might be sufficient to point out here that this view argues that motivation is essentially egotistical and *consequentialist* in that it proposes that the moral rightness of an act is determined by its effects on the acting agent, and not from any sense of obligation to others. It is argued below that this is a view largely rejected by Western society as being ethical.

During the same era that Smith authored his economics and moral philosophy, the great enlightenment philosopher Immanuel Kant composed his considerable seminal contribution to modern ethics. (See Chapter V.) Kant argued that an action can only be classified as ethical if it originates with the proper motivation, and that motivation, what Kant termed the *pursuit of the kingdom of ends of a moral community*, must not be narrowly egotistical, but rather broadly social. If we accept Kant's dictum, then how can actions motivated by the profit motive, which appears to be narrow and egotistical, ever be considered ethical? Could the free-market and its narrow profit motive, a motive that might well serve the overall end-goals of society, be inherently unethical because of the individual egotistical motivations necessary for this profit motive to work? This text forcefully argues that the profit motive can be consistent with the ethical motivation as required by Kant's pursuit of a moral community. Such a pursuit, however, requires ethical constraints on the seeking of profits. Exploration and understanding of these constraints form the basis for business ethics as an academic subject. To the extent that an economy of business agents follows these constraints, the free-market price system for resource allocation is fundamentally ethical, at least conceptually.

The author's motivation for writing this text originated in a college ethics debate in 2003. The subject of the debate concerned whether a particular online game was addictive, whether it was designed to be so, and whether the large corporation that ran this online game was unethical in its conduct. The debate took place in a large, filled lecture hall, and was one of several activities that took place during a School of Business sponsored *Ethics Awareness Event* at a sizeable Midwestern university. A distinguished faculty member from the Philosophy Department and I were the debaters. He professed to be an Aristotelian, meaning he believed that the appropriate school of thought was *virtue ethics*, a branch of ethical philosophy that believes in developing a set of personal characteristics which will then guide individuals to moral decisions and behavior.

I am a Kantian. I am convinced that the ethical vision set forth by the 18th century *Enlightenment* philosopher Immanuel Kant provides the appropriate framework for practical ethical decision- making, especially in business ethics. My debating opponent argued that more evident information would be needed to make an ethical judgment on this online gaming problem. I fully anticipated this response from an Aristotelian in that they tend to be unable to make practical decisions unless faced with circumstances of perfect clear-cut certainty, a situation seldom encountered when making ethical judgments in the practical business world. What I did not anticipate, however, was the audience's response to my pointing out that if the management of this company were to pursue the goal of maximizing the total market value of the corporations' equity, the usual goal cited in business schools for publicly traded corporations, then public boycotts of the company's products and financial securities would force society's sense of ethics onto the corporation. I expected that both the audience's response, and my opponent's response to my claim that through boycotts, society would force the company to behave according to society's sense of ethics, would focus on the moral weakness of *cultural relativism* as the fundamental problem of this public boycott vision [2]. This did not appear to be a concern even when I pointed it out to the audience. The issue that raised the ire of this predominantly student and faculty audience was the issue of shareholder wealth-maximization as the goal of the corporation. This goal, they wanted to argue, would motivate unethical behavior.

In response to the audience's declaration of outrage, I pointed out that this goal has always been considered as constrained by both law and society's sense of ethics. I also pointed out that other alternative goals essentially enable and encourage management-welfare pursuit. These other goals rely upon management's own sense of ethics, which one could argue is not obviously superior to the ethical standards of society. In fact, society's boycotts, as motivated by ethical outrage over some business practices, have a long history, including a robust recent history, of effectively changing the behavior of business, of channeling this behavior to meet objective and broad ethical standards. Finally I pointed out that recent corporate scandals tended to involve actual management stealing from the shareholders, not for them.

The issue of shareholder-wealth maximization motivating unethical scandals has frequently been raised over the last few decades. (Some of this history is reviewed in this text.) My own strong view is that this anti shareholder-wealth claim completely misunderstands the issue, especially the issue of agency (separation of

---

[2] As a school of ethics, cultural relativism argues that the rightness or wrongness of an act should be judged solely by the standards of the surrounding social culture, and not by some philosophical absolute objective-standard of right and wrong. This proposition is examined throughout this text.

ownership between management and owners). Furthermore, mainstream Western ethical thought is entirely consistent with the shareholder wealth goal, as I shall effectively argue in this text. I strongly believe that the anti-shareholder wealth motivation is not founded in reasoned ethical logic. Providing this argument, and providing a robust organization for analyzing ethical conundrums in business, motivates this text.

Other texts on business ethics are generally authoredby those without an academic economics background [3]. As such, they often do not fully appreciate the democratic benefits of the marketplace, and its association with maximizing individual freedom provided the agent does not impinge on the freedom of others, i.e. the *universal principle of justice* proposed by philosophers John Rawls and Immanuel Kant.

This text, however, is built around exploring both the benefits and deficiencies of free markets. It explores the ethical constraints on free-market competition for the firm, and does so in a Kantian context, i.e. in the context of the duties business agents owe to society. This exploration is largely centered on Kantian-Rawlsian notions of fairness, and their application to negotiation in business. These negotiations should be considered broadly as forming both explicit and implicit contracts that form the basis for market interactions. In this context, this text is also an exploration of neoclassical economics and its linkage to societal welfare.

Other explorations of the ethical foundations of neoclassical economics, such as Hausman and McPherson (2006), focus on the moral implications of public policy. The goal of this text, however, is to explore the moral foundations of internal firm management, and to do so in the context of the neoclassical theory of the firm. This text is Kantian in its approach, but this Kantian analysis is extended well beyond the depth of other Kantian approaches to business ethics, such as Bowie's (1999), *Business Ethics: A Kantian Perspective.* [4] In this context, this text may provide a substantial contribution to the pedagogy of the subject.

---

[3] The author holds a PhD in Economics.
[4] Mark White's (2011) recent scholarly treatise is an exception.

The economic context of this text is presented at the level of an introductory micro-economics course, i.e. the exposition relies substantially on graphical analyses for explorations of concepts such as utility functions, marginal-costs, -revenues and –products. Some calculus is presented in footnotes in a few chapters, except for Chapter IX where it is used for the development of the concepts of market power. Since elementary calculus is required in the undergraduate curriculum for both economics and business students, this mathematical and associated graphical analysis is appropriate for this exploration. Those wishing to avoid this mathematics, however, should still benefit from the material of pages 1 – 6, and 22 – 30 of Chapter IX, where mathematical expositions are not present. It should be recognized that the mathematical sophistication utilized in this text does not exceed that usually found in intermediate microeconomics texts.

Of course not all of modern ethical philosophy as it applies to economics and business decisions could be included in any single text. In particular, I have not included the considerably important explorations of the Nobel Laureate Amartya Sen because his work is largely focused on the public policy implications of economics rather than the foundations of individual decision making. The latter is the subject of this text although public policy implications are also partly reviewed. Perhaps a more extensive analysis can be authored in the future so that disappointed instructors can be better served.

Richard Robinson, PhD
Professor of Business Administration
SUNY at Fredonia
September, 2012

Table of Contents

———— ⊰❈❈⊱ ————

Chapter I

ETHICS AND BUSINESS PRACTICE

Chapter Abstract: Western philosophical ethics is based upon logical applications of fundamental principles. It is the basis for effective codes-of-conduct for business, and examples of avoidance of this philosophical approach generally explain the failures of some business codes to restrict unethical behavior. This introductory chapter outlines this logical approach which is fully explored in this text.

1. Introduction

The author of this text has a long-term friend who is a dean of arts and sciences at a major university. From time-to-time, we discuss each other's ongoing work. When informed that I began work on a business ethics text, he joked that there is no such subject, that business was devoid of ethics, and a text on that subject would be both brief and in low demand. He thought of this subject as a brief review of what is right and wrong, as in "do not break the law, at least in an easily discoverable way."

This dean's view is certainly consistent with a more general view of business education frequently held by those outside of this branch of academia: that it is a shallow study not well-grounded in the more traditional academic subjects such as philosophy, economics, mathematics, and the other social sciences. This is a view of business education that is far from reality. Business education has evolved greatly over the last five decades, and is increasingly well- grounded in the traditional academic subjects. This text provides a practical demonstration of this claim.

Business ethics concerns the most fundamental aspects of how a business is organized, the general behavior of business interaction, the very motive for business activity in general, and the basis for logically-reasoned action in business. It is a very broad subject of such great societal importance that business ethics should be considered the most important subdivision of the broader category of applied ethics (which includes subjects such as medical ethics, sexual ethics, societal welfare considerations and the like). To explore this subject, this text is built upon the traditional academic subjects of philosophy and economics. All of these bold claims are substantiated by the expositions presented in latter chapters.

2. Ethics and Normative Economics for Business

The title of this text, *Ethics, Economics and Business Management*, links the notion of ethical to a norm for management, i.e. a standard management should meet. This is hardly a surprising linkage since of course we want business to meet, at minimum, the moral standards of society. To state that this text also explores normative economics, however, may be surprising for many. This text argues that economics has generally understood that the universally offered goal for the firm, i.e. the profit motive, is a constrained goal, with the constraints being law and society's sense of what is ethical. Our microeconomic pedagogy of the theory of the firm, however, does not explore these constraints in any depth, so it is easy for the more casual student to ignore this very normative side of the subject.

In fact our microeconomic theory of the firm is generally presented as a *positive theory*, i.e. a theory of what actually exists rather than some norm to be pursued. The profit motive is presented as the actual existing motive force in the neoclassical economic model. Following this approach, we could explore the constraints that actually exist on this profit motive. These are essentially legal constraints which, along with legally reached contracts, dictate much of society's imposed restrictions on the profit motive. Taking a positive viewpoint, we could explore these constraints from an *industrial organization* approach. Exploration of how business should ethically behave would be avoided in this more scientific and detached positive view. We would not be exploring ethics as a norm.

Nevertheless, this text argues that normative ethics is at the heart of the economic theory of the firm, and as such, its implications for management practice are profound. Since Smith (1776), we have recognized the strong ethical

implications of the marketplace, but following Smith's lead, we generally rel-
egate our explorations of these implications to the domain of public policy. We
explore the public welfare implications of regulating market structure, of the
existence of externalities, of income and wealth redistribution, and the like. [5]
 The implications of the marketplace for societal welfare are generally recognized in microeconomics and industrial organization courses, but still we seldom
explore the importance of ethically-based managerial decisions on the internal
efficiency of the firm or of society. The economic tradition is to view the manager
as ethically neutral. Our neoclassical economics approach argues that through
market competition, society's sense of ethics will be instilled in the firm; that
managers must respond to society's sense of what is ethical or suffer boycotts
and consequent firm decline.

In economics we generally avoid exploration of what this exogenously-determined
societal sense of ethics might be, of how it could affect managerial decisions
and firm behavior. This latter subject is, however, explored in this text where
the Western ethical tradition is reviewed, and the Kantian components of this
tradition are especially explored. (This Kantian ethical philosophy is reviewed
in detail in latter chapters.) Following this, the ethical managerial leadership
and decision making, as they affect firm efficiency, are explored in some depth.

This text does suggest a particular norm that is different from consequentialist
egoism – which is defined as the theory that the moral rightness of an act is determined solely by the goodness of the results for the individual. Very much the
opposite is the case here. This text argues that Kant's social goal of harmonious
pursuit of generally-accepted moral maxims (Kant's *kingdom of ends*) must be
the proper motivation for ethical decision making for management. It argues that
this is appropriate for the firm, and for society, and that this motivation is solidly
within the Western ethical tradition. It is also, the text argues, the motivation that
leads to firm and market efficiency. It provides the workable ethical constraints
on the profit motive, constraints that lead to this efficiency, i.e. the competitive
marketplace is likely to favor these properly motivated Kantian moral constraints.
These are bold claims to be substantiated by the strength of the arguments of

[5] As an example of a recent example of exploration of economics, ethics and public policy see Hausman and McPherson (2006).

subsequent chapters. Nonetheless, we can offer as a partial argument here that our most fervent moral outrage at those managerial decisions we consider to be illegal or unethical occurs when we believe the generally accepted norms of our society have been violated contemptuously. When only an obscure regulation is violated without apparent contempt, the fervor of our moral outrage is so much the less. This moral fervor certainly affects stakeholder relations of all sorts, and therefore the economic performance of the firm.

Furthermore, this is not a philosophical egoist argument since consistent assurance of the pursuit of society's agreed-upon moral maxims only results when we do what is right not for our own narrowly defined benefit, but because we wish to be members of a moral community. This is the appropriate and reliable motivation for moral decisions; our own personal benefit may well also result, but this is an ancillary benefit.

This text explores these ethical propositions in some detail, particularly the Kantian propositions concerning the structure of fairness (following the Kantian-oriented philosophy of John Rawls as reviewed below), and it shows applications for fairness in managerial negotiation with stakeholders of the firm. These requirements for *fairness in negotiations* should essentially provide the rules-of-the-game for marketplace interactions. They have strong implications for firm and marketplace efficiency. In this sense, this text provides a normative guide for managerial leadership and decision making.

3. The Ethical

Ethos is the ancient Greek term for "custom." Webster's dictionary defines this as "the distinguishing character, moral nature, or guiding beliefs of a person, group, or institution." *Ethics* is the philosophical study of morality, our useful customary system for decision making particularly with respect to what we term "good or bad," or "right and wrong." It is not a shallow subject. It extends way beyond simple notions of right and wrong, notions such as "Do not cheat, or steal, or harm others!" This subject has ancient roots, and it has always been a subject of reason, reflective thought, and logic. It concerns both "What is right?" and "What is good?"

Notions of "the right" and "the good" form the foundational axioms for what rational people derive as the moral principles that govern our decisions. We pursue this or that action as based upon what we perceive as "right," and/or what we perceive as "good." It is an immutable property of existence, a law of physics, that time does expire; that we cannot experiment so as to do over our decisions. It is better to have a set of moral principles to guide us prior to these decisions, although as we shall discover, reflective reasoned-thought is always one of these necessary principles. For these reasons we study ethics as a preparation for moral decision making. The very practical subject of business ethics is no different. Indeed, we shall see that this subject is not only of extraordinary importance for society, but it is perhaps more interestingly complex than many other subjects in practical ethics.

To provide some introductory examples, consider the manager interacting with employees, or even potential employees. Ethical norms must be followed, norms of honesty and fairness in negotiation and arrangement of workplace rules. It is obvious, and it is clear, that violation of these norms can have strong current and subsequent consequences for the existence of the firm and the welfare of employees, owners and managers. What is not so clear is that the very motivation that managers take to these negotiations frames and often dictates the results. Clarity as to ethical motivation is necessary for achieving what we term below as an harmonious organization, and this is necessary for achieving any reasonable interpretation of success for both the organization and the individuals involved. This is also true for interactions with customers and society in general. I argue in this text that managers with the proper ethically-based motivation are likely to achieve results generally preferable to what can be achieved from a more narrow egotistical motivation. Nonetheless, following the Western philosophical tradition, I argue that the ethically-based motivation is worthy in itself, and this worthiness is explored in detail in this text.

4. Teleological Ethics

The term "teleological" stems from the ancient Greek word "teleios," which means "complete" or "perfected." It concerns the end goal of a thing, so that "teleological ethics" concerns the end goal that we seek from our ethical system. Philosophers have typically treated the subject of "what ends," i.e. "what goals," we should pursue as either "the flourishing life" or some notion of what is "intrinsically good."

We can apply the idea of the "flourishing life" to either ourselves as individuals, or to our business organization, or to society. We, of course, can also link all three of these entities as interdependent. As far as the individual is concerned, we could define the flourishing life as hedonistic, that we merely pursue pleasure, particularly in the form of consumption. Generally, however, we define the flourishing life well beyond consumption. Among the things philosophers have included as necessary for happiness are knowledge, friendship, freedom, beauty and harmony, and this list can be considerably extended. Indeed, many philosophers have sought the commonalities of the attributes we might include in this list so that we can better define what we mean by the "flourishing life." If we could adequately define what we mean by "flourishing," then we might be able to organize our notions of morality around what we perceive as the most effective pursuit of this life.

If we seek to investigate "the flourishing life" of an organization or of society in general, then we might take a *utilitarian* approach to what is moral, i.e. whatever maximizes the sum total of the happiness of all individuals within society, is what we should do. Hence, our ideas of morality would be organized around the pursuit of this limited notion of the general welfare of society. We shall find, however, that this is not a very satisfactory way of organizing our moral thought. It is not very practical since notions of general societal welfare are nebulous at best. We shall need a sharper logical framework in order to form our concepts of morality so that our system is robustly functional in business.

We could, of course, root our moral code in some religious scripture. Even if we do not believe in the religious foundation of the scripture, for example even if we do not believe in some notion of God, we could still accept this scripture as historically based, and hence an expression of historically accumulated wisdom about how to live. This could be a powerfully persuasive argument. Of course we also note that religious conflict has led to a very destructive history, as these conflicts even today are extremely destructive. For this reason we hesitate to base our notion of "the right" on religious texts. Individually, we could follow a religious text for our personal lives, but not insist that others follow our personally accepted scripture just because it is scripture. Others may have their scriptures, or personally different interpretations of the same scripture, and therefore the conflict begins. A reasoned approach to forming a moral code for society, or our business organization, must be built upon logic, upon the basic notions of what is right and wrong that can appeal to all. This approach is sound even for the pursuit of the flourishing life as it applies to our business or society.

5. An Axiomatic System of Logic

The study of "what is right" seeks to establish principle axioms from which we can logically derive a moral code to guide our actions. This moral code places the notion of "duty" at its center [6]. This is a system built upon self-evident axioms that act as first principles from which deductive logic can be used to build our moral code. That these axioms are true to begin with must be agreed upon after reflective thought.

For example, consider one of the fundamental problems in ethical philosophy, the lying promise and why it is wrong. It should be obvious that this is an important problem in business ethics since a wide variety of contracts (both the explicitly legal obligation, and implicitly moral obligation that is not necessarily legally enforceable) are necessary to conduct modern business. Many might try to justify the lying promise as allowable under certain circumstances such as those required for survival. One might argue,

"My business, and its ability to employ others, will not survive unless I obtain this loan, although I know it is unlikely that I will be able to repay it. As a result, I will deceive the lender into believing I am financially sounder than I really am. My business survival is at stake, however, and so I am justified in this deception."

Why is this deception wrong?

To logically analyze this problem, consider the axiom,

"We should not deceive others into doing what we want them to do, if by this deception, we frustrate their pursuit of their own goals!"

The lying promise clearly violates this axiom. But why would this axiom be necessary, that is why would it be readily adopted as part of the foundation of a business code? A logical answer is that business cannot flourish in

---

[6] "Deontological" ethics concerns the study of duties, both positive obligations and absolute prohibitions.

a world where this sort of deception is acceptable. If one person can morally deceive, so can others. This is not the business world we want, and in fact a business world that accepts deception of this sort will implode [7]. Hence our social goal of seeking a flourishing business environment justifies this axiom as based upon reflective reasoning.

In our society, we seek to express a variety of self-evident axioms as fundamental laws which we generally accept after democratic discourse. The authority for this expression lies in the sovereignty of the individual who votes for this legal code either directly or indirectly through representatives. Still, not all of our moral problems can be handled by society's law. We also need a code to handle non-legal ethical problems, a code we might adopt for our business organization. Even for this code, the axiomatic approach as part of reasoned discourse is appropriate as we will explore in great detail in this text.

This formal-logical approach is best exemplified by the ethical philosophy of Immanuel Kant (1721-1804), often cited as the founder of modern ethics. This philosophy establishes some basic universal principles from which pure reason (logic) can operate. Consequently, the derived moral principles become an ethical duty as a result of logic. As Kant put it, these laws are those that we, as rational human beings, give to ourselves. They are laws for a republic of reason, a *kingdom of ends of a moral community* whose legislature comprises all rational beings. Through this ideal, Kant makes understandable the argument that moral principles should be derived from reason. This Kantian approach is investigated in detail in latter chapters where it is argued that it forms the logical basis for practical business ethics.

6. The Social Contract

Those who argued that our moral code essentially stems from what is generally agreed upon in the form of a social contract (contractarians), were inspired by Hobbes, Kant, and Locke. The philosophy of John Rawls (1921-1991) is the most influential of modern Kantian- contractarians. Our moral principles, he argued, represents the ideal terms of social cooperation for those who regard each other as equals, and who live in fellowship, perhaps in the form of a business-partnership

[7] The reader might note the role of the *lying promise* in the financial debacle that imploded our market system in 2008, especially the *lying promise* role in the sub-prime mortgage market.

organization. Rawls' vision, however, is that of an ideal agreement among such people, an agreement they would adopt if they met as an assembly of equals to decide collectively on the social arrangements that govern their relations. These arrangements are envisioned as agreed upon after open debate and rational discourse. The authority for these moral principles relies upon the fairness of the procedures by which this agreed-upon social-code is reached. We assume that any rational individual who wants to live cooperatively with others in this society would, in view of the fairness of the procedures, assent to its results.

Rawls suggests a number of requirements in order for a social-contract deliberation to be considered *fair*. If these procedures are followed, then the resulting agreement manifests what he terms *justice as fairness.* We can, and do in latter chapters, use Rawls' notions of fair deliberation to establish requirements for *fairness in negotiation*, a problem that we shall see is of great importance for business ethics.

7. Business Codes of Conduct

Many professions and occupations, such as medicine, law, accounting, engineering, journalism, business, and education, have established codes of conduct that guide professional behavior. This is a subject of applied ethics. Standard philosophical history and methods are used to develop and reform these codes. Given the rapid technological advance of our society, reform of these codes is frequently necessitated.

One of the frequent questions for investigation of these codes concerns the reasons for their development, modification, and abandonment. Why do our moral codes sometimes fail to prevent unethical behavior, or even prevent the more extreme behavior we term *evil*? Why does this *evil* permeate some business organizations and cause the moral scandals we associate with cases such as Enron, or Bernard Madoff? Why are these codes apparently readily abandoned from time to time?

We suspect the answer to these questions lies in either (1) a lack of clarity in understanding either the meaning or (2) the importance of the code. Rational reflection concerning the reasons for the code may be lacking, and so belief in their importance can be shallow. For example, consider those who keep the code only out of fear of being discovered if they do not keep it. Are they likely to be persuaded that under certain circumstances they can violate the code and not be discovered? The answer is probably "Yes!" Also consider those who believe the code is just old-fashioned and silly, that it has little social importance. This person also is likely to readily abandon what might be a very important code.

Prevention of both of these cases occurs if the importance of our moral code is continually examined in a reasoned way, if reasoned and reflective discourse is used to reform the code so that rational individuals have the opportunity to contribute to the debate, and to understand the importance of what is adopted. Latter chapters examine this issue in detail.

8. Schools of Ethical Thought

Ethical thought can be divided into innumerable schools, although these frequently overlap. Various divisions are proposed, and it appears that the number three is particularly popular for these divisions. One such threesome is (1) Kantian social-contract ethics, (2) utilitarianism, and (3) virtue ethics. This text examines the first of these schools in considerable detail, and shows its practical application to business management. This text also, however, examines the second school with some detail, and even the third school with a lesser degree, but still substantive detail. All three have practical applications to business ethics.

There are, however, other ways of approaching ethical theory. One way is to pose a natural theory of ethics; that ethics have a natural origin in the ways humans evolved, interact, and attempt to coexist. Systems that fail are historically abandoned. Certainly there is truth to this natural proposition. This is one illustration that these artificial divisions may well be useful. In fact, many of these divisions are useful, but the usefulness stems from their ability to extend practical applications. Stating that ethics may have a natural basis may be stating truth, but does it give us practical insights?

I find the Kantian approach to be the most useful for business ethics. It gives us insights into practical methods of organization, of the leadership skills to be developed, and of negotiating rules and methods. We seek practical applications, but nonetheless, we still primarily seek a system of moral codes based upon ethical motivation. Our ultimate motivation is Kantian. We seek a moral code that exhibits clarity of understanding, and harmony in pursuit within our business organization and overall society. This is the norm we logically explore in latter chapters as the primary ethical basis for business interactions. The economic implications for economic efficiency are explored in detail.

9. The Noble Nature

Reflective thought about the social morals we live by is an essential component of our moral life. It has been the basis of our Western ethical tradition since the ancient Greek philosophers. But more than this is required if we are to live a moral life, pursue "the good," and participate

in a moral society or organization. The 20th century philosopher Hanna Arendt (1906-1975) argues that we must have a "noble nature" of willingness to speak out socially about our moral judgments. We must participate, and even stimulate, logical social discourse involving reflective thought about our moral problems and codes. We must not merely drift with our times, and refuse to think critically about our actions.

Reflective reason is essential to our understanding of our moral codes. We cannot just accept these codes as based upon some form of authority, be it religious, government, or business authority. If we do not understand the social reasons for our moral code, we will not internalize the code. We will readily abandon the code when it appears personally beneficial. An education in ethics is a start towards understanding, but this is just a start. Frequent reasoned reflection is also required, but this also is not enough. We must also be willing to engage in social discourse, to say "No! This is wrong!" or "This is the moral thing to do!" Moral courage is therefore also necessary for an organization and society to flourish. All of these concepts are reviewed in detail in latter chapters.

10. The Design of the Text

This text explores the answers to a series of important interrelated questions. The subsequent chapters roughly, but not precisely, follow these questions:

- Does the traditional business goal of profit motivate unethical greedy behavior? What ethical constraints should be imposed upon management to limit this profit motive? What are the conditions necessary for this profit motive to actually be considered ethical by society?

- Where do our notions of ethics originate? Do we have a Western ethical tradition?

- Are there any useful lessons from utilitarian philosophy? Can we form any practical moral maxims from utilitarian analysis?

- Does the Kantian approach lead to useful moral maxims for business? Can these maxims be a foundation for leadership?

- Does virtue ethics lead to practical applications in business? What are the common personal characteristics of the moral manager if any are to be found?

- If management receives their compensation from owners, does this create a conflict of interest in dealing with non-owner stakeholders? If so, how can management ethically, or fairly, deal with this conflict?

- Is it possible for product and capital markets to reflect society's sense of ethics and force business to conform to this societal sense? Is this societal sense itself worthy?

- Why are moral codes of conflict established and abandoned? Why does evil permeate some business organizations but not others?

- If there is a Western ethical tradition, how is it changing especially in the context of modern globalism?

The exploration of the answers to these questions forms a substantial investigation and text.

Questions for review and discussion:

(1) What is the difference between normative and positive economics? How might this difference apply to the differences between normative and positive ethics?

(2) Beyond material well being, what do you consider as the necessary elements of the good life? Can doing what is right conflict with what you consider being your pursuit of the good life?

(3) Besides the example of the lying promise, what other business decep-
     tions might violate our suggested axiom?

(4) Can you suggest any requirements for negotiations to be fair?

(5) Find the professional code for accounting auditors. Hypothetically, if
     you did not understand some aspect of this code, what would moti-
     vate you to follow it? Is this an ethical motivation? What aspect of
     public accounting education follows from your answers?

(6) What do we mean by the *noble nature*? How could you manifest this
     in your professional career?

Chapter II

---— ❧ ——---

ETHICAL MOTIVATION AND THE
GOAL OF THE BUSINESS FIRM

Chapter Abstract: The business goal of shareholder wealth maximization, properly constrained by society's laws and by negotiations with stakeholders, is shown to be potentially consistent with Kant's categorical imperative and associated moral maxims. As such it potentially justifies a claim to being ethical. This interpretation fits the constuctivist school of social contracts. The stakeholder-balance approach, an opposing business goal, is shown to be consistent with the rational intuitionists' view of ethics, where the manager acts as intuitionist in balancing the interests of stakeholders. Ethical weaknesses that stem from the stakeholder-balance approach are demonstrated. This introductory chapter establishes the debate between these two approaches to the ethical goal of the publicly traded corporation. It also reviews the subsequent chapters, which are aimed at establishing the Kantian approach, and also the necessity of the intuitionist approach when the Kantian conditions cannot be met.

1. The Shareholder-Wealth Maximization Debate

Michael Porter (2002), the founder of the management subject of business strategy, blamed shareholder wealth maximization (SWM) as the root cause of unethical managerial conduct associated with various corporate scandals such as those of Enron, Tyco, Adelphia, WorldCom and Global Crossing. (Note that the linkage between shareholder wealth and expected profit is fully developed in the appendix to this chapter.) He argued that pursuit of this goal motivates the sort of earnings manipulation associated with accounting fraud. He asserted that the stakeholder-balance approach motivates better ethical conduct. Business students should realize, however, that the shareholder wealth goal is a powerful tool for ethically resolving the agency conflict inherent in the modern corporation's separation of ownership from management. It is the goal generally cited in courses in managerial finance as appropriate for the publicly traded corporation with diversified ownership[8]. As such, it leads to the business world's generally accepted methodologies for capital budgeting, capital structure decisions, dividend policy, working capital management, and for resolution of a myriad of other business problems.

Consider, for example, one of these business problems, the capital budgeting decision. SWM requires that the expected rate of return on a capital project be compared to the rate of return required by investors on the finance they contribute to funding the project. This required rate of return has the investors assessing the risk of the project and incorporating a premium that reflects this risk into the rate of return on the securities they purchase. This is essentially a democratic process that has the investor-owners voicing their assessment of the risk of the firm through the financial markets and the prices established for the firm's securities. The management's preference for bearing risk plays no role in this system; it is not their preference that counts but rather that of the investor owners voiced through financial markets. The risk is therefore analyzed by a much wider segment of society than management. If it were otherwise, then since management is notoriously more risk averse than the typical shareholder, conflict between the owners and their agents (management) would exist[9]. Stakeholder-balance theory poses no similar solution to capital budgeting other than utilizing the personal preferences of management. Capital budgeting via some sort of balancing of the heterogeneous preferences of stakeholders is hardly a practical solution. It demands unrealistic management capabilities. Stakeholder-

[8] Narrowly owned private business (those not publicly traded on stock exchanges) do not suffer from significant agency problems. Private companies are generally owner managed to a large degree, and the goal of owner wealth may be replaced by other goals such as the steadiness of income particularly since an active equity market may not exist for that firm.

[9] Shareholders typically have highly diversified portfolios, as in shares of mutual funds. In this sense, the typical shareholder owns only a very small portion of the firm in question. The diversified portfolio enables shareholders to bear much more firm-specific risk in that the failure of any single firm would not significantly impact their wealth. Management, however, has much human capital tied up in the financial success of the firm. Financial distress could severely disrupt their careers and have a large significant impact on their wealth. For this reason, management is more averse to firm risk than its many shareholders.

balance theory also poses no solutions for the other common business problems listed above.

Porter's criticism, however, warrants a rigorous review, one that draws on mainstream philosophy to more properly analyze the ethics implicit in the pursuit of SWM versus the stakeholder-balance goal. In this text, the moral-philosophical perspectives of *ethical constructivism* [10], as drawn from the enlightenment philosophy of Kant, and its chief modern extender, John Rawls, is juxtaposed against the *rational intuitionist* approach, with its Socratic roots and post-intuitionist proponents, McDowell and Nagel. Porter's criticism in favor of the stakeholder approach is shown to be implicitly intuitionist in origin. The shareholder wealth goal is shown to be consistent with the Kantian philosophy.

This text argues forcefully for the Kantian approach to management. It shows that Kant's *categorical imperative,* and its derived moral maxims, provide the very foundation for an effective business-leadership style aimed at producing an *efficient and harmonious organization* based on ethical conduct. Furthermore, this text argues that for the modern publicly-traded corporation with diversified ownership, SWM is ethical within this Kantian system provided that society's legal constraints are maintained along with certain constraints of fairness in negotiation with all stakeholders. These are the issues fully explored.

The debate over the ethical implications of the stakeholder-balance versus the SWM goal has strong implications for the structure of education in business ethics, that is whether the subject should seek to develop a "moral sense" among would-be managers (the intuitionist approach), or whether a proactive and fair negotiating ability should be developed (the constructivist approach). It is argued below that both approaches are necessary. It is a goal of this text, however, to provide some clarity concerning when each applies.

---

[10] *Ethical constructivist* is a term coined by John Rawls to describe his approach, but others call this school *contractarian* because it envisions the moral maxims as derived from the social contract.

---

2. Preface Concerning the Ethics of SWM

Often cited reasons why SWM is believed to motivate a firm's management include:

- As the owner's agents, management has a legal obligation to primarily pursue the owner's interests or they may be fired, i.e., shareholders have sole authority to hire and fire upper management,

- The market for corporate control (the takeover market) motivates management to drive the market value of equity to a level at least as high as potential buyers estimate it should be.

- Managers usually own a portion of the firm so that pursuing shareholder wealth is in their interests.

- SWM should properly be viewed, however, as a constrained maximization, where there are two particularly effective categories of constraints:

- law as represented by the democratically established social contract, and

- negotiated agreements with stakeholder constituents such as workers, suppliers, debt holders and the community.

Those mathematically uninitiated may be confused over the notion of constrained maximization. For this reason, the stakeholder-balance approach may appear *prima facie* more accurate or less abstract. People who hold this view, however, should be more open to the benefits of the more precise statement of maximizing the objective function of shareholder wealth, as constrained by the interests of other stakeholders.

For example, consider Figure 1. It illustrates a two-dimensional maximization process in the mathematical sense, where Y, the objective variable to be maximized, is a function of X, the decision variable. If allowed, the solution is given by XMax. Assume that legal constraints, however, will not allow X to be greater than XCon; then this is the constrained maximization solution. Of course, shareholder wealth is a function of many variables, some of which are legally constrained, some are constrained by negotiation with stakeholders, and some factors include the more familiar and mundane notions common to marketing, finance, and production. Shareholder wealth maximization must occur in many dimensions, some with constraints and some without [11].

To reinforce the SWM idea, some of the constraining negotiated agreements should be recognized here. Agreements with workers form both implicit and explicit contracts, the latter being union and service contracts; the former represented by the more informal agreements that often compose the rules of the internal labor market, rules such as seniority privileges, schedules for annual reviews and raises, and the like. Community negotiations often specify employment commitments, environmental contributions that may occur in return for tax breaks, and similar arrangements. Debt indenture agreements specify priority of claims, and other firm obligations to bondholders. All of these stakeholder agreements are negotiated and arranged within the democratic institutions of adjudicated law. The other laws that act as constraints (product safety, worker safety, contract, property, equity, employment, tax, security, and environmental law), are all established democratically, and as such, they have the potential to embody society's notions of ethics. This text argues that if our explicit and implicit contracts are negotiated under certain specified rules-of-fairness, and our laws are established democratically under certain guidelines, then they contain strong ethical content which should not be ignored for personal managerial preferences.

[11] This is essentially a notion from neoclassical economics that follows the mathematics of constrained global maximization via Lagrangian multipliers, or similar mathematical approaches.

Figure 2-1: Illustration Of Constrained Maximization

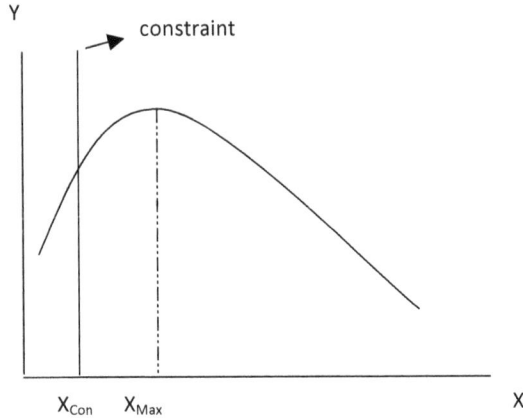

This is the *ethical constructivist* approach. From time-to-time, however, there may occur some ethical conundrums that fall outside of these implicit and explicit contractual agreements, and also outside the law. In these cases, managerial intuition may provide the ethical solution. This represents the proper role of the *ethical intuitionist*.

The great *Enlightenment* philosopher Immanuel Kant (1724 -1804) originated much of modern ethical philosophy. He argued that society should utilize logi-cally reasoned discourse to establish a set of *moral maxims* that we should all aim to follow. He further provided an overall guide for deriving these *maxims*. He termed this guide the *categorical imperative*, and it has three linked forms:

(1) We must intend that any maxim we form be followed by everyone.

(2) Our *maxims* should dictate that *we treat people as an end, never only as a means to our own ends.* This requires that we allow others to pursue their own lawful goals; that we do not lie, deceive or coerce others into serving our goals while preventing them from serving their own.

(3) The motivation for following our *moral maxims* must not be self serv-ing. Our motivation must be broadly social, that we seek a society

in which all, including ourselves, seek to harmoniously follow our derived *maxims.* For example, we should not steal because we fear being discovered, but rather because if we allow ourselves to steal, then we must permit or expect others to do the same. Society could not function harmoniously in these circumstances.

Kant's *categorical imperative* is essentially a guide for deciding if our actions and agreements are moral. Kant argued that through social discourse, practical *moral maxims* should be derived that are consistent with what he termed the *categorical imperative* (reviewed in depth in a later chapter). This is essentially a democratic process aimed at coincidentally developing social commitment to these *maxims.* The 20th century philosopher John Rawls (1921-2002) is Kant's most recent and important extender. As reviewed in detail in latter chapters, Rawls (1958, 1971) developed Kantian principles into a system in which our democratic discourse would also be fair. If followed, then our democratic process would reveal a system of *justice as fairness*. In latter chapters, we apply these Rawlsian principles to establish *rules for fair negotiation*, from which we can say that our implicit and explicit contracts are ethical. This is at the heart of our Kantian analysis, i.e. the constraints on SWM must be ethical in a Kantian-Rawlsian sense.

Our corporate legal form, where management represents the legal agents of the shareholders, was established democratically. Following a Rawlsian approach, this text shows that if the Kantian conditions are met, then SWM becomes part of society's expression of *justice as fairness.* In this sense, it is therefore fully ethical. Any effective argument against SWM being ethical requires an analysis and articulation of the conditions that violate our notions of fairness. If and when these conditions are effectively violated, then SWM is inappropriate, and alternative solutions must be presented. This text also attempts to present these alternative intuitionist solutions, along with delimiting the conditions for when they are appropriate.

3. Preface Concerning the Ethics of the Stakeholder-Balance Approach

Juxtaposed against the shareholder wealth goal is the so called *stakeholder-balance approach* (SB), where stakeholder interests are not just expressed by society's laws, even in combination with negotiations, but rather these interests must be continually balanced by ongoing judgments of the manager through using his/her own intuited sense of fairness. Management's judgment as to the priority of stockholders' claims (lower priority than under SWM) supercedes society's process of fairness. Rawls terms this approach *rational intuitionism* (the manager intuits the applicable ethical maxims, perhaps after consultation with others), while the Kantian enlightenment approach is termed *moral constructivism*.

A complete statement of the principles of stakeholder theory is presented by Clarkson (2002). (Note that Clarkson is one of the originators of this theory.) For the debate at hand, one of the more interesting aspects is Clarkson's treatment of the role of the shareholder. He recognizes the stockholder's role of being the residual claimant. This is somewhat better than the stakeholder-balance theory of Solomon (2000), who only recognizes the shareholder's right to a fair return. Clarkson, however, is woefully deficient in not recognizing the other principle ownership-characteristic that shareholders possess: *namely the right to hire and fire management*. Common- stock owners select the members of the board of directors, usually by annual vote, and this board selects the top management team. In addition, stockholders often vote on major corporate decisions concerning such important matters as significant acquisitions or sale of subsidiaries. Their votes are binding. They are fully recognized by law as owning the firm, although as with ownership of any other asset, there are legal restrictions on this right.

It is often argued that shareholders usually have too little at stake in any single corporation to fulfill their ownership responsibilities. This is generally true of most large modern corporations. Nevertheless, an era of shareholder activism started in the 1980s and is still with us. Most shares are held in pension funds, mutual funds, and in other institutional forms, where they are controlled by port-folio managers acting as agents of those who own the funds. Large institutions, such as public retirement systems, have organized at annual meetings to elect boards more amenable to the desires of the shareholders, and less amenable to the personal welfare pursuits of management. In addition, management is gen-erally bonded to the interests of the owners through the grant of shares in the firm. The purpose of this is to align the interests of management with the share-holders as much as possible. Also, the *market for corporate control* is active, so management fears for their positions if they do not pursue the interests of the owners, i.e. the corporation may be taken over by outsiders, which usually means that the management team is changed. For these reasons, shareholders do have some degree of control over management, and this control is strong enough to assure that either SWM is pursued, or that management exposes itself to the wrath of owners.

Once the ownership role of shareholders is recognized, the logic of treating them as just another stakeholder who deserves no priority of treatment is seen as fallacious. Of greater importance, however, is the realization that the authority to hire and fire management, and as a result to guide the destiny of the firm, results in SWM, as properly constrained, to be the goal of the firm. Negotiated stakeholder interests form much of the constraints on the SWM process, and there lies the proper role for stakeholder theory.

Note that Jensen (2002) also points out the impossible position of stakeholder theory when not placed in the context of constraints on SWM. As he argues, the firm needs an objective function to maximize (as constrained by law and stakeholder negotiation) in order to objectively resolve business problems; otherwise it will likely sink into the morass of management welfare pursuit, although no doubt with lots of rhetoric about serving the interests of other stakeholders provided as a screen to mask management's self-serving decisions. The ethics of management welfare pursuit is explored in detail in latter chapters.

The formal philosophical foundation of the intuitionist approach is Socratic. In Plato's (1961) *Socratic Dialogues*, Socrates' discussion with Euthypro logically establishes that "good is not good because the gods approve it, but the gods approve it because it is good." In addition, through discussion with Meno, Socrates establishes that moral truths are eternal, perhaps discovered by the soul in previous lives. These dialogues establish *rational reflection* as a basis for discovering the eternal truths of ethical behavior[12]. This rational reflection is, however, also the foundation Kant uses for rational constructivism. Note that the Socratic *Dialogues* are reviewed in Chapter 3.

The fundamental difference between the intuitionist and the constructivist is subtle, but extraordinarily important for business ethics. The intuitionist discovers ethical axioms after rational reflection. They are seen as laws of the

---

[12] What is obvious from the entire set of *Dialogues*, however, is that despite a considerable effort towards discovering these eternal truths, only slight progress is made.

natural order of things; they may be theologically derived. The constructivist has these laws formed through human discourse (the social contract), during which rational reflection is also necessary, and the process by which the axioms of ethical behavior are reached is of particular concern. If the process is correct, then the laws restricting social conflict are correct by definition. Service to humanity is always at the center of enlightenment philosophy [13], and social discussion of these ethical axioms is also required to provide a democratic filter that might expose some of the posed axioms as extreme, impractical and inappropriate.

The intuitionist approach can be particularly worrisome in practice. The view of manager as intuitionist, combined with the problem of agency, can leave SWM-opposing business decisions theoretically justified. This view has the potential of allowing management-welfare maximization to hide behind some stakeholder-balancing rationale. The manager is seldom a disinterested party; he/she may benefit or suffer from the decision. For this reason, society should be suspicious of ethical claims by managers, at least when they are unmotivated by law or other fairly reached agreements with management representing the interests of owners in bargaining with various stakeholders.

4. The Intuitionist Approach to Business Ethics

The intuitionist approach asserts fundamental principles as axiomatic, such as "Do not hurt another person unnecessarily! [14]" Principles of this sort beg further definition of terms such as "hurt" and "unnecessary," as well as specification of the tradeoffs that are invariably implicit. Choices between who is to be hurt may be inevitable, and comparison of degrees of hurt may be necessary for the ethical decision. Uncertainty as to outcomes further complicates the analysis. This is particularly frequent in business problems.

For example, a new production process might lower the cost of production, but might also increase the incidence of worker injury. Generally accepted business practice demands that expected values for both possibilities should be measured,

[13] While this is certainly not a perfect statement of the differences, it does serve the purpose of this discussion. See Frazier (2000), Walzer (1995), O'Neill (2000), and Dancy (2000) for a discussion of each.

[14] The intuitionist approach, though being Socratic in origin, has its current developmental origins in Sidgwick (1874), Ross (1930) and Prichard (1949). These authors popularized the approach as a restatement of Platonistic philosophy. See Dancy (2000) and Frazier (2000) for reviews.

as well as the variance of the probability distributions as an indication of risk. Resolving the tradeoff is complex. Should this resolution be left to management via pursuit of SWM, or by negotiation with workers, or by societal constraints manifested through law? Intuitionist solutions require management judgment, a stakeholder balancing approach. The constructivist approach requires that management represent shareholders, but with constraints established by society, and/ or negotiations with workers.

The most relevant question for the intuitionist is "What initiates the intuition?" Modern intuitionists, Nagel (1986) and McDowell (1985), argue that an individual's "moral sense" must be developed. This requires development of a sympathy for the pain of others; otherwise the morality implicit in situations may be missed. Nonetheless, the moral axioms, asserted by philosophers or society or by other individuals, must be fully grasped in order to understand what should be done. Note that Chapter 3 explores this notion of what initiates intuition in some detail.

The intuitionist-axiomatic approach asserts applicable ethical principles as universal; that these principles should be obvious to all rational beings (even if one group disagrees with another so that each group, believing it to be right, claims to behave ethically). To operationalize the axioms, certain definitional details and rules for tradeoffs are demanded. For the problems presented above, quantitative rules are demanded. Even if the broad principles are generally accepted as true, the detailed operational specifications may be in dispute. More importantly, managers who must specify the tradeoffs and apply the principles cannot be viewed as disinterested, a necessary requirement for moral judgments, as established by Rawls (1951) and explored below. It is for this reason that practical application of the intuitionist approach to business ethics is hardly robust. Parties to disputes (consumers, workers, other stakeholders) must be suspicious of the manager as intuitionist, or even of the manager who applies intuitionist principles asserted by others. Such a system is inevitably judged as dysfunctional.

Consider again the intuitionist approach of applying axioms under uncertainty to problems of product safety, worker safety, income and wealth-generating investment selection where stakeholders are expected to benefit unequally. Application of an axiom generally demands the almost unending gathering of more information before final resolution can be decided. Information gathering, however, is costly in time and resources, and this constitutes an expense for owners, and perhaps the sacrifice of the interests of some others since firm growth may suffer. Also, the decision criteria for the necessary degree of certainty are generally far from implicit in the axioms. To explore some examples, consider the following quandaries faced by the manager-intuitionist:

i) How strong should a soft-drink manufacturer make a glass container considering that children will certainly be consuming the product, and there will be some inverse relation between the probability of child injury (however slight the probability might be) and the strength of the glass container? The manager intuits the rule "Do not hurt another, especially a child, unnecessarily!" The soft drink is certainly not a necessity; but there is no certainty of hurt either. Should the firm experiment with how children handle the various bottle designs? It is likely that the firm should, but when is information from experimentation sufficient to make a decision, and what probability of injury is tolerable? These questions are answered in our society by the democratic process of establishing product-safety law; they are not recognized as within the domain of the intuition of the manager.

ii) How safe should a production process be for the workers involved? What probability of injury is tolerable, and what extent of injury is tolerable? Again assume the manager intuits the axiom "Do not hurt a worker unnecessarily!" As in the consumer safety issue, there is no certainty of any worker injury, but there are probability distributions that can be discerned from experimentation. Our society, however, does not accept answers for these questions to be decreed by the manager, but rather established by either the democratic rule of establishing worker-safety law, or by labor negotiation.

iii) New production processes may increase the expected revenue stream for the firm's owners, but lead to fewer employment and advancement opportunities for workers. The manager intuits the axiom "Do not hurt either workers or owners unnecessarily!" What tradeoff is acceptable, and given that the outcomes are uncertain, what degree of certainty must be established prior to deciding the appropriate tradeoff? Again, our society expects that the decision lies in the democratically established corporate law, or perhaps in labor negotiation, but not decreed by the manager.

iv) A new production facility inherently generates an externality in the form of carbon monoxide. The manager intuits "Do not hurt the environment unnecessarily!" and attempts application of this axiom to establishing the degree of pollution abatement warranted. Again our society expects the decision to be in democratically established environmental law, or perhaps community negotiation, but not subjectively decided by the manager.

One might argue that the dilemma posed by these illustrations lies in the stated axioms, and not in the intuitionist method. For example, one could pose the *golden rule* axiom of "Do unto others as you would have done unto yourself![15]" But would this rule solve any of the tradeoff problems reviewed above? If asked, the worker is likely to demand an absolute right to work and to advance, and to enjoy almost certain worker safety; the consumer is likely to demand extreme product safety at low cost[16].

In addition, this *golden rule* axiom is silent concerning self respect, or benevolence towards others. It is based solely on reciprocity, and as such, it certainly requires a great deal of extension and elaboration to be reached only after great amounts of rational reflection. As with "Do not hurt unnecessarily!" the *golden rule* axiom also appears problematical in business application.

A possible solution to these conflicts lies in the utilitarian approach, i.e. the manager could select the solution that apparently yields the greatest total satisfaction (utility) when summed across all affected parties. (Note that Chapter 4 provides an extensive review to *Utilitarianism*.) Under conditions explored by neoclassical economists, a perfectly competitive marketplace without externalities is capable of yielding this solution assuming homogeneous utility functions and equal initial endowments. Short of this, however, the agent-manager would have an impossible task in identifying the preference functions of affected parties. A neo-classical economist would argue that the manager in control would seek the solution that maximizes his/her own happiness; that a clear case of agency conflict exists. Absent the competitive, non-externality conditions required of a

[15] Hare (1981) poses this axiom as universal, as does Darwin (1859). See Midgley (1991) for a review of Darwin's assertion.
[16] Habermas (1999) argues that negotiation where each party places himself in the other's position is necessary to resolve these sort of problems

market solution, the utilitarian solution must be imposed by society in the form of law or negotiation.

It is particularly important to realize that for all four of the ethical dilemmas posed above, the manager would not be trusted to make the ultimate decision for two reasons:

(1) the manager is not viewed as disinterested since he/she is likely to benefit from the outcome in the form of bonding compensation, and

(2) we view the filtering process of democracy and negotiation as fairer in establishing the complex rules regarding uncertainty and tradeoffs; that is a sort of insurance principle that applies under democracy and negotiation, a principle akin to Aristotle's rule of the mean [17].

So it becomes obvious that individually established axioms, however universal they might appear to the individual, provide a rather weak foundation for systematically establishing business ethics, especially as compared to a democratically established system of fairness embodied in rules of justice, i.e. the Rawlsian system. Nonetheless, if one does hold to the stakeholder approach, then the very nature of balancing stakeholder interests, without reliance upon *a priori* negotiation, requires the notion of manager as intuitionist. We argue later that there is a limited role for the manager intuitionist.

Kant (1785) also points out that it is difficult for us to accept our own moral axioms based only on our own rational reflection without considerable interactive and reflective consideration by others. For this reason, axioms derived through proper democratic discourse are more acceptable even to the individual intuitionist.

5. Problems of Cultural Relativism

One advantage of the intuitionist approach is that it does not appear to suffer from the criticism of cultural relativism. How can absolute truth, if ever found, suffer from culture-specific

problems? We state "appear to suffer" because in practice, as agents reveal their applicable

---

[17] Act as the average of wise people act. (Aristotle, 1953, Book II, *Morals*.)

intuited axioms of decision making, they may impose culturally specific biases. The Kant-Rawlsian approach is certainly vulnerable to the same criticism, but only insofar as the bias passes through the filter of democratic review and decision.

It must be kept in mind, however, that as illustrated by Figure 2-2, of the entire set of culturally specific systems of justice, democratically established systems represent only a subset, and that systems developed from the initial social-discourse conditions of equality, fairness and rationality, represent a smaller subset, as depicted by the unshaded area of Figure 2-2. As reviewed in detail in Chapters 5 and 8, the Kant-Rawlsian political-ethical system of social discourse initiated from a position of equality and manifesting logical rationality can establish a set of moral maxims (laws) that manifest *justice as fairness*.

Figure 2-2: Systems Of Morality That Exhibit Cultural Relativism

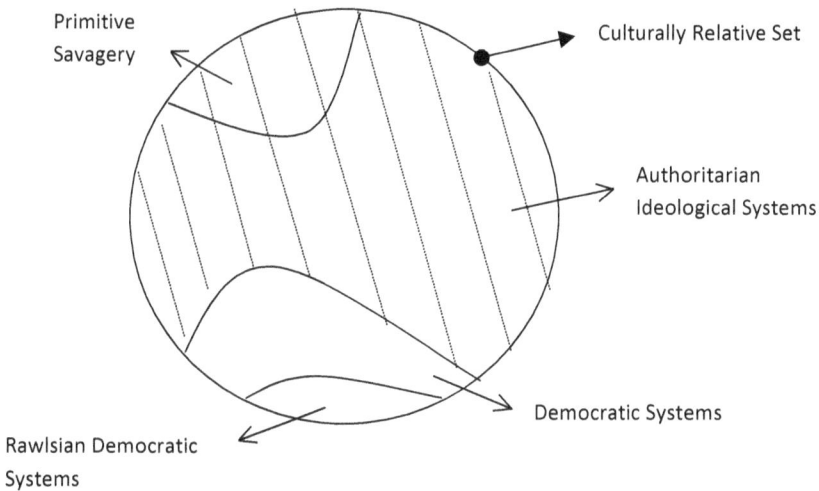

This also requires imposing other suitable restrictions on the initial societal position (restrictions concerning the method of democratic discourse), creates a smaller subset, one that is capable of maximizing the likelihood that the absolute truths of ethics, if they exist, are embedded in the system of justice that constrains liberty for business and non-business. In this sense, the Rawlsian approach does not preclude the intuitionist approach as an end. In fact it opens the door to its widest possibilities by allowing the democratic discourse. The intuitionist approach as a precondition, however, precludes the Kant-Rawlsian constrained-democratic end.

6. The Market and Ethics: SWM as the Completion of the Neoclassical Model

As reviewed above, the most commonly cited appropriate goal for the diversified corporation is SWM, defined as maximizing the market value of equity [18]. The SWM goal, however, is often attacked as either *prima facie* unethical because it is motivated by greed, or as eliciting unethical conduct [19]. Balancing the interests of all stakeholders is often offered as the ethical alternative. Those who argue this appear unaware that the shareholder wealth goal is one of constrained maximization where the constraints consist of law, and negotiated settlements with other stakeholders such as workers, the community, and debt holders. In addition, those who argue the stakeholder approach appear unaware of three other important aspects, i.e. it requires either

- an arbitrary declaration of the weights used in the balancing equation, or

- a pure utilitarian approach with all its inherent contradictions [20], or

- an intuitive approach that requires considerable intuitive insight in order to balance the stakeholder interests.

As explained above, however, the strongest implication of the Rawlsian democratic system lies in its potential for the perfect expression of justice as fairness embodied in the rule of law. Since SWM is constrained by society's law in all its forms, or by negotiation with stakeholders, management need only follow the law and previously reached agreements to exhibit ethical conduct. The existence of any problems not covered by these arrangements implies that deliberations are incomplete. The business manager should not impose her/his intuitions because

[18] As an example of a goal for a non-diversified ownership company, privately held small firms frequently sacrifice firm value for steadiness of income, employment for family members, or even hobby interests of the owners.

[19] As reviewed above, Michael Porter (2002) provides an example of this criticism. He links the shareholder wealth goal to recent accounting disclosure scandals, and corporate fraud. This claim is particularly ironic in that these scandals (Enron and other scandals) invariably involve theft from the shareholders, not for them. Managers who steal do so from the shareholders, and other stakeholders, not for them. In addition, all of the fraud scandals of the last few years involve massive erosion of owner wealth.

[20] By the pure utilitarian approach, it is conceivable that the interests of the worst off could be sacrificed for the interests of the those most well off provided that total societal utility rises.

stakeholders will suspect bias since the manager cannot fit the requirements of the disinterested judge.

All business problems of corporations with diversified ownership suffer the potential of agency conflicts in their resolution. The goal of constrained share-holder-wealth maximization provides applicable decision rules (the standard method of NPV for capital budgeting is an example) within which management-welfare pursuit becomes difficult to hide. If boards of directors do their job, then these decisions must be relatively transparent upon board review. Claims of satisfying multiple stakeholder interests, or of satisfying intuited ethical consider-ations, can easily become masks behind which the biased interests of management welfare can be hidden. In addition, when one realizes that properly distributed wealth implies considerable diversification of ownership among the population (including ownership for employees), then pursuing owner wealth interests does not imply some sort of class conflict [21].

7. The Invisible Hand of the Market, Ethics and Justice as Fairness

What is not generally perceived is that the Kant-Rawlsian system of democratically established justice as fairness is entirely consistent with the goal of shareholder wealth maximization, and may require this as the ethical solution for business problems. The argument for this last proposition is fully established in Chapters 8 and 9, but is briefly reviewed here.

Chambers and Lacey (1996) point out the democratic nature of managerial pursuit of the shareholder wealth goal. As envisioned by Smith (1776), the marketplace is essentially a voting place where the invisible hand moves participants to respond to meet society's needs. Under conditions of sufficient knowledge about the workings of the firm (especially about any externalities generated), the product market will democratically voice the concerns of the populace about perceived ethical lapses. Firms that pursue shareholder wealth as a goal must respond to society's sense of moral rightness. As evidence of this, note the numerous prod-uct market boycotts such as the California grape boycott in support of Migrant Farm Workers'

---

[21] Most US corporate wealth is currently held by pension funds, mutual funds and other broadly owned institutions.

Union during the 1960s, the tuna boycott of Bumblebee during the 1970s and 80s, the 1990s'

Nestle Foods boycott due to its powdered baby-formula problems involving exports to Africa. Although not formerly an organized boycott, the rapid reduction in demand for Calvin Klein's products that occurred as a result of the public's negative view of that company's use of children in sexually provocative advertisements during the late 1990s can be categorized as an informal or implicit boycott. That company's policies changed too rapidly for any organized boycott to be formed. All of these boycotts, whether formally organized or unorganized, were effective in causing behavioral changes in firm policies. Perhaps the informal boycotts are the most effective in eliciting a quick response, and these are frequent occurrences in the marketplace.

Capital market boycotts also voice society's demand for moral reform of business behavior. Note the effective pressure exerted by the capital market boycott of firms doing business with South African companies during the apartheid era of the 1970s.

For boycotts of this type to take place, society must have knowledge of the perceived ethical lapses, but information concerning serious problems does have a way of surfacing in a free and open democracy. The pursuit of shareholder wealth as the overriding goal of the firm forces business behavior to conform to the democratic pressures of the marketplace and its declaration of moral reproach. If the Kant-Rawlsian requirements for the initial position are met, then the democratic marketplace is the complete expression of the person-centered notions of justice as fairness. The manager-as-intuitionist plays no role. This is an important argument of later chapters.

8. The Categorical Imperative and SWM

Business serves its own ends through serving customers, but by serving its own ends, it is meant that it serves its owners. Shareholders invest in corporations with other diversified owners in order to serve their own wealth interests [22].

---

[22] One should understand the principle of Fisher separation, i.e. by the firm maximizing the value of current equity, the individual investor can allocate her/his time preference for consumption (consumption now versus later), by either borrowing against this wealth, or further investing at the market rates of interest.

As a result, it can be argued that the other business constituents are used as a means toward pursuing the business ends. Given the freedom of occupation and movements of employees, freedom of capital movement by debt holders (secondary capital-debt markets are very fluid, free and active), and given the freedom of communities to tax, legislate and regulate business, constituents use business toward meeting their own ends. If constituents possess the requisite freedom, then interfering with their pursuit of their own ends through business interaction should only occur in cases of fraud or deception about purpose or effect. It is for these reasons that laws regulating business behavior are democratically established, and negotiations with constituents are conducted, the purpose of which are to avoid exploitation, and assure that the intended ends of constituents are served. This follows from society's sense of fairness as an expression of the categorical imperative of Kant. These Kantian principles are examined in detail in Chapter 5.

One of these Kantian principles is the *universal principle of justice* (UPJ), which requires maximizing the freedom of the individual, providing that laws constrain an individual's impingement of the freedom of others. The UPJ should be considered as a requirement for society, and is a necessary foundation for any democracy we would desire to live in. Establishment and preservation of freedom is as ethically important as provisions for sustenance or shelter. Its pursuit, subject to the UPJ, is clearly an ethical demand for both the individual and society. This important principle is fully developed in Chapters 5 and 8.

9. Ethical Basis for the Stakeholder View

Solomon (2000) presents a complete statement of the stakeholder-balance approach as an ethical system. He states that business is part of culture, part of society, and as such has ethical obligations to all stakeholders. He states, "The purpose of the corporation, after all, is to serve the public." (p. 361) In addition, he declares that the profit motive for business is a "myth," (p.356), that profits are just a way of keeping score, and that business serves higher purposes of society; that "The pursuit of profits is not the ultimate, much less the only goal of business. It is rather one of many goals and then by way of a means and not an end-in-itself." (p. 357)

Solomon does not recognize Smith's "invisible hand of the market" as leading business to serve the interests of the public (for which profit is the motive force).

As such, he also does not recognize the "invisible hand's" role in transferring society's sense of moral reproach to the firm, as in Chambers and Lacy (1996). Most importantly, as with all those who have the stakeholder view, he does not recognize the primary legal obligation of management to shareholders, as constrained by law and other agreements. Solomon's refusal to recognize this is willful, and certainly deceitful, since it is our current legal system. Shareholders are the legal owners of the firm; they are the residual claimants. They are not, as claimed by Solomon, entitled to just a "fair return" (except for those firms in regulated monopolistic-industries such as utilities), they are entitled to the residual claim, whether it be high or low or nonexistent.

Solomon's essay is an excellent example of stating the stakeholder-balance view while not recognizing that SWM is constrained by law and stakeholder negotiations, that the social compact embodies society's sense of ethics and imposes this on the firm. The fact that those who hold the stakeholder view avoid recognition of the constructivist's complete argument is distressing in that it exhibits a lack of intellectual honesty. Denying legal realities of our system further compounds their ethical lapse.

By quoting the left's favorite whipping boy, Milton Friedman (1971), Solomon is consistent with those who hold his views. Friedman claims that viewing management as not having the fiduciary responsibility established in our legal system, i.e. denying management's primary responsibility to owners, and denying the profit motive, is socialistic. This was not used as a pejorative term, but rather as an attempt at a factual observation by Friedman. Solomon, however, resists this claim as embodying his own view. We should view Friedman's statement, however, as being based upon the common and objective definition of socialism: either society owns the means of production or individuals do, no matter the constraints on their actions established by the social contract. The former is by definition socialistic, but this does not fit the view of stakeholder theorists. They allow ownership to be private, but the owners' interests are not fully served. Because of this, however, the benefits from the invisible hand as it influences consumer satisfaction and owner wealth, and allows society to voice its moral reproach against any particular lapse of ethics, would not fully occur. Balancing all the interests of stakeholders in the way viewed, especially by Solomon, impinges on the firm's response to market pressures.

Solomon lists several concerns of business behavior: charitable contributions, environmental problems, product safety, truth in advertising, labor problems. He then states the supposed benefits of the stakeholder theory for resolving those concerns. Latter chapters also review these problems, and some others, but they show the superiority of the constrained SWM method for resolution.

How do we explain the recent academic view that maximizing shareholder wealth elicits unethical behavior? This is a particularly troubling claim since moral motivation is a subject well explored in the history of Western philosophy. Kant argued that the proper motivation for moral action is the pursuit of the *kingdom of ends*, a social goal where society democratically establishes, understands, and pursues a set of moral maxims that respects the dignity of individuals (as briefly reviewed above and reviewed in detail in later chapters). To be moral, individual actions must be motivated by the pursuit of this harmonious social goal, and not by self-interested goals. One should not commit fraud because of the fear of being discovered, but rather because if society accepted fraud, it would be dysfunctional. Management pursuit of SWM, as properly constrained by democratically established law and fair constituent negotiation, need not violate the Kantian moral motivation, especially since respecting the dignity of others by not committing fraud, deception, or coercion is generally in the interests of SWM. Indeed, it is argued in latter chapters that, under certain robust conditions, SWM may be required as the moral motivation for managerial decisions.

It is therefore argued in this text that SWM is entirely consistent with Rawls' *justice as fairness*. As such, it is entirely ethical when pursued under appropriate constraints. These constraints include society's laws plus negotiated agreements with stakeholders, plus society's expression of reproach through product and capital-market pressures. All of these provide appropriate ethical guidance for managers, a guidance that passes the filter of democratic discourse. Unlike the intuitionist approach, the constructivist approach of SWM provides a robust system for business ethics by solving a wide variety of current problems.

Rawls' system is still criticized by various neo-Marxist perspectives such as that offered by the so-called Frankfurt School[23]. This School sees a democratically

---

[23] See Baynes (2000), McCarthy (1999), and Honneth (2000) for reviews of this school of neo-Marxist philosophy.

established system of *justice as fairness* as vulnerable to the Marxian assertion that *political consciousness is determined by economic position*. It is for this reason that Habermas (1999) rejects Rawls' democratic conditions as being sufficient to assure fairness, and sees this democratic bargaining as biased. Habermas claims that, in addition to the Rawlsian conditions, empathy for each other's position is also required in order to reach fairness. This presumably would overcome any bias due to economic position.

The author views this neo-Marxian position as an overly strong and unjustified condition placed on democratic discourse, that the economic determinism doctrine of the Marxists is faulty, and that in fact Rawls' constraints are overly strong. Equality in bargaining does not require equality of position, but only equality in power of the countervailing sort similar to observations of Galbraith. Our current democratic system does offer a series of countervailing powers (unions, community groups, strong legal representation for debt holders and various SEC laws offer some examples that balance the powers of bargaining). For this reason, the SWM system, with legal and negotiated constraints, has and currently does exhibit remarkable stability, even under the recent strains of the current financial crisis and also recent accounting-disclosure frauds.

Faults in our democracy's view of business fairness are observed from time to time, and democratically established institutional remedies emerge from our discourse. The system of fairness is strengthened as a result. For examples, consider the Sarbannes-Oxley Act of 2002 that seeks to remedy the accounting and auditing problems with stricter liability for providing misleading accounting statements, and a new oversight board to regulate auditors and punish malpractice. Also note the NYSE and NASDAQ recent requirements that a majority of boards be composed of outsiders, and the Dodd-Frank Act of 2009 that seeks to remedy the banking problems that led to the 2008 financial crisis. All of these illustrate that the democratic system does reform.

During times of crisis, there are always those that argue they know truth via their own intuition, that our system of democratic establishment of *justice as fairness* is fundamentally flawed. Those unknowledgeable of the constructivist approach will always find the intuitionist approach as their panacea; it is always appealing to intuit truth, however delusional the intuition might be, than to trust the democratic discourse and decisions of fellow citizens. Porter's claims that SWM is inherently unethical, that it is the root cause of the recent accounting frauds, that the stakeholder-balance approach is the ethical alternative, is an example of delusion.

10. SWM with Legal and Ethical Constraints

To fully argue that pursuit of constrained SWM is ethical in the Kantian sense, one must examine the nature of the constraints. Management is bonded to the interests of shareholders via our legal corporate structure (shareholders decide the corporate board of directors who in turn hire and fire managers), and also through compensation packages that are generally linked to shareholder wealth (the market value of equity). Managers are therefore not disinterested parties to the decisions they make; they are frequently directly affected by these decisions. Therefore in dealing with non-shareholder constituents, managers must be viewed as representing the interests of shareholders. Constituent negotiations, however, can still be viewed as fair by all parties provided certain prohibiting conditions involving fraud, deception and coercion, and similar problems, are met. Fairly reached constituent agreements should form a large body of the constraints on SWM necessary to justify it as ethical in the *Kantian constructivist* sense. Furthermore, these agreements can be either explicit (legal contracts), or implicit (not necessarily legal, but still morally binding). This *fairness in negotiation* is the subject of Chapter 7.

Fairness in negotiation, however, is not always possible. The necessary conditions for its existence are often unavoidably violated in business. When this occurs, the *intuitionist approach* must be pursued. This is also examined in Chapter 7 .

Review Questions

(1) What are the key differences between the SWM and the SB approaches to the managerial goal for the publicly traded corporation with diversified ownership? Review two ethical quandaries that illustrate the superiority of SWM as compared to SB? What is the fundamental ethical problem with the SB approach?

(2) Can product and capital markets influence the ethical behavior of business? Explain with some illustrations?

(3) What is Solomon's argument with respect to SB? Is this argument flawed?

Appendix: Profit and Shareholder Wealth

Introductory courses in microeconomics argue that profit maximization is the goal of the firm. Introductory courses in managerial finance, however, argue that shareholder wealth maximization (SWM) is the appropriate goal of the publicly traded (shares traded on stock exchanges) corporation with diversified ownership. The reason for the difference between these visions lies in the different purposes these courses have. Introductory microeconomics seeks to explore notions of economic efficiency, of the differences between competitive markets and monopoly, and the implications for social welfare. To do this, the course universally assumes certainty and no real future time. There is only a now and a later. These are the assumptions of the simple neoclassical micro model.

The managerial finance course, however, is generally a more advanced course that requires intro microeconomics as a prerequisite. This course is aimed at explaining a variety of more real-world firm decisions such as capital budgeting, capital structure (debt versus equity), dividend decisions, working capital decisions, and more. The models examined are multi-period with an indefinite future, and incorporate risk.

Consider Figure A-1, where a hypothetical expected profit stream is envisioned. The question concerns, "How does this expected profit stream translate into shareholder wealth?" For a corporation, profits are entirely owned by the shareholders (stockholders). As is always argued in the managerial finance course, a firm's profit can be used by the firm in either of three ways: (1) it is either reinvested into capital projects so as to generate future profits, or (2) it is invested into working capital so as to enhance the equity value in some way, or (3) it is paid out to shareholders as dividends. The first purpose generates an increase in equity value, and indeed, the SWM goal requires that it not be reinvested unless it is expected to enhance the total value of equity.

Figure 2-A1: The Expected Profit Stream

Expected Profit

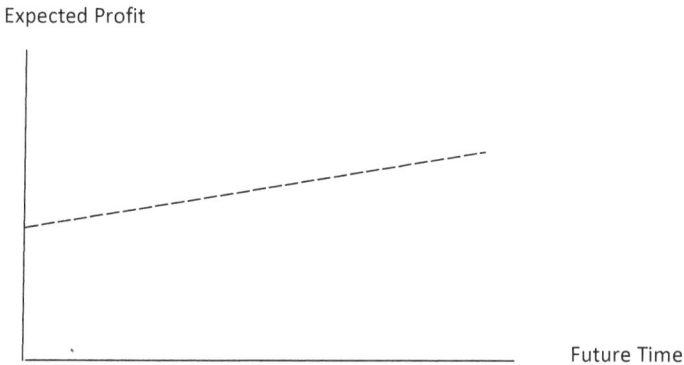

Future Time

In general, if management decides to retain profits (or net cash-income), it is expected to raise the future profit stream. We can place a value on any expected stream by using elementary time-value of money algebra. This is not reviewed here, but readers can review this algebra in any elementary financial algebra course. It measures the value that financial investors would pay in order to purchase this expected cash-flow stream. As a result, the expected profit stream is capitalized into the firm's total value of equity (total value of outstanding shares).

There are, however, problems associated with this valuation process. The first is risk. In order to place a value on this profit stream, the riskiness of actually obtaining this stream must be assessed. In particular, the greater financial markets assess this risk, the lower the value. There is a substantial science behind how this risk should be assessed, particularly in a diversified portfolio sense. The conclusion of this methodology is that only market related risk, not firm specific risk, is relevant for this valuation. The latter risk is diversified and eliminated. The subject is reviewed in every managerial finance text.

The second problem associated with risk concerns the effectiveness of communication of prospective managerial decisions to financial markets. This must be accomplished in such a way as to allow effective assessment of the risks involved. Deception is generally discovered ex post, and future communication discounted by financial markets as likely to also be deceptive. This ex post discovery is likely since future earnings will eventually be revealed. Corporations communicate their prospects to financial analysts who are generally educated in accounting, finance and the industry's characteristics within which the firm operates.

As a result of this analysis, the goal of maximizing the total value of outstanding equity (shareholder wealth) is essentially the maximization of the present value of the expected profit stream, where risk is incorporated into this valuation process.

Chapter III

―――― ❦ ――――

A BRIEF INTRODUCTORY REVIEW OF THE WESTERN ETHICAL TRADITION

Chapter Abstract: *The Western ethical tradition is rooted in ancient Greek philosophy. This tradition extends through the enlightenment and up to modern social contract theory. Knowledge of the origins of this tradition is necessary for organizing the applied subject we term business ethics.*

1. Introduction

What are our ethical traditions? Where does our sense of moral obligation originate? Are traditional moral obligations relevant and practical for modern business management? Are they relevant for our pursuit of a successful and satisfying life? These basic questions are actually addressed by a serious investigation of the Western philosophical tradition. A reasoned exploration reveals appropriate answers that form an essential academic subject worthy of exploration in any respectable business curriculum. An introductory review is presented here, but more serious explorations are left for later chapters.

The word ethic (or *ethos*) stems from the Greek word for "custom," or "method of living." The ancient Greek philosophy concerned how to live the good life, not merely in the sense of material well being, but in the sense of a successful and fulfilled life, especially as that life interacts with its surrounding community. Our moral requirements are linked and designed towards achieving this life.

2. The Greek Origin of Rationalism

The Western academic subject of ethics is categorized as part of philosophy. It is rooted in logic, and largely originated by the ancient Greek philosophers: Socrates (467-399 BCE), Plato (427-347 BCE) and Aristotle (384-322 BCE). Their lives, and their philosophy, overlap. In each case, the younger was the student of the older. This ancient philosophy forms the foundation of much of Western ethical reasoning and tradition over the past 2,500 years. The basic questions they investigated still lie at the core of our ethical concerns: (i) how do our moral laws originate, (ii) how are they related to our personal lives, and (iii) how are they related to a functioning society?

Warren Ashby (2005) points out that the Greeks formed their philosophy around four basic ideas: (1) individual lives have a purpose, and this purpose is to pursue the good life, (2) this good life requires a certain harmonization of human attributes or virtues, (3) rational inquiry is the distinctive and primary aspect of anyone's life, and therefore dedication to its development must be one of these virtues, and (4) the individual is interdependent with the community. The first three of these ideas can be reduced to the fundamentally linked concepts of *eudaimonia* (achieving a happy life), and *arête* (the personal virtues of excellence necessary to achieve a happy life). Aristotle lists these virtues as wisdom, justice, courage, moderation, piety towards the gods, and the capacity to pursue reasoned argument. The essential question explored was "How should a person live in order to achieve *eudaimonia?*" The answer requires reflection about what is essentially desirable and necessary to live a successful life. To Socrates and Plato, this required living a good moral life, i.e. one linked to the pursuit of *arete*. Aristotle adds that both the intellectual life and the moral life must be linked to pursue *eudaimonia.*

This ancient Greek ethical philosophy, however, depends upon some prior notion of what it is to be human, of what it is to pursue the good life, what is the end (*telos*) or purpose of life. In this sense, the Greek moral system is said to be *teleological*. It concerns purposeful living, but since there can be different views about human nature; there can be different views about what is necessary to live a good life. Is intellectual pursuit essential as Aristotle argues? Is a physically active life of interaction with nature essential? Is a social life involving a large family, or civic involvement essential? These are questions posed by this notion of "pursuing the good life."

Socrates, an Athenian Greek of the first half of the fifth century BC, wrote no philosophical works, but still powerfully affected the history of philosophy, particularly ethics. He discussed his ideas with admirers who gathered around him, one of whom was Plato. His personality and method were recorded in his *Dialogues*, written by his admirers after his death. Socrates' discussions took the form of face-to-face interrogations of others, generally about the nature of some virtue such as courage or justice. The interrogations universally generated confusion about the nature of these virtues. Socrates always concluded by indicating the need to think harder and longer about the problems raised. Socrates never argued that he knew the answers to the questions posed, but he did argue that virtue requires knowledge of its nature, otherwise it cannot be pursued. How can one pursue courage without knowledge of what it is? He argued that comprehensive knowledge of virtues is essential for pursuing the good life.

At the age of 70, Socrates was charged by the Athenian popular court with "impiety," not believing in the Olympian gods, and of corrupting young men through his constant questioning of everything. He was found guilty and condemned to death. In Plato's *Apology*, Socrates presents an impassioned defense of his life and philosophy. It is a classic of Western literature. In part, it explores the nature of one's obligations to society.

As stated, our knowledge of Socrates stems from his characterization in a series of dialogues written by his student Plato (and others). These dialogues are recorded discussions (questions and responses) between Socrates and one or more other Athenian characters. In one of those dialogues, *Gorgias*, Socrates explores what an unjust or shameful act is, and why such an act should be avoided. Is behaving unjustly better for the agent? It is recognized that each individual has obligations to his or her civic group, associates and friends, and that these are often competing obligations. It is further recognized that the so-called rules of justice are limitations on one's freedom to act as imposed by society. Are they merely imposed by those in power so as to further their own interests? When is self sacrifice performed in order to further the interest of others justified?

The pursuit of *eudaimonia* is the key to answering this conundrum. Socrates argues that no one does wrong deliberately (knowingly), that doing the right thing is always in the one's best interest. Sufficient reflective reasoning prevents willingly doing what is wrong because such an action violates pursuit of the good life. It involves hurting oneself, not necessarily in a material sense, but in a broader sense of conscience and happiness. The problem with this approach, however, involves the notion of reason [24]. Plato and Aristotle point out that not every action allows time for sufficient examination and logical analysis. The limitation to this Socratic approach lies therefore in the requirement that the agent be properly prepared to respond to ethical dilemmas, that sufficient reflective examination of ethical problems has occurred prior to the experience. This is itself a powerful argument in favor of a reflective study of ethics. One ought to be prepared to face the myriad of ethical dilemmas one encounters. This preparation is necessary for pursuit of *eudaimonia*.

The rise of Greek ethics occurred perhaps because of their view of the conflict between the individual ethos and the co-operative behavior required by society. For the Greek, society would be the family and the civic organization. Man was viewed as political. Rational participation in the community was required for pursuit of *eudaimonia*. Mores and expectations concerning individual behavior arose because of the necessity of this involvement. As a result, the source of moral knowledge became a major exploration of the Greek philosophers.

In the Socratic dialogue *Euthyphro,* the essential question explored concerns whether truth is what the gods say it is because they decree truth, or whether truth exists independently so that the gods merely repeat what they know to be independently true. Greek philosophy asserts the latter, but this poses the problem of how we are to discern this independent and objective truth, especially the moral truth [25]. If the gods (or God) do not merely decree it, then can we find moral truths by other means than from religious texts? If truth has independent existence, then perhaps

[24] The diseased mind, one that is perhaps incapable of reason, or incapable of empathy for the pain of others, is not considered here. The diseased mind is not capable of pursuing *eudaimonia*.

[25] Christians will note that in the first chapter of John's Gospel, truth (or the Greek notion of logos, i.e. the motive force of existence) is identified with God. This is also a Greek notion. It resolves the problem of the separation of truth and God, i.e. Christians claim they are one and the same. This is one of the two Greek philosophical pillars of Christian Theology, the other being the Socratic notion of the soul.

it can be discovered from reflective thought, i.e. logical means. (In the Appendix to this chapter, a Tabular synopsis of these Socratic *Dialogues* is presented.)

In our scientific age, we have no difficulty envisioning a discovery process for truth. In chemistry and physics, we pose hypotheses, experimentally test them for prediction of results, and discern truthful theories from this process (the so called scientific method). Moral truths, however, have additional difficulties associated with their discovery. The experimental process is rather limited. The only experimental process we can utilize is to pose hypothetical moral maxims, and through the filter of democratic reflective discussion, discern whether there is general agreement as to their worth. This is essentially the Socratic process exhibited in the Dialogues, although Socrates is always encountering a limited number of individuals to discuss the problem at hand [26]. Socrates poses the possibility of a pre-existing and everlasting soul as the source of what is apparently an intuition that provides the source for the originally posed moral maxim to be examined. This is the source of what is termed the "intuitive approach" to ethics. It is essentially, the Greek approach, i.e. intuition gives us the idea, but logical examination through social discourse gives us the affirmation. The idea itself is essentially innate, with which our soul has experience prior to birth [27]. The original idea and logical discourse should be a common intuition to all who seek it. Hence, the moral truths are not hidden from us.

This innate notion of truth is reiterated in Plato's *theory of forms,* presented in his *Republic*. Here, Socrates asks, "What is X?" This question is particularly important for concepts such as beauty, goodness and justice. What are the common characteristics of all the things we term beautiful, just or good? These commonalities are difficult to define, but this led Plato to suppose that there must be unambiguous examples of each of these concepts, perhaps not in this world, but in some other. He reasoned that we must have been acquainted with these unambiguous examples termed the "*forms* of beauty, goodness and justice." As argued by Socrates and Plato, it is our soul which carries these vague memories of each into our current life. Plato argued that we are born into this world with

---

[26] We shall see later that the enlightenment philosopher Immanuel Kant poses a similar process, but with guidelines for a broader democratic examination of the posed moral maxim.

[27] The notion of the soul also finds its way into Christian philosophy. Socrates and Plato are the origins of this Christian idea.

dim recollections of these forms. This is why we have some dim notion of these concepts, but cannot readily define them.

Philosophers, Plato argued, reactivate this truth, which is recollected from pre-birth memories. Is this account of how we discover moral truth helpful in practical life? When faced with moral conundrums, is this intuitive process helpful in-the-now? Must we intuit possible solutions, and then engage in social discourse prior to action? If this is the case, then we have obvious practical problems. Aristotle tries to pose more practical solutions to these conundrums.

Aristotle (*Nicomachean Ethics, Eudemian Ethics*, and *Magna Moralia*) rejects the *innate theory of intuition* in favor of an *experiential theory*. To Aristotle, knowing how to act requires a combination of training and direct experience which together should develop the correct habits of dealing with ethical problems. He poses a *doctrine of the mean* which requires two steps: (1) those without sufficient experience should follow those who are considered wise and experienced, and (2) actions should always avoid excesses in either direction. For example, courage should be a balance between cowardice and confidence. Aristotle's approach is therefore also accessible to all as is Plato's, although for both, we envision few achieving *eudaimonia* since few will properly apply logical reasoning to discern solutions to the problems at hand (as in Plato), and/or few will learn from experience (as in Socrates). This is Aristotelian virtue ethics, and it forms much of the basis for Chapter VI.

3. From the Ancients to the Enlightenment

Between the second and fifth centuries CE, Judeo-Christian scriptures were joined with Greek and Roman philosophy to develop Christian theology. Christian Church patriarchs, such as Clement of Alexandria (150-215 CE), recognized that the Greek philosophers posed moral views about how to live that were consistent with Christian scriptures. Indeed, concepts such as the soul, conscience, truth (or *logos* as in John's Gospel), virtues and their perfection (or at least development) were all necessary for a full formation of Christian theology and philosophy. Much of Christian philosophy is therefore Greek [28]. In particular, the Church adopted the Greek tradition of logical reasoning in deciding the right way to act,

[28] Chaim Potok (*Wanderings*, 1978) provides an historical review of Jewish attempted resistance to a similar Helenization of Hebrew philosophy.

particularly with respect to moral decisions. It adopted the position that every-one has the capacity for moral reasoning (almost everyone), and therefore all have *free will*, and have the ability to either commit sin or to achieve salvation.

This Greek philosophical tradition, however, inherently questions the necessity of the Judeo-Christian scriptures (or any other religiously revealed scriptures) for salvation since this tradition poses an innate ability for making moral decisions. If people are endowed with the capacity for logical reasoning, then starting from certain premises which are not dependent upon religious revelation, they can logically deduce correct moral decisions. This is the Greek *rationalist* approach. Alternatively, people might be endowed with the necessary intuition for moral choices, as in the *intuitionist* approach. Either poses the possibility of salvation without scriptural knowledge. In response to this challenge to Christian reli-gion, the Church offered various theories of *the grace that goes before*, a divine inspiration or gift from God that stimulates this logical or intuitional capacity for moral decisions. This notion of *grace* aimed to save the role of religion and the Church in morality.

St. Jerome (347-420 CE) argued that *a spark of conscience (synderesis)* allows one to discern right from wrong, or good from evil, and therefore to avoid the Christian definition of sin.

According to Augustine (354-430 CE), God endows everyone with a conscience so that each can know the correct moral action. This knowledge is, however, not sufficient for virtuous conduct. Correct conduct requires that a person's free will must be aimed at *the good*, which is revealed to humanity through God's per-fect goodness. Through experiencing God's goodness, the soul turns upwards towards joining this revealed goodness, and away from worldly matters, a process termed *the flight of the soul*. This is also a vision of God-provided grace that is required for correct moral conduct. Through St. Jerome and St. Augustine, the religious notion of godly revelation was re-established in moral philosophy, but not necessarily in deciding what was correct, but rather in stimulating individu-als to pursue correct moral decisions.

Of particular importance to the modern ethical philosophy is St. Augustine's exploration of ethical merit as stemming from and being required for correct motivation. (This is a broad philosophical subject of later importance for Kantian analysis.) St. Augustine argued that a love of God, and a wish to perfect oneself to get closer to God, are necessary motivations for any action to be morally correct. "To live well is nothing other than to love God with all one's heart, soul and mind." (*De Moribus Ecclesiae Catholicae, I, 25, 46.*) This focuses on the state of mind of the individual, not on the actual act itself. Some action can be moral if the motivation is correct, but the same action can be unethical in the absence of the correct motivation. For example, a self-righteous desire to be thought of well is not the correct motivation for charity, and fear of being discovered is not the correct motivation for not committing fraud. According to St. Augustine, only a desire to join with God (a desire to join with the good) is a proper motivation.

As we will explore in later chapters, Kantian analysis argues that only the pursuit of a final social goal of *harmony*, what Kant termed the *kingdom of ends*, is the appropriate motivation for moral action. This notion of *harmony* consists of society's knowing pursuit of a set of generally recognized moral maxims. All of this is explored in detail in later chapters, but one can see now how this pursuit of a secular version of *kingdom of ends* is an extension of the religious idea of the goal of joining with the ultimate good, be it interpreted as heaven, nirvana, paradise or some other non-worldly achievement. Hence this notion of motivation as important to ethical decisions has its roots in post-Greek religious philosophy, and it extends through the enlightenment to modern ethical thought. It also extended from Greek philosophy's emphasis on *eudaimonia's* requirement that we fit with our community, especially concerning our moral obligations.

Dionysius, the fourth to fifth century philosopher, argued a strict theory of moral assessment: the category, the motive and the outcome of some action must all be moral or the action is worthy of blame. Beneficence, for example, must be both properly motivated and have a charitable result. One should know that any charitable giving will reach the deprived, or it is without moral merit, it is not *good*. As with St. Augustine, Dionysius also argued that *evil* is just the privation, or destruction, of *good*. (This notion of *evil* is an important consideration for later exploration.)

In the fifth century CE, the Western Roman Empire succumbed to the Teutonic invasions from the north. In the next century, the Eastern Roman Empire was invaded by Arabs during the Islamic invasions. The Roman educational systems were destroyed as a result. The only centers of education remaining were in isolated rural monasteries, which attempted to preserve the ancient knowledge of ethics and natural philosophy. This medieval period is marked by the age of *scholasticism*, the age of this monastic preservation. The age was not so much concerned with the content or logic of moral concepts as with their categorization into which virtues should be cultivated (as in Aristotle), and the relation of morality to divine revelation (as in Socrates). Even during this period, however, there were substantive philosophical-ethical examinations published.

In the sixth century, the scholastic philosopher Boethius argued that some moral principles are self evident (axiomatic). In *Cur Deus Homo*, he writes that it shows "negligence if after we become established in the (Christian) Faith we do not strive to understand what we believe." By "understanding" Boethius means to first assert the moral axioms, and then through logical analysis to reach conclusions concerning moral decisions. This is certainly an affirmation of the Socratic-Platonic *intuitive* process, although with a religious link.

Thomas Aquinas (1225-1274) [29] argued that the first principle of thought about conduct is that good should be pursued, and evil avoided. He termed this the *synderesis rule,* similar to Augustine and St. Jerome's approach. Aquinas argued that this is a self evident principle, or axiom. He also argued that conscience provides the practical reasoning necessary for correct moral decisions. Aquinas linked Greek philosophy to religious doctrine to form a Christian philosophy, generally termed *Thomastic philosophy* or *Thomism*. In this process, however, Thomas Aquinas developed a *natural law* version of ethics that stands independent of religious doctrine. He benefitted from concurrent republishing in the West of Aristotle's writings. Thomas argues that a *natural law* of things, even ethical laws, can be discovered through rational thought. By *natural law*, Thomas refers to the general natural order of things which involves humanity and its progress towards perfection.

In *Summa Theologiae,* Thomas Aquinas shows the parallels between the Greek classical virtues and those recurrent in Christian perfectionist thought. He therefore utilizes the classical virtues as a foundation of ethical philosophy. Right action, Thomas argued, promotes human flourishing. There exists an essential

---

[29] Thomas of Aquino was an Italian Dominican priest of the scholastic era. See Wikipedia for a brief biography that indicates his considerable importance in the history of philosophy and Christian theology.

human nature, and associated with it, a set of values that constitutes excellence in life. Virtues are those habits that are conducive to fulfilling a person's life, i.e. a version of *eudemonia*. *The natural law referred to stems from the natural human tendencies to preserve one's life, raise children, co-operate with society, and generally to flourish happily.* The law of God (Mosaic law and other extensions) is not independent of this *natural law*, but just another version of it according to Aquinas.

The religious basis of ethics was re-inserted by Thomas through the notions of divine revelation and inspirational grace, which aid in the pursuit of virtue so that a state of blessedness (*beatitudo*), an eternal joining with God, can be achieved. Hence *eudemonia* is replaced with *beatitudo*, but the classical idea of virtues being desirous of pursuit remains [30]. As in the Greek philosophy, these virtues have a natural basis founded on the pursuit of the good life. This good life, however, is not just a broad state of happiness, but rather a final joining with God. This is the core of *Thomastic philosophy,* and this formed the basis for subsequent Roman Catholic religious philosophy (theology).

4. The Enlightenment to Modern Ethical Philosophy

The ancient Western philosophical thought concerned the pursuit of the highest good, i.e. a life that is most fully and lastingly satisfying. Virtue, although central to our managing social relations, was primarily concerned with attaining the optimal life (*eudemonia).* Western Christianity imposed notions of salvation as the purpose of life (*beatitudo*), which necessitated divine involvement. With increasing religious conflict, however, knowledge of the requirements for the pursuit of virtue and the pursuit of the godly became increasingly complicated. The philosophy of the enlightenment period sought to clarify and simplify by founding ethics in non-religious reflective thought. The reliance on logical reasoning certainly stemmed from the Greek, but the non-reliance on perfectionist virtue was an *Enlightenment* idea. The *Enlightenment* placed humanity, and its social relations (the *social contract*), at the center of ethical reasoning.

---

[30] The author Jack Kerouac (1922-1969) pioneered the beat literary movement of the 1950s and 1960s. He coined the term *beat* to reflect beatitudo. His most significant literary novel, *On the Road* (1957), explored the notions of virtue among his friends

Perhaps the basic theme of the enlightenment was declared by Kant in *Answer to the Question: What is Enlightenment?* (1784, 8:36 and 8:37):

Enlightenment is man's exit from his self-incurred minority. Minority is the incapacity to use one's intelligence without the guidance of another. Such minority is self-incurred if it is not caused by lack of intelligence, but by lack of determination and courage to use one's intelligence without being guided by another. "Have the courage to use your own intelligence!" is therefore the motto of the enlightenment. All that is required for this enlightenment is freedom; and particularly the least harmful of all that may be called freedom, namely, the freedom for man to make public use of his reason in all matters.

The development of and use of this "intelligence" is the purpose of our education, particularly of higher education. The phrase "make public use of his reason in all matters" is particularly important and explored in this text. It is a critical element in business ethics where emphasis must be placed on the word "public." This *public use of reason* is the foundation for what the 20th century philosopher Hanna Arendt termed *the noble nature*. This is explored in considerable detail later in this text.

Ethical philosophy originated with the idea that laws of morality, like the laws of natural science, exist independently of human preferences, that they are objectively real. Violation of these moral laws means that *eudemonia* is inevitably frustrated. *Enlightenment* philosophy, however, placed morality at the center of human self-governance, or personal *autonomy*. This philosophy was more socially oriented, centered around political notions of the social contract.

In the sixteenth century CE, Europeans were increasingly literate and self-reliant. Protestantism split Europe into religious wars so that Christianity became increasingly viewed as incapable of providing moral guidance. It was obvious that secular, as opposed to religious sectarian, principles were necessary. Although universities offered reasoned versions of morality independent of religious scripture, this scripture still provided some guidance. Christians believed that God's law provided this individual guidance, and that it benefitted all in a social sense. It was a matter of *free will* whether this law was followed or not; to not follow God's law meant committing sin, to separate oneself from God's community. The seventeenth century extended this version of Thomastic natural law.

Philosophers Hugo Grotius, Thomas Hobbes, and John Locke began the modern social contract theory of ethics. Hugo Grotius (1583-1645 CE) originated modern natural law theory (post Thomas Aquinas). He argued that individuals are entitled to determine their own objectives, but that the purpose of ethics is to pose the conditions under which these objectives can best be pursued. In *Law of War and Peace* (1625), Grotius argued that people are sociable by nature, that we form political societies only if we believe that our individual rights will be protected, although some rights might be traded for political security. These rights are, Grotius argued, a natural attribute of the individual and independent of any social contribution they might provide, i.e. all posses these rights no matter their societal position.

In *Leviathan* (1651), Thomas Hobbes argued somewhat differently than Grotius while further developing the social-contract natural-law idea. Hobbes denied that people are naturally sociable. People, he argued, relentlessly seek power to achieve self-interested aims. The inherent conflict that inevitably results forces us to agree to some sort of sovereign rule capable of enforcing peace while we pursue our individual goals. The natural laws of morality are no more than the most essential steps we must take so that an orderly society can exist. The theory that political society emerges from this social contract makes man the source of these secular laws rather than any objective natural law.

John Locke (1632-1704) argued in opposition to Hobbes. Locke argued that some rights are inalienable, and this places natural limits on government. Nevertheless, Locke claimed that most people do not know what morality requires; they must be instructed and controlled by the threat of punishment. Even though the natural law is meant to guide us to both individual and social well being, and even though we are capable of, and should be involved in, forming our political order, we need to have morality imposed upon us. Much of seventeenth and eighteenth century political philosophy essentially argued this necessity of the imposition of morality.

In opposition to this rather dim view of humanity, i.e. that morality must be imposed, in *Inquiry Concerning Virtue* (1711), the Earl of Shaftsbury claimed that people have a moral faculty that enables them to judge their own motives. We are virtuous only when we act upon those motives we approve, and we approve only our benevolent or sociable motives. In this sense, Shaftsbury argued, morality is an outgrowth of human feelings, and not intuition or logical reasoning. This originated the modern debate between whether morality should or could be the result of the higher faculties of moral reasoning, or merely the result of human feelings.

Both sides of this debate argue that benevolence and morality benefit society. The question concerns whether morality stems from human feelings or intuition. In either case, moral rules would be accessible to all since all are capable of both this reasoned intuition and of moral feelings. Unlike Hobbes, many argued that people naturally desire the good of others, that they usually do not need the threat of penalty to behave morally. Immanuel Kant (1724-1804) and David Hume (1711-1776) began their considerable contributions to ethical philosophy at this point. Both challenged the notion that morality depends only upon achievement of the good result. In their philosophy, they posed the notion that motivation should be at the center of morality, as Saint Augustine argued. The philosophy of Kant and his modern extenders is left for a subsequent chapter, but both Hume and Kant are reviewed here in brief. Both rejected natural law theories of morality.

Hume argued that a virtue-centered theory best accounted for our moral convictions, and these virtues are rooted in our feelings towards others, emotional feelings necessary to move us to moral actions. Reason, he argued, is incapable of this motivation. We are often self interested, but we still desire the well-being of others. Our actions in pursuit of the well being of others constitute virtue. Motivated by a sympathetic appreciation for the feelings of others, we observe societal rules that pursue what we term *justice*. These rules are generally accepted practices, but they originate in human feelings or empathy for the suffering of others. Hence, according to Hume, all our ethical standards stem from personal feelings.

Kant argued very differently from Hume. Kant placed reason, and not feelings, at the center of his notion of the ethical. He argued that the central point about morality is that it implies personal duties, and these duties can only arise from the reasoned maxims we pose on ourselves. When we know that morality requires us to do some action, we know that we can perform this action. This can only be true if we are free to do this. This excludes requirements imposed by forces outside of ourselves; these requirements must be determined by something within our own nature, i.e. our ability to think and reason. They cannot be imposed by a god, or by some external natural law, or we are not free (or *autonomous* as he termed it).

According to Kant, the moral law must consist of maxims that tell us to act in ways that we would have everyone act (the property of *universality*). Each of us, Kant argues, can analyze whether some maxim is moral or not by asking whether we would will that everyone behave according to it. If we make a personal exception for ourselves, then it cannot be a moral maxim, and we have a duty to obey all qualifying maxims. This is not, however, a view that each of us should have our own personal moral code different from others. The democratic filter of reflective social discourse (as in the Socratic dialogues) should be used to establish our moral maxims or duties. Hence we are fully able to participate in this moral legislation, and this should give us a high degree of respect for obeying the maxims we impose. In this sense, we are fully autonomous.

To guide our moral thinking and formation of our agreed moral maxims, Kant posed a set of simple rules which he termed the *categorical imperative*. As we shall examine in a later chapter, Kant posed three of these rules, which he saw as really just different versions of one another, that to assert one logically implies the assertion of the other two. The first rule, *universality*, is examined above. The second form of this rule is *respect for the dignity of others*, i.e. allow others to pursue their own purposes without deception, fraud or coercion. This implies that one ought not to deceive someone else into pursuing our own ends while subverting their own intentions. As an example, if we hire someone then he agrees to work for us for some specified wage. His purpose is to earn income. If we knowingly intend to not pay this wage, then we frustrate his purpose, and we engage in deception. We have not respected his purpose.

We can readily discern that *universality* implies that our moral maxims are constructed about the principle of respect for individuals, the second form of the *categorical imperative*. The third form of Kant's *categorical imperative* concerns the proper motivation for our moral maxims. He termed this motivation *the pursuit of the kingdom of ends*, where this *kingdom* is a social goal of all clearly understanding and pursuing our democratically established moral maxims, i.e. pursuing a moral community. Our motivation for being moral should be a social motivation. We seek an *harmonious society*. For example, if we decide to violate a maxim against theft, we (1) violate our requirement for universality since if theft is generally acceptable, then society would breakdown. At the same time, (2) we would certainly not be respecting the dignity of whomever we steal from. In particular, (3) our motivation for not committing theft should not be because we fear possible discovery, but rather because we wish society to be *harmonious*. When we examine this Kantian approach in more detail, then we shall explore the very practical nature of this ethical philosophy for business.

Kantianism forms one of the major schools of ethical thought, along with intuitionism, the natural law school, and utilitarianism (examined below). Each has commonalities with the others, but each emphasizes a different organization of our ethical thought. For example, Kantianism must rely upon some origination of posed moral maxims, which are to be examined for possible acceptance according to the *categorical imperative*, and according to democratic discourse. We can see the very roots of this process in the Socratic dialogues, which forms the basis of the intuitionist approach. Indeed, the posed maxim can be viewed as originating in intuition, a notion that Kant would not object to, provided the maxim passes the filter of open and logical discourse.

Still, Kantianism had its opponents. Thomas Reid (1710-1796) argued that morality was common sense, essentially intuitive. We just know our obligations towards others, and logical systemization of these moral principles is neither needed nor possible. We shall argue extensively in later chapters the opposite view of this. We shall show the usefulness of this systemization within the Kantian framework, especially for business ethics and management.

Jeremy Bentham (1748-1832) originated modern utilitarianism, a theory that moral principles should be those that benefit overall society the most. This is a hedonistic-consequentialist theory where human good is to be served, and this human good results from the sum of individual happiness. Our Western society does not accept this theory in that it believes that there are fundamental individual rights which must be respected despite the overall total-sum of the happiness of society's members. This utilitarian theory is examined extensively in a later chapter where it is argued that utilitarianism is not especially useful as a practical method of organizing business ethics.

John Stuart Mill (1806-1873) pointed out that common-sense morality, which we learn as children, represents a lengthy historical accumulation of wisdom about desirable and undesirable consequences of actions. He argued in *Utilitarianism* (1863) that basing moral principles on a desire to maximize societal satisfaction would not lead to common sense solutions to ethical problems. The wealthy miser might still derive great pleasure from an additional small amount of cash, while the poor person might not. Does it fit common sense to have the poor redistribute to the wealthy?

5. A Western Tradition

We have briefly reviewed this history of Western moral thought in an attempt to understand some sources of our ethical tradition. This Western tradition indicates several fundamental principles:

(1) Ethics needs no religious or authoritative basis other than general agreement after reflective thought and logical reasoning. There is no need for basing ethics upon divine scripture from any source. Truth can be viewed as either independent of the divine, or one with it, but in either case, divine revelation is not necessary to know truth. Perhaps to know truth is to know the divine

(2) Ethics is a subject of logic even if we accept the view that intuition is the source of ethical ideas. Practical applications of ethics stem from logical analysis from which moral duties can be derived.

(3) The Kantian system of social discourse in which we derive moral maxims from fundamental guides (the *categorical imperative)* is very much at the heart of modern Western ethical philosophy. It is inherently a democratic system that is rooted in Greek philosophy. It is centered upon the individual as an autonomous, rationally reflective individual legislator.

(4) Ethical motivation must not be based upon personal consequences, but upon the pursuit of a broad social ideal. The individual is the moral agent, but social harmony must be the ultimate motivation (Kant's *kingdom of ends*). This also is deeply rooted in the Socratic tradition.

Review Questions

(1) Define *ethics*? Where does the concept originate?

(2) According to Ashby, what are the basic concepts of Greek ethical inquiry?

(3) What are the significant contributions to philosophy presented in the *Gorgias* and *Euthyphro* dialogues?

(4) According to Socrates, where do our ethical ideas originate?

(5) Explain the importance of Plato's *theory of forms*, and of the *soul* in ethical philosophy?

(6) Briefly review Aristotle's *doctrine of the mean*?

(7) Briefly review the *Thomastic* notion of the *natural law*, and the role it plays in religious notions of ethics?

(8) What is the core idea of the Enlightenment? Are moral laws exogenous to humanity?

(9) Explain the role of *public* in the Enlightenment idea of *public use of intelligence*?

(10) How do the notions of *free will* and *autonomy* contribute to ethics?

(11) Explain how Grotius extended Thomastic *natural law*?

(12) What are the essential differences between Humeian and Lockeian extensions of *natural law* philosophy?

(13) According to some *Enlightenment* philosophers such as Hume, what is the role of *feelings* in ethics?

(14) What is the essential difference between Kantian and Humeian ethics?

(15) According to Enlightenment philosophers, explain the central role of *motivation* in ethics?

(16) Briefly review Kant's use of the *categorical imperative* in ethics, and Reid's objection to this use?

(17) Briefly review Kant's *kingdom of ends* and *harmony* in his ethical theory?

(18) What is J.S. Mill's objection to Bentham's version of *utilitarianism*?

Appendix: The Socratic *Dialogues*

Table A-1: A Brief Synopsis of Eighteen of the Twenty-Three Socratic Dialogues

Dialogue	Subject
Apology	Socrates is accused of corrupting the youth of Athens by encouraging idle discussion, and disrespect for the gods. His defense is that he encouraged search for the truth, and that he sought to kindle the spark of good in every man. When he encountered blind obstinacy and bias, he did not condemn those at fault. The Apology also presents an early example of the Western ideal of a trial: prosecutor, defense, jury, judge, evidence, cross examination and procedure.
Crito	Examines civic duty, and the wrongfulness of returning evil for evil.
Phaedo	Socrates argues that the eternal soul, which exists prior to birth, discovers and continues truth in the next life. It alone discovers and knows the eternal truths of goodness and beauty.
Charmides	The ancient Delphic notions of "Know thyself!" and "Nothing in excess!" are explored. Arrogance and insolent self assertion are explored as detestable.
Laches	Examines the notion of courage. To act bravely without knowing what bravery is constitutes ignorance. To be virtuous without having a clear idea of virtue is of small importance. Socrates argues that "The unexamined life is not worth living!"

Lysis	Socrates questions two boys about the meaning of friendship. He seeks to kindle the spark of reasoned discourse and examination so they can discover the flame of good within.
Euthyphro	Socrates argues that "Good is not good because the gods deem it, but rather the gods approve what is good!"
Ion	Art is not dependent upon emotion, but rather upon knowledge.
Gorgias	"To do wrong is misery; to suffer wrong is nothing in comparison."
Protagoras	"No man does evil voluntarily, that is, thinking it to be evil!" Virtue, Socrates argues, is one with wisdom; wickedness has its root in ignorance.
Meno	"Everyone desires good; no one ever desires evil!" For what else is unhappiness but desiring evil things and getting them?" The Socratic method of reasoned discussion is also illustrated as a method of recalling truth known in prior life.
Cratylus	Socrates argues that to reason that god initiated something is to merely offer an excuse for having no reason. Also goodness and beauty exist and are permanent, but the words we use to try to express them are never adequate.
Phaedrus	Explores the various notions of love.
Symposium	Explores a variety of views of love. It forms a basis for Christian notions of love.
Republic	The just man, not the unjust, is the happy man. There is eternal truth beyond the changing world, and by reason, man can find it. The world will never be justly ruled until rulers are philosophers who know and pursue the good. Even if this just rule is never achieved, a man should order his life in pursuit of it.
Theaetetus	Virtue stems from knowledge, and to be wise is to be good. The faults of the busy business life are examined in opposition to the contemplative life.

Statesman   Statesmanship is an art, and the true statesman can bring the minds of men into union. The rule of law is practically necessary for the best state.

Philebus   Things of the mind are superior to sensual enjoyment. This motivates the pursuit of the truth, and doing all things for the sake of the truth.

Chapter IV

UTILITARIAN PHILOSOPHY AND UTILITY THEORY

Chapter Abstract: *Various versions of utilitarian philosophy are reviewed along with fundamental Western philosophical objections to it. Utility theory as a basis of individual choice is also reviewed, and is used as a basis for bargaining, social welfare considerations, and behavior under conditions of uncertainty. As such, this utility theory forms the foundation for much of our ethical consideration of marketplace transactions, including negotiations over trading arrangements.*

1. Utilitarianism

Utilitarianism is a consequentialist branch of ethical philosophy that claims that our moral rules should be so designed as to maximize the total sum of society's happiness. By this we mean the total sum of the happiness of all individuals in that society. This definition of utilitarianism is actually rather limited in that in its extreme form it could justify the gross violation of the rights of some in order to benefit the whole of society. As such, we would never accept this extreme form of consequentialist theory as the basis for morality.

For example, the 1961 movie *Judgment at Nuremberg* concerns a fictional post-WW II trial of German jurists who had warped the legal structure of 1930s Nazi Germany so as to allow the wrongful persecution of various political and ethnic minorities, a persecution that evolved into what we ultimately describe as the *holocaust*. The two main characters in this cinema-play are Judge Hofsteder, played by Burt Lancaster, who is being tried for crimes against humanity, and presiding Judge Haywood, played by Spencer Tracy. One of the critical acts that Judge Hofsteder is accused concerns a particular trial that occurred early in the Nazi era. Hofsteder is accused of knowingly allowing an innocent man to be convicted, and presiding in such a way as to enable that conviction. Judge Hofsteder is found guilty, and when Judge Haywood reads the sentence, he states "We declare now that we stand for truth, justice and the value of a single human being!" At the end of the movie, the two judges meet in Judge Hofsteder's jail cell. Hofsteder pleads he had not known that his undermining of the judicial system would lead to the horrors of the *holocaust*. Judge Haywood responds, "Judge Hofsteder, it became that when you knowingly first convicted an innocent man!"

This *Judgment at Nuremberg* story actually illustrates both the fault with the extreme consequentialist form of utilitarianism, and its two variations explored below, each of which is more practical, but not necessarily applicable and useful. In Western society, the rights of the individual are held as a sacred ideal. This philosophy is the foundation of Western democratic constitutional arrangements, i.e. there are limits to the democratic rights of the majority.

The three branches of utilitarianism referred above are

- Hedonistic utilitarianism: People seek pleasure and avoid pain so as to maximize the difference between these sensations. Whatever actions maximize the sum of these differences across society should be adopted as our moral rules.

- Rules-based utilitarianism: We should adopt whatever rules we believe will maximize our expectation of societal happiness.

- Social-welfare based utilitarianism: We should adopt actions and rules we believe will maximize our expectation of a societal welfare function, which considers not only societal happiness, but also to some specified extent, the rights of individuals. In this case, the specified rights of individuals can be considered as constraints on our attempts to maximize societal happiness.

This third case of utilitarianism is considered in greater detail when we consider *The Ethic of the Marketplace* chapter. The first two utilitarian theories originated with Jeremy Bentham (1748-1832), and were extended by John Stuart Mill (1806-1873) and Henry Sidgwick (1838-1900), all three of whom were English philosophers. The economics of the social-welfare function extends back to 19th century philosophy. Bator (1957) Lange (1942), Arrow (1951), and Samuelson (1956) review and extend this theory.

At first glance, utilitarianism can appear to be based upon common sense. It fits common slogans such as "the greatest good for the greatest number," which some argue should be our guide for action and rule making. The problem is that in application, this sort of slogan is problematic in measurement of this "good." Are we to try to apply utilitarianism as a norm in establishing rules and actions, or are we to use the theory as an explanation of how our rules evolved, i.e. did they evolve so as to maximize societal welfare? If it is the former, then we must answer "Who is the "we" who will be deciding the rules and actions?" Will this be by democratic vote? Will we sacrifice the interests of minorities to benefit the majority? Will we sacrifice the welfare of future generations to benefit the welfare of the current generation?

We can illustrate the problems with utilitarianism by considering the conundrum of income redistribution. To what extent is it in the interests of social welfare to redistribute income from the wealthy to the poor? There is no doubt that if we tax the income of the wealthy, they will be less happy as a class (although perhaps some individual wealthy people will not be less happy). If we redistribute this income to the poor, there is little doubt that as a class, the poor will be happier, but how much happier as compared to the loss of happiness of the wealthy? How much redistribution should we undertake? Our society decided that some redistribution is in order since we have progressive income taxes, but should we not redistribute income so that it is equal? If the relation between income and happiness were identical for all individuals, then this sort of income equality would maximize current overall societal happiness.

There are, however, two problems with this income equality argument:

- The relation between income and happiness may not be identical for all, and interpersonal comparisons would be faulty. As an example, some individuals might prefer less income and more leisure, while others prefer the opposite. As a result, the income transfer benefit to the leisure class would be small, but the hurt it would cause the high-income class could be relatively large. Net societal happiness would decrease. We should also consider that some high-income employment could be very necessary for society to function but stressful and unpleasant for those who perform it. Also, some low-income employment could be much less stressful and more pleasant. As a result, an income transfer could result in a large scale shift away from the stressful and less pleasant employment and therefore ultimately hurt overall economic performance and societal happiness.

- Income transfers of this sort could hurt savings, capital investment and entrepreneurship. Future generations could suffer as a result.

A positive claim that our current rules and actions evolved so as to maximize anticipated social welfare might be accurate, but is hardly testable. As such, this claim is of little interest. We are always interested in exploring new actions and rule modification. This is the democratic process. We are always interested is posing new actions and norms for our democracy to consider, but shouldn't ethical considerations such as Kantian moral-maxims and duties act as constraints to these newly posed actions?

In the sections below, we explore utilitarianism in more detail. Establishing our foundation for further analysis of this and other subjects, however, requires that we separate the notions of utility functions from the philosophy of utilitarianism. We do that below. We can then use notions of the utility function as a tool to explore several analytical problems other than maximizing overall social welfare. For example, one of these problems concerns fairness in bargaining. Others concern the efficiencies of markets and associated ethical problems in business strategy. Our utility analysis is therefore a very useful tool.

2. Utility Functions and Individual Choice

Utility is defined as the happiness or pleasure derived from some set (or combination) of goods where "goods" are broadly defined. We can classify goods as either positive or negative, where the former are goods we enjoy, and the latter are goods we wish to avoid. Examples of the former include food of various sorts, leisure and recreation, housing and medicine. Examples of the latter include pollution of all sorts, the expectation of crime, time spent in traffic jams and the like. We could always consider reductions in these negative goods as being positive additions to utility.

Consider two positive goods, X and Y. Allow U to be the utility function that measures the utility of consuming various amounts of X and Y, as given by equation (4-1) where U(X,Y) indicates some general but unspecified function except in broad categories described below. In

$$U = U(X,Y) \tag{4-1}$$

addition, since X and Y are positive goods, increases in consumption of either increases U. This direct relation is termed the principle of *positive marginal utility*, i.e. marginal means increase in the sense that increases in X or Y increases U. We also assume both X and Y exhibit *diminishing marginal utility* in that the greater the consumption of X or Y the smaller the increase in utility associated with further increases in their consumption. Figures 4-1a and 4-1b illustrate the *principle of positive but diminishing marginal utility* [31].

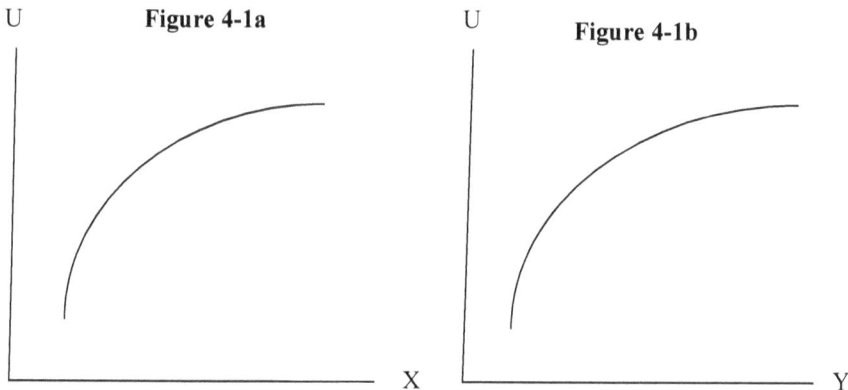

Figure 4-1a

Figure 4-1b

[31] Using the calculus, we describe positive but diminishing marginal utility as dU/dX > 0, d²U/dX² < 0, dU/dY > 0, d²U/dY² < 0.

Graphical analysis can also be used to illustrate the concepts of *complimentary goods* and *substitute goods*. If goods X and Y are *complimentary*, then increases in consumption of X increases the utility enjoyed from Y at each level of consumption of Y [32]. This is illustrated by Figure 4-2a. If X and Y are substitute goods, then increases in the consumption of good X decreases the utility enjoyed from Y at each level of consumption of Y. This is illustrated by Figure 4-2b.

An example of complimentary goods would be the condiments that we use for our summer grilling of hotdogs and hamburgers (condiments such as relish, and other seasonings that we might add). Perhaps the more condiments we have, the more we enjoy our hamburgers and hotdogs, i.e. they complement one another. An example of substitute goods are the very hotdogs and hamburgers we have at our picnic. One substitutes for the other. If we consume a hamburger first, then the consumption of a hotdog yields less utility than if it were consumed in isolation.

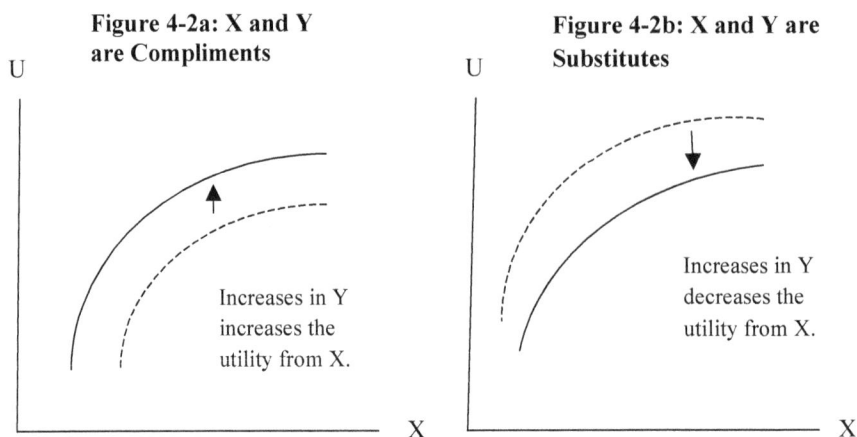

Figure 4-2a: X and Y are Compliments

Increases in Y increases the utility from X.

Figure 4-2b: X and Y are Substitutes

Increases in Y decreases the utility from X.

3. Indifference Curves

Since both goods X and Y are positive goods, we could decrease the individual's consumption of X while increasing the consumption of Y by an appropriate amount so as to leave the consumer indifferent that is at the same utility level. There must be some amount of increase in Y which compensates for the reduction in X so

[32] For complimentary goods, $d^2U/dXdY > 0$. For substitute goods, $d^2U/dXdY < 0$.

as to leave the consumer's utility level constant. This is illustrated by Figure 4-3 where the curves depicted are termed "indifference curves" because the consumer is indifferent between being at one or the other point along any particular curve.

The indifference curves depicted in Figure 4-3 are labeled IC-1 and IC-2. Each curve represents different utility levels with the utility level of IC-2 being greater than that of IC-1. Consider the two positions "a" and "b" along indifference curve IC-1, "a" has more of good Y and less of X than does position "b." Since these positions are along the same indifference curve IC-1, they indicate combinations of goods Y and X that yield the same utility level. Since position "c" has more of good X than position "a," but it has the same amount of good Y, it must yield a higher level of utility since both goods are positive goods. The utility level associated with IC-2 must therefore be greater than that of IC-1.

Figure 4-3: Indifference Curves

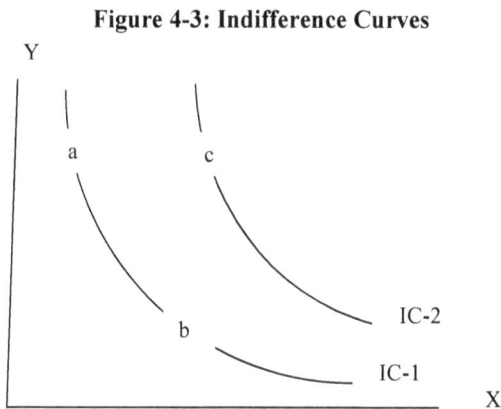

The curvature of the indifference curves shown in Figure 4-3 is also important, i.e. they are concave from above. Figure 4-4 illustrates the reason why these indifferences curves are concave from above. Consider positions 1 and 2. Consider the question, "If we start at position 1 and decrease the consumption of good Y, how much must we increase consumption of good X so as to leave the consumer at the same utility level?" This involves moving to position 2. Since the initial position 1 has more of good Y and less of good X, and since we assume diminishing marginal utility, we can compensate the reduction in Y by a much smaller increase in X. This is because the consumer has little of X to begin with. If, however, our initial position is 3 where we have only a small initial amount of Y but a relatively large amount of X, then a similar reduction in Y must be compensated by a larger increase in X. This occurs because of diminishing marginal utility, and results in the curvature of the indifference curve to be concave from above [33].

Figure 4-4: Concavity of Indifference Curves

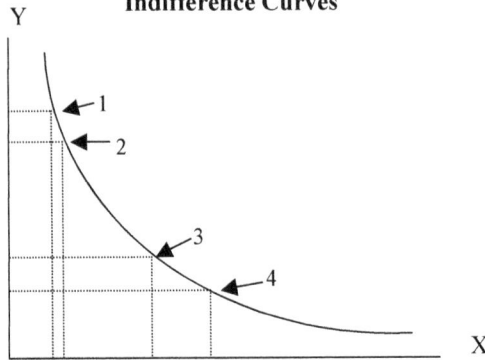

We can identify three rules (or theorems) for indifference curves:

(1) Indifference curves are everywhere dense in that every point in the allocation space of Y and X is on one, and only one, indifference curve. Indifference curves do not intersect.

(2) For positive goods, indifference curves are concave from above.

(3) Increases in consumption of one, or both of these positive goods (X and/or Y) implies a higher utility level and therefore a higher indifference curve.

---

[33] Taking the total differential of U in equation (1), and setting it to zero so utility is constant along the indifference curve, gives $dU = U'_x dX + U'_y dY = 0$. This implies $-U'_x/U'_y = dY/dX$ where dY/dX is the slope of the indifference curve. U'_x is interpreted as the marginal utility of X, and U'_y is the marginal utility of Y. Both marginal utilities are assumed positive so that along the indifference curve, $dY/dX < 0$. The term $-U'_x/U'_y$ is termed the "marginal rate of substitution." As X increases and Y decreases, U'_x/U'_y decreases so that the magnitude of dY/dX decreases, i.e. the indifference curve in Figure 4-4 becomes flatter.

We have already explained theorems 2 and 3. To explain and illustrate theorem 1, consider Figure 4-5. It must be that point "c" yields a higher level of utility than point "a" since point "c" has a larger amount of both goods than "a."

Figure 4-5: Intersecting Indifference Curves Implies a Logical Contradiction

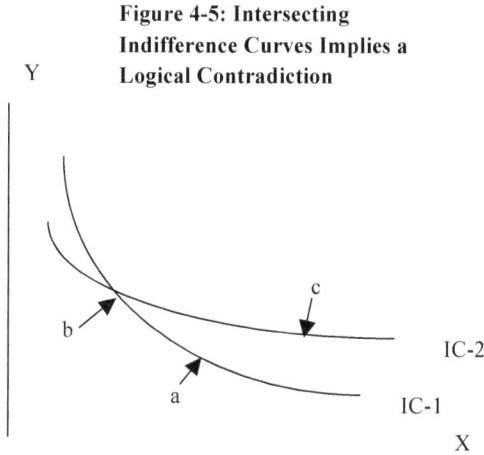

Since the two indifference curves, IC-1 and IC-2, intersect at point "b", however, we are left with the contradiction that the consumer is indifferent between points "a" and "b", and also between points "b" and "c". This is a logical contradiction since "c" must be preferred to "a". For this reason, we must conclude that indifference curves cannot intersect. An intersection would be illogical. Every point in the allocation space can only be on one, and only one, indifference curve.

Figure 4-6: IC-3 Yields Higher Utility than IC-2, which Yields Higher Utility than IC-1

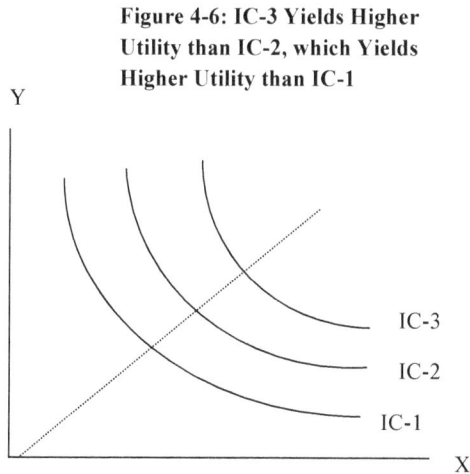

Figure 4-6 illustrates the property that increases in consumption of both goods (outward movement along the ray from the origin) implies movement to higher indifference curves, i.e. the utility level of IC-2 exceeds that of IC-1, and IC-3 exceeds that of IC-2.

Equation (4-2) gives the slope of the indifference curve at any point where MUX is the marginal utility of good X, and MUY is the marginal utility of good Y. The ratio of these marginal utilities is termed *the marginal rate of substitution*. This is a convenient concept, and is depicted by $MRS_{X\ for\ Y}$[34].

Slope of indifference curve $=-MU_X/MU_Y =-MRS_{X\ for\ Y}$ (4-2)

4. Budget Allocation

Indifference curve analysis can be used for exploration of the consumer budget allocation. This poses a methodology we utilize in our latter chapter on market efficiency. To do this, consider the budget constraint represented by equation (4-3) where P_X is the price of X, P_Y the price of Y, and B is the total amount the consumer has to spend on these two goods. This budget is linear in the space of X and Y, and is depicted by Figure 4-7. This budget function acts as a constraint on the consumer's budget allocation in that she/he can afford any point along the function, or any point within the function, but cannot afford any point outside the function. For example, position "d" is outside the constraint and is therefore unaffordable.

$B = P_X X + P_Y Y$ (4-3)

Figure 4-8 combines the consumer's indifference curve map with the budget constraint. In this analysis, we consider four different combinations of goods X and Y, depicted as "a", "b", "c" and "d", three of which are affordable (within or on the budget constraint), and one is not (outside the budget constraint). The consumer would find points "a" and "b" to be suboptimal since she/he can afford to be on a higher indifference curve (a higher level of utility) by selecting affordable point "c". Indeed, although both points "b" and "c" are on the budget constraint, point "c" is on a higher utility level, and so it will be selected as compared to any other point on the budget constraint. At this point, the tangent point, the slope of the

[34] See footnote #3 for the derivation of $MRS_{X\ for\ Y}$.

budget constraint equals the slope of the indifference curve, i.e. equation (4-4). We note that point "d," although it has a higher utility than points "a", "b", or "c", is not affordable. It is outside the budget constraint so it cannot be selected.

Figure 4-7: Consumer Budget Constraint

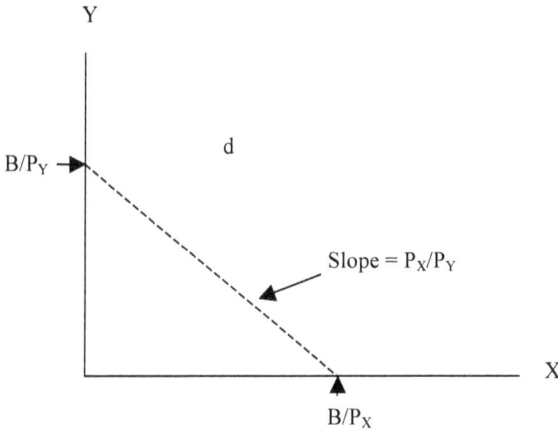

$MRS_{X \ for \ Y} = MU_X/MU_Y = P_X/P_Y$

**Figure 4-8: The Optimal Allocation
of the Consumer Budget**

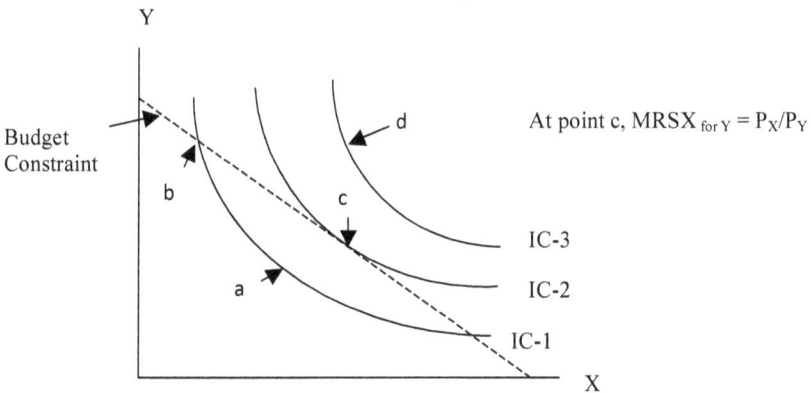

To gain further insight into this optimal point "c", consider rearranging equation (4-4) to obtain (4-5), which also describes this optimal point. Consider the inequality $MU_X/P_X > MU_Y/P_Y$. This

$$MU_X/P_X = MU_Y/P_Y \qquad\qquad (4\text{-}5)$$

inequality would correspond to point "b" in Figure 4-8. By reallocation of $1 of expenditures on Y to gain more of X, the overall utility of the consumer would increase in that the increase in utility per $1 of expenditure on X exceeds the decrease in utility per $1 on Y. Utility increases as a result of this budget reallocation. The consumer would continue to make this reallocation until point "c" is reached, and equality (4-5) holds.

5. The Nature of Goods X and Y

The expenditures on the two goods analyzed above should be considered broadly in that X and Y could be broad categories such as leisure, recreation or savings. As an example, if Y were leisure, then the price of Y, the opportunity cost of leisure, would be the wage rate. An additional hour of leisure would cost an hour lost of income, the hourly wage. Good X could then be interpreted broadly as consumption where PX is the cost of consumption, i.e. its price index. The budget amount B would be the maximum amount of income the consumer could earn. The optimal point of consumption versus leisure would occur at the point where equation (4-6a and b) holds.

$$MRS_{\text{Consuption for Leisure}} = \text{Price Index for Consumption/Wage} \qquad (4\text{-}6a)$$

$$MU_{\text{Consumption}}/P_{\text{Consumption}} = MU_{\text{Leisure}}/\text{Wage} \qquad (4\text{-}6b)$$

Equation (4-6b) is a rearrangement of (4-6b). The more the worker devotes time to employment, the greater the income and consumption. At an optimal point, the allocation of time between leisure and consumption (via hours worked) so as to maximize utility is illustrated by Figure 4-9. The consumer moves along the income budget constraint to maximize utility at C* and L*. The "maximum consumption" is the level achieved with no time allocated to leisure. At a level of zero for income, leisure time is maximized.

Figure 4-9: Income versus Leisure Allocation

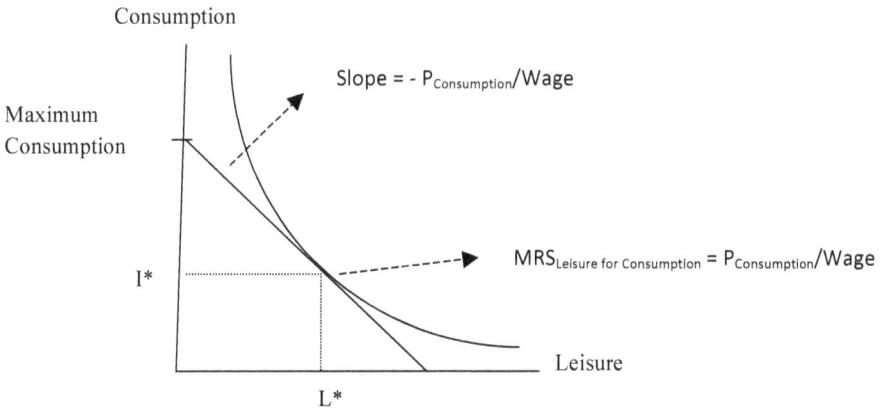

6. The Terms and Benefits of Trade

We might also use indifference curve analysis to examine the benefits derived from and the establishment of the terms of trade between individuals. This analysis is generally termed *the Edgeworth Box analysis*, and it will be utilized extensively when we consider *fairness in negotiation* issues in a later chapter. Envision two people, persons 1 and 2, who consider trading goods A and B. We plot a set of indifference curves for each as shown in Figure 4-10, where the indifference curve map for person 2 is rotated upside down. The rectangle shown for this Edworth Box diagram has dimensions that consist of the sums of both parties' initial endowments of goods A and B. Their initial position before conducting trade is at position "i".

We ask the question, "Is it possible that trade among persons 1 and 2 would be in the interests of both?" Before trade takes place, individual 1 is on indifference curve IC-1a, and would like to move up to a higher indifference curve, say IC-1b. Likewise individual 2 starts at indifference curve IC-2a, and would like to move to a higher utility level, say that depicted by IC-2b. If individual 1 gives up some of good A, and individual 2 gives up some of good B, then trade can move both from position "i" and to position "ii". Both are better off in that the utility levels of both are higher. The slope of the arrow from position "i" to "ii" is called the *terms of the trade* in that it represents the amount of A that individual 1 gives up to obtain the particular amount of B, and vice versa for individual 2.

Figure 4-10: Edgeworth-Box Diagram

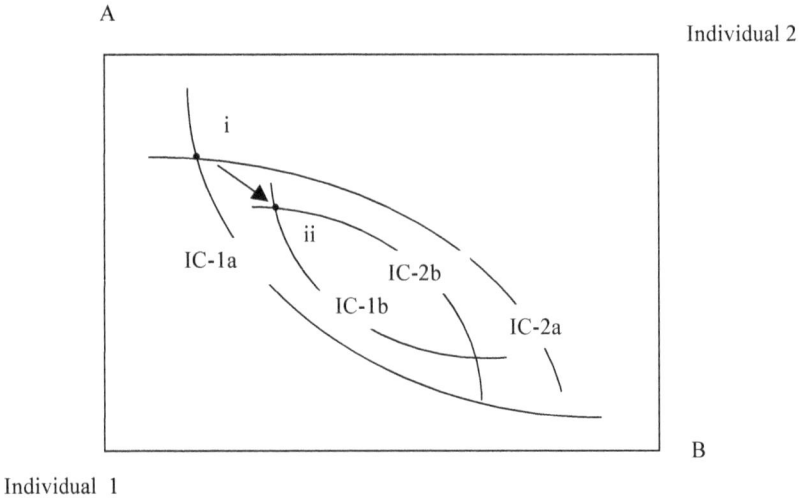

We can call the area between indifference curves IC-1a and IC-2a the *trading space* in that trade that achieves any position between these two initial indifference curves leaves both better off. Any position outside of this interior area would leave one worse off and the other better off. A new position on either of the initial indifference curves would make one better off and leave the other no worse off.

In fact, a position such as "ii" in Figure 4-10 is clearly better, but suboptimal in that further trade could make both still better off. Until the traders reach some position of tangency between their indifference curves, there is further potential trade which would make both better off. This tangency point is illustrated by point "iii" in Figure 4-11.

There are multiple tangency points within the trading space, as illustrated by Figure 4-12. (For purpose of visual ease, Individual 1's indifference curves are depicted as dashed.) If trade reaches any one of these tangency points, further trade will make one of the individuals worse off, although it will benefit the other.

Figure 4-11: Edgeworth-Box Diagram With
Tangency

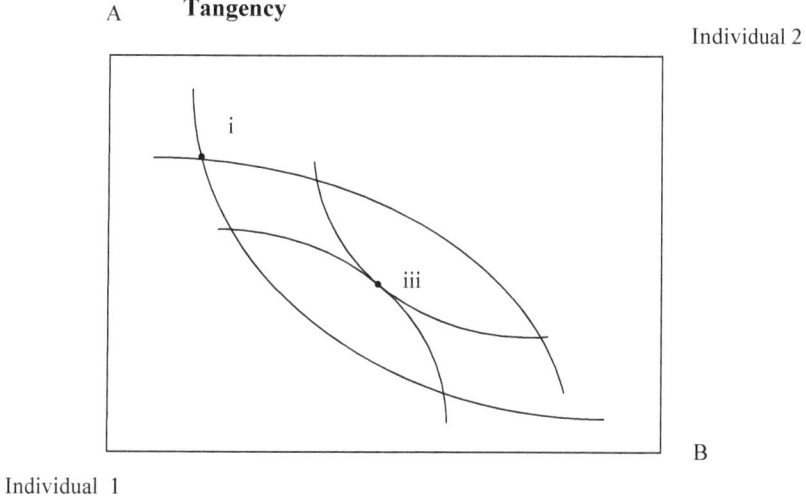

The locus of these tangency points within the trading space is termed *the contract curve*. Once it is reached, further trade that benefits both is not possible. The exact position on the contract curve that is ultimately reached by trade depends upon the relative bargaining abilities of the individuals. Also, this final position determines the terms of trade, i.e. the relative amounts of A and B that are traded.

Figure 4-12: Edgeworth-Box Diagram

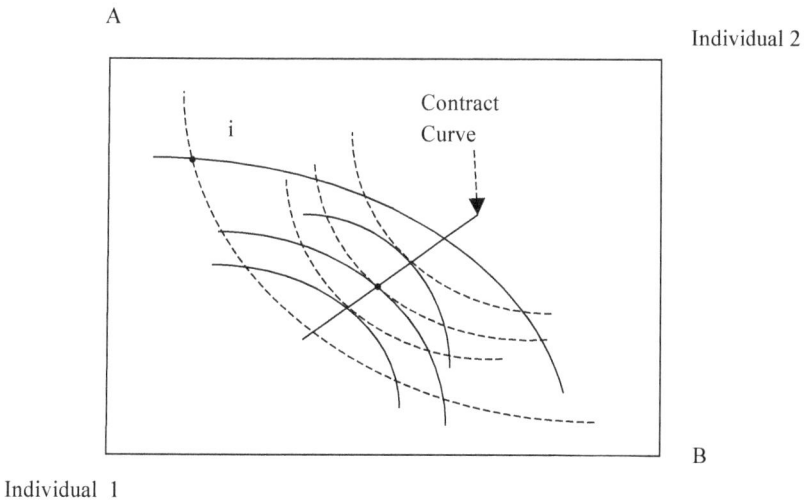

There are certain principles we can discern from the Edgeworth-Box analysis:

(1) Our Edgeworth-Box analysis indicates that free trade between two individuals benefits both. If both did not benefit, then at least one or the other would not engage in the trade. This begs the question, "Is trade always beneficial to everybody?" Could there be third party effects in which others who are not party to the bargaining suffer as a result of the trade, as might be the case with any pollution that is generated by the transaction? Also, could there be fraud involved where one of the trading individuals deceives the other as to the intended results? These questions, and others, are examined in later chapters.

(2) Our Edgeworth-Box analysis also allows us to examine the potential detrimental effects of externally imposed controls on the terms of trade, as might be the case with government imposed price controls. Consider Figure 4-13, where government imposes a control that if any trade does take place, it must be along the ray "i" to "ii." The slope of this ray determines the price of the trade. As we perceive, trading along this ray would make individual 2 better off (move this person to a higher indifference curve), but individual 1 would be worse off. As a result, person 1 would decline any trade at these government imposed terms, and the opportunity to make both better off by moving to a position on the contract curve is lost.

A classic example of the deleterious effects of government price controls is the rent controls imposed on much of New York City. Note that there might be socially desirable benefits of these controls, benefits such as having a more income diverse population within certain neighborhoods, but there are also considerable social costs. If the landlord and tenant were allowed to negotiate, a higher rent might result in capital improvements and better maintenance, a situation where both could benefit. Setting a maximum to the rent, however, prevents this sort of negotiation so that maintenance and improvements are limited. This has often been cited as a cause for deteriorating housing conditions in New York City.

The ethical implications of free-trade versus government controls on trade are rather strong. These are explored in some detail in later chapters.

Figure 4-13: Edgeworth-Box Diagram with Externally Imposed Terms of Trade

A

Individual 2

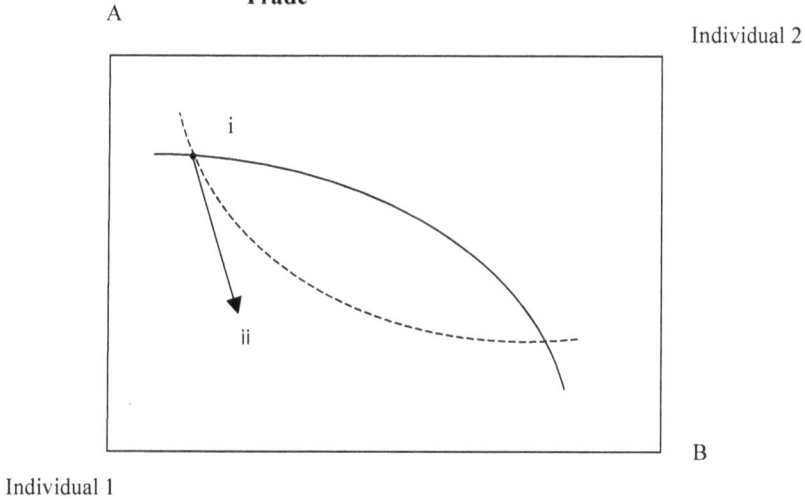

i

ii

B

Individual 1

7. The Social Welfare Function

It might be asserted that the happiness of a society is just the sum of the happiness of all the individuals in that society. This is a Bentham-based utilitarian proposition. Suppose society consisted of only the two individuals analyzed above so that we could find a social utility function by merely summing the utility functions of each. Indeed, we might term this summation *the social welfare function*, although we might also use formulae other than simple summation for this welfare function. Of course, however we define this function, we would wish to use it for policy prescriptions for solving potential problems such as income and wealth distribution, pollution abatement, price controls, etc. The definition of this function is therefore ripe with moral implications, and we will examine these implications in detail in later chapters. Here we examine some of the difficulties associated with forming such a function.

Consider a very primitive society that consists of the individuals 1 and 2 analyzed above. Allow us to consider a simple summation of their respective utility functions for the social welfare function of this society. Furthermore, allow the two goods we wish to examine to be leisure and consumption, where the latter consists of a single homogeneous good that is strictly produced by a team effort on the part of both individuals. This team effort requires that they work simultaneously together at any moment. If one does not contribute at any moment, then there is no production at that time from either. For this reason, both individuals must enjoy identical amounts of leisure, and also have identical times in production.

We also initially allow each individual to have the same utility function for leisure and consumption. The social welfare function is therefore just twice the individual's level of utility. Both are depicted in Figure 4-14.

Figure 4-14: Utility and Social Welfare
Functions for Two Individual Societies

Consumption-Production

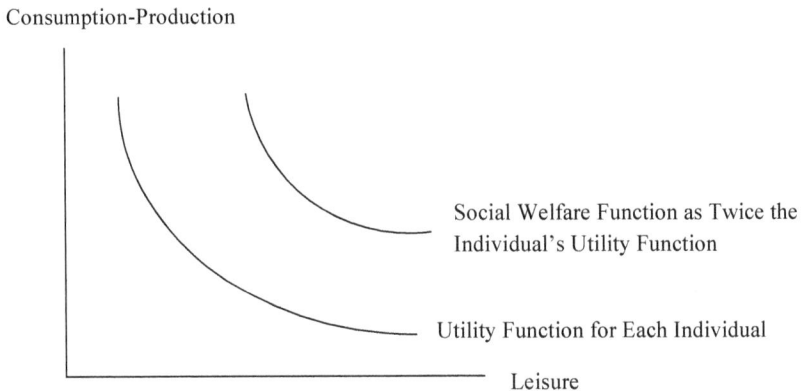

Social Welfare Function as Twice the Individual's Utility Function

Utility Function for Each Individual

Leisure

To further our two-person analysis, envision a production constraint that specifies the tradeoff of production versus leisure. To keep things simple, envision a production function where for each hour spent by our team of individuals in producing, they generate one more unit of consumption. Hence the tradeoff is one for one. Whatever is produced is to be divided up equally. This production tradeoff function is shown in Figure 4-15 along with both the social welfare function and the individuals' utility functions. The optimal amounts for each to consume is shown as C*, and the optimal amount of leisure for each is L*. This occurs because each of the two individuals have identical utility functions. Our social welfare optimality is at 2C*, and 2L*.

Figure 4-15: Social Welfare Function,
Production and Leisure

Consumption-Production

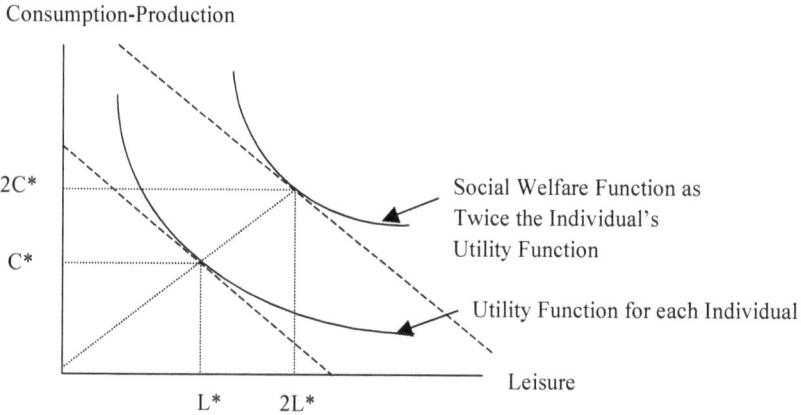

$2C^*$ .... Social Welfare Function as
Twice the Individual's
Utility Function

C^* .... Utility Function for each Individual

Leisure

L^* $2L^*$

In this analysis, the social welfare is easy to discern. Our two individuals have the same preferences for consumption and leisure, and production is team oriented with each putting forth identical efforts. Consider however, Figure 4-16 where the indifference curves indicate that individual 1 prefers more consumption and less leisure, while individual 2 prefers the opposite. As in our above analysis, the social welfare function is defined as the sum of our two individuals' utility functions. Given the one-for-one tradeoff of production versus leisure, individual 1 prefers C1 and L1, while individual 2 prefers C2 and L2. The problem is that these heterogeneous utility functions and production function do not allow these combinations given our team production function. Our individuals must bargain, and achieve a position on the contract curve that specifies the homogeneous amounts of leisure to be enjoyed by each, and the production level to be divided by each. Heterogeneous preferences do not allow an easily formed social welfare function.

This problem of heterogeneous preferences, but with team production, highlights a typical problem in welfare analysis, i.e. as a team, society produces *public goods.* These are goods available to all, but are either produced by society, or in some cases such as clean air and water, their provision are assured by society through its laws and regulations [35]. These goods tend to not be entirely subject to market based production, but must be controlled by, if not provided by, society through government action. Since all must typically participate in their production, perhaps through tax expenditures or some other regulation, but preferences for their consumption differ, a political problem exists concerning their provision.

Figure 4-16: Utility and Social Welfare Functions for Two Individuals with Different Utility Functions

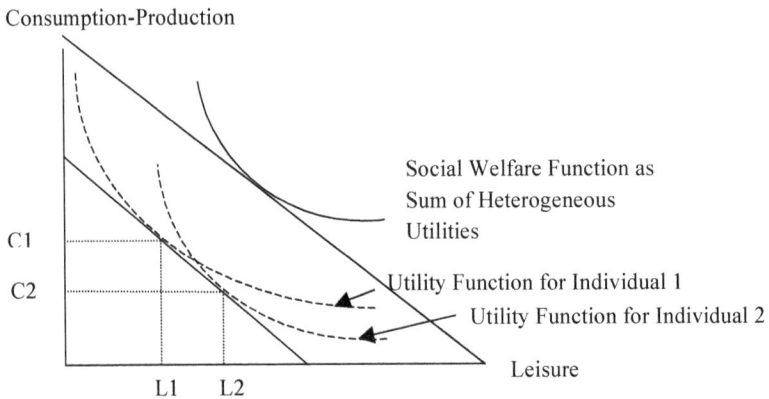

For example, park-like recreation lands are provided through the public domain. People might enjoy these by varying degrees according to taste. It may be hoped that a variety of different public goods are provided, even a variety of different sorts of parks, and it is hoped that although all have different preferences for enjoyment of one versus the other, in the last analysis, the entire package is enjoyed equally by each individual, some enjoying one thing and others enjoying another. It should be therefore obvious that there are strong social welfare implications associated with the mix and extent of the public goods provided.

For private goods, i.e. those goods that can be enjoyed in isolation by single individuals or groups, the marketplace can respond through the profit motive and the price rationing system. Producers who seek to profit provide the goods to those

[35] *Pure public goods* are those for which if one person can enjoy it, so can all people. Clean air and police protection are good examples.

willing to pay for them. In the absence of externalities such as pollution, this free market generation of goods will enhance welfare[36], but many valuable goods are public goods. There are strong ethical implications associated with their provision especially in the context of a society with income and wealth inequality. This problem is explored in much more detail in later chapters.

8. Expected Value and Risk

Risk, and who bears and manages it, is another problem that is full of social welfare and ethical implications. Generally, risk is considered a negative good. We should recognize that choices in the real world, especially choices involving moral questions, often involve uncertainties or risky situations. We must make a decision, but we do not know the final outcome with certainty. We have an expectation of an outcome, and an assessment of the risk associated with obtaining it.

A good example of the ethical implications of risk concerns problems involved with product safety. We might want to produce a product that would never harm a consumer. This might, however, be impossible. A glass container, however strong, might break and harm somebody. A metal container might also break and harm someone. The contained good might also be healthful if used in moderation, but harmful otherwise. We can only form an expectation of the result, but we must also properly measure the risk associated with obtaining this expectation.

The appendix to this chapter reviews the mathematical-statistical measures utilized for expectation and risk, i.e. the expected value and variance measures. Variance is generally used as a measure of risk, and it can be considered a negative good. These formulae are utilized here and in later chapters. Those in need of reinforcement in the utilization of this elementary mathematics should review this appendical material before proceeding to the next section.

9. Notions of Risk Aversion

Consider the utility of wealth where U(W) is the utility function, and W is the wealth level. Further assume that this utility function is concave from below as illustrated by Figure 4-17, i.e. there is diminishing marginal utility to wealth. Allow W4 – W3 = W3 – W2 = W2 – W1 so that as we move from left to right on

---

[36] This does not say that such a provision maximizes social welfare. A variety of interferences in the free market system may be justified in that they enhance societal welfare. Monopoly regulation provides one such example.

the wealth scale, the increments in wealth are equal. We note, however, that utility increases but by decreasing increments. We suspect that this is the situation for most (normal) people. This is what we mean by a "concave utility of wealth" function, i.e. we have diminishing marginal utility to wealth. Wealthy people, we expect, do enjoy further additions to their wealth, but not as much as poor people.

Figure 4-17: Concave Utility of Wealth Function

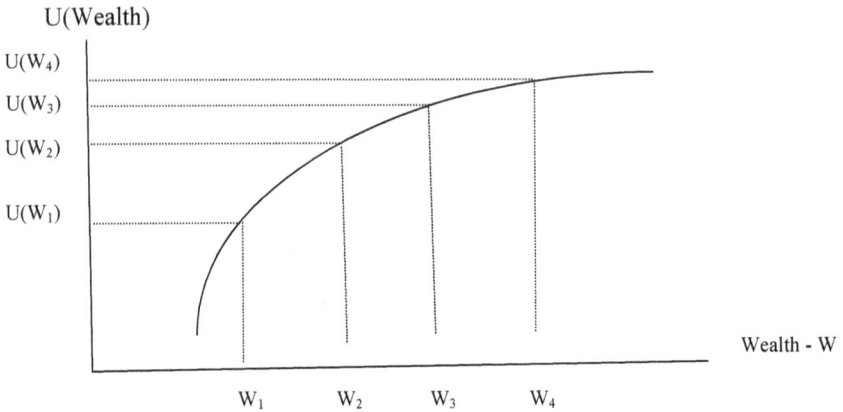

Allow us to consider gambles where the odds of winning and losing are 50%–50%, as in a coin-flip bet. A gamble of this sort is said to be *fair*, or *actuarially neutral* if the amount to be won equals the amount to be lost, i.e. the expected value of the gamble is 0. People with concave utility functions for wealth will not accept fair bets. They are said to be *risk averse*, and this risk aversion results from concave utility functions for wealth.

To establish this notion of risk aversion, we need two axioms (propositions that appear self evident).

Axiom (1): More wealth is better than less:For any levels of wealth $W_0 < W_1 < W_2$, then $U(W_2) > U(W_1) > U(W_0)$.

Axiom(2): Fair utility: For a binomial gamble of 50%–50% odds involving a wealth loss of B or win of A, where A > 0, and B > 0, then the individual is indifferent between taking the gamble or staying at initial wealth W0 if the utility to be gained equals the utility to be lost as in (4-7).

$$U(W_0) - U(W_0 - B) = U(W_0 + A) - U(W_0) \qquad (4-7)$$

Axiom 2 states that the gamble must be fair utility wise in order for indifference. This is illustrated by Figure 4-18 where the possible increment to utility of $U(W_0 + A) - U(W_0)$ equals the possible decrement of $U(W_0) - U(W_0 - B)$.

Definition of risk aversion: Axioms 1 and 2 imply risk aversion if $A > B$.

Note that (4-8) algebraically follows from (4-7). In (4-8), the right side is the *expected utility* of the 50%–50% gamble for stakes A and B. For indifference, this expected utility must equal the utility of initial wealth, W0, with certainty.

$$U(W_0) = (1/2)U(W_0 + A) + (1/2)U(W_0 - B) \qquad (4-8)$$

Figure 4-19 illustrates this expected utility notion presented by equation (4-8).

Figure 4-18: Sweetening the Winning Stakes by A – B

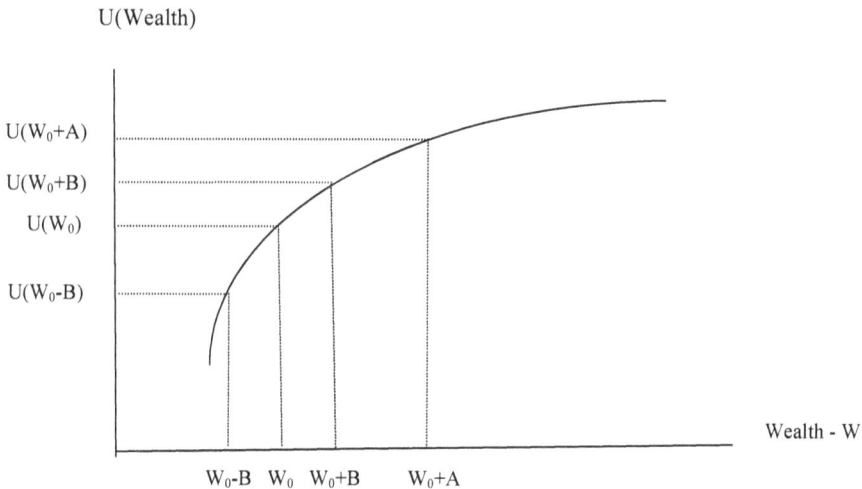

Note that (4-8) is a simple algebraic derivation from (4-7). The expected utility of the gamble follows directly from the *fair utility axiom* as expressed by equation (4-7). Expected utility is in fact embedded into *axiom 2*. This is the simplest derivation of expected utility possible and is derived from coin-flip type gambles [37].

Figure 4-19: Expected Utility and the Markowitz Risk Premium of $W^* - W_0$

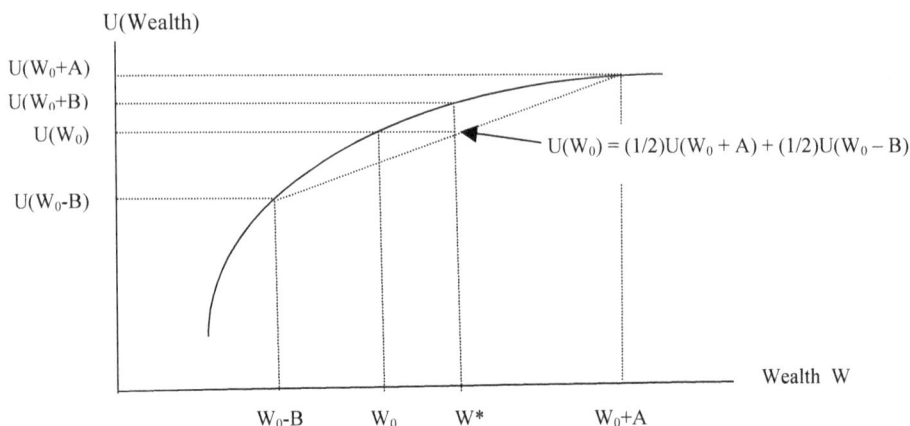

10. Expected Utility and a Simple In-the-Large Risk Premium

Figure 4-19 is adequate to illustrate the expected utility notion. It can also be used to illustrate the Markowitz risk premium. Given the 50%–50% odds, the expected wealth level W^*, as given by (4-9), and it also lies at the expected utility point. It is an elementary geometric exercise to show that this intersection must occur as indicated in Figure 4-19. [38]

$$W^* = (1/2)(W_0 + A) + (1/2)(W_0 - B) \tag{4-9}$$

To derive the Markowitz in-the-large risk premium, one need only redefine the level for initial wealth to W^* rather than W0. The individual should then be forced to undertake the binomial gamble of being at either W0 + A, or W0 – B each with 50% probability. Since our initial wealth is W^*, then this gamble is actuarially neutral since $W^*- (W0-B) = (W0+A) – W^*$ with the left side being

[37] The derivation when probability distributions are continuous, and also when multiple goods are at stake, is much more complex. See Haley and Schall (1973).
[38] Note that (4-8) and (4-9) require this intersection.

the possible amount to be lost, and the right side being the possible amount to be won. [39] The right side of equation (4-8) still measures the expected utility of this gamble, but W0, being on the left side of (4-8), now becomes the certainty-equivalent wealth level for this gamble. By certainty-equivalent wealth we mean the level with certainty that yields the same utility as the expected utility of the gamble with expected wealth W*.

As indicated, W0 allows the expected utility, given by (4-8), to equal the utility of the actuarially neutral gamble of starting at initial wealth W* and resulting at either W0+A or W0-B. The Markowitz risk premium measures the difference between the expected wealth (W* for this actuarial-neutral gamble) and the certainty equivalent wealth (W0 in this example). As a result, (4-10) measures the Markowitz risk premium π associated with this gamble given that W* is the new initial wealth. Further insights into this risk-related measure is given in Appendix B.

$$\pi = W^* - W_0 = (1/2)(W_0 + A) + (1/2)(W_0 - B) - W_0 = (A - B)/2 \qquad (4\text{-}10)$$
$$= \text{expected wealth} - \text{certainty-equivalent wealth}$$

11. A Concavity Measure, Risk, and the Risk Premium

For the 50%–50% gamble examined above, the standard deviation is given by (4-11). [40]

$$\sigma = (A+B)/2 \qquad (4\text{-}11)$$

Given (4-10) and (4-11), the relation between π and σ is given by (4-12), which has a particular interpretation with respect to the concavity of the utility function.

$$\pi = \sigma(A - B)/(A + B) \qquad (4\text{-}12)$$

The difference A – B is the amount that must be added to the winning stakes in order to induce indifference between the individual either taking the gamble or remaining at initial wealth W0 with certainty. The sum of A + B is the spread between the gamble's outcomes. The ratio

(A-B)/(A+B) is a natural concavity measure in that the more concave the utility function is, the greater the amount that must be added to the winning stake as

---

[39] Equation (4-9) requires $2W^* = W_0 + A + W_0 - B$ which results in $W^* \cdot (W_0 - B) = (W_0 + A) - W^*$.

[40] Note that $Var(W) = (\frac{1}{2})\{W_0 + A - (W_0 + (A-B)/2)\}^2 + (\frac{1}{2})\{W_0 - B - (W_0 + (A-B)/2)\}^2 = (\frac{1}{4})(A+B)^2$.

a portion of the total stakes. This ratio is always positive for a risk averse individual (by the definition above, A > B for risk aversion).

12. Numerical Illustrations with Revealed Preference

For an illustration of our risk premium analysis, assume an individual's utility function is logarithmic where U = ln(W), and assume that the initial wealth is $100 [41]. Also assume a 50%–50% gamble with losing stakes of B as given in Table 4-1. We envision asking this individual for the corresponding levels for A that leave the individual indifferent about staying at the initial wealth level of $100, or undertaking the gamble. Assuming the specification of the logarithmic utility function, the necessary values for A are also presented in Table 1. Given the values for A and B, then the resulting values for the risk premium π, the risk level measured by σ, and the concavity measure (A-B)(A+B), are also presented.

Table 4-1: Values for π Given U = ln(W), and $W_0 = \$100^1$

B	A	Π	Σ	(A-B)/(A+B)
$ 2.00	$ 2.04	$ 0.02	$ 2.02	.0100
10.00	11.11	0.56	10.56	.0530
20.00	25.00	2.50	22.50	.1111
40.00	66.67	13.33	53.34	.2500

^{1} $\pi = (A - B)/2$; $\sigma = (A - B)/(A + B)$

In Table 4-1, the initial wealth level stays at $100, but as the losing stake B increases, we note that the risk premium also increases, and more importantly for our analysis, the concavity measure also increases. For each point in Table 4-1, equation (4-8) is maintained at

U(W0) = U($100). It is appropriate, therefore, to interpret each point as being along a constant utility indifference curve in the space of π and σ. In addition, the concavity measure π/σ = (A-B)/(A+B) is the slope of the ray from the origin to the particular point along the indifference curve. As Table 4-1 shows, the increasing slope illustrates that the indifference curve is concave from above. This is illustrated by Figure 4-19.

---

[41] U = ln(W) exhibits positive but diminishing marginal utility.

Figure 4-20: Indifference Curve for EU = U(W₀) = U($100) With Increasing Stakes B

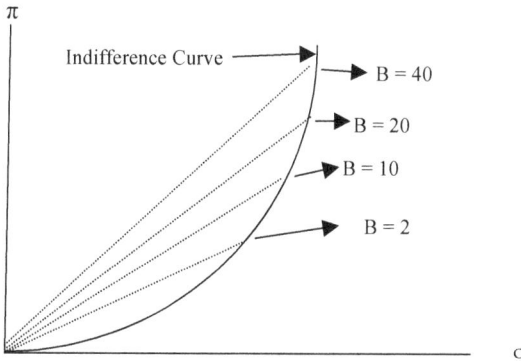

It is important to note that a series of revealed preference questions can elicit data such as that presented by Table 4-1, but without the specification of the individual's initial wealth or utility function. This can be conducted as an exercise by asking appropriate questions. One need only ask a selected individual, "Given a 50%–50% gamble where you could lose $2, how much must the winning stakes be in order to induce you to undertake the gamble?" [42] Once this answer is elicited (the value for A in Table 1), then the losing stakes can be varied, and for each elicited pair for A and B, equations (4-10), (4-11) and (4-12) can be used to complete the table. Knowledge of W0 and the functional form for U are not necessary. The consumer's response implicitly incorporates this information. [43]

Since in Figure 4-20, is the expected value of the gamble, we can reinterpret the indifference curve depicted as in Figure 4-20. Here the indifference curves shown exhibit an increase in utility as E(Wealth) increases while holding σ constant as in moving from a point on IC-1 to

IC-2. This analysis can be utilized in later chapters when we consider bargaining over who bears the risk associated with various contracts.

---

[42] It may be necessary to try more than one consumer in order to find one that is risk averse.

[43] As an econometric exercise, one can use least squares to fit a particular functional form, such as the logarithmic, quadratic or exponential utility functions through the elicited data.

Figure 4-21: Indifference curves for Risk

E(Wealth)

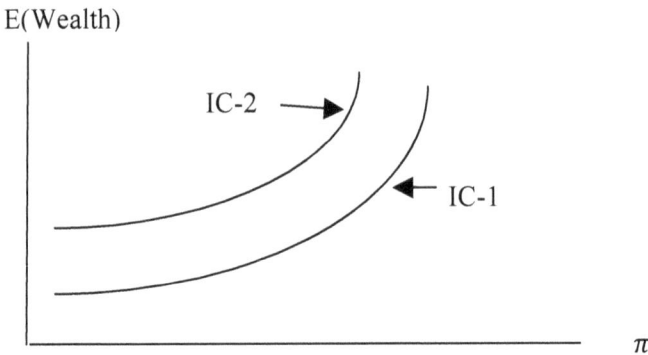

π

Review Questions

- (1) What are the three versions of *utilitarianism*? What is the fundamental Western philosophical objection to *utilitarianism*?

(2) What are the problems with the *utilitarian* theories of the social welfare benefits of income inequality?

(3) What are *positive goods* and *negative goods*? Explain the notion of *positive but diminishing marginal utility*?

(4) What is the difference between *complimentary* and *substitute* goods?

(5) What are the rules of *indifference curves*?

(6) Use the concept of the MRS$_{\text{x for y}}$ to explain the concavity of indifference curves for positive goods?

(7) Explain how if MUX/Px > MUY/PY then the consumer will reallocate her budget so that equation (4-5) is established?

(8) Fully explain why equation (4-6) must hold?

(9) Using the Edgeworth-Box diagram, indicate those trades that benefit both individuals, and also those trades that benefit only one?

(10) Explain the nature of the contract curve? Explain why once on the contract curve, further trading must hurt at least one individual?

(11) Does free trade between two individuals always benefit social welfare in a utilitarian sense?

(12) Use the Edgeworth-Box analysis to explain the implications of government control of the terms of trade?

(13) What are public goods? How do they differ from private goods? Why do public goods cause political problems involving social welfare and their provision?

(14) Explain how society's production of private and public goods differ especially in their ethical and social welfare implications?

(15) What do we mean by risk aversion? How do we measure expected utility for coin-flip type gambles?

(16) Explain the *Markowitz risk premium* for a coin-flip gamble? Must this always be a positive amount if the individual is risk averse?

(17) Compose a table similar to 4-1 but with $U = W_{1/2}$? Does this utility of wealth function exhibit risk aversion?

Appendix A: Probability Distributions and Their Parameters

The probability distribution shown in Figure 4-21 is the "normal" distribution, a distribution frequently encountered. Values for the variable X are measured on the horizontal axis, and the probabilities of obtaining these values are measured on the vertical axis. The parameter termed the "expected value" is a measure of central tendency, and is symbolized by $E[X]$. This distribution, like many others, is a symmetric distribution in that the left half of the distribution is a mirror image of the right half. For symmetric distributions, the expected value is in the center. Also, for the normal distribution, the expected value has the highest probability associated with it.

For symmetric distributions, if one marks off equal distances above and below the expected value, for example the values $E(X) + c$, and $E(X) - c$ where c is just some fixed number, then the probability in the tails are equal. This stems from the "mirror image" nature of symmetric distributions referred to above.

Figure 4-21: The Normal Distribution

Probability of X

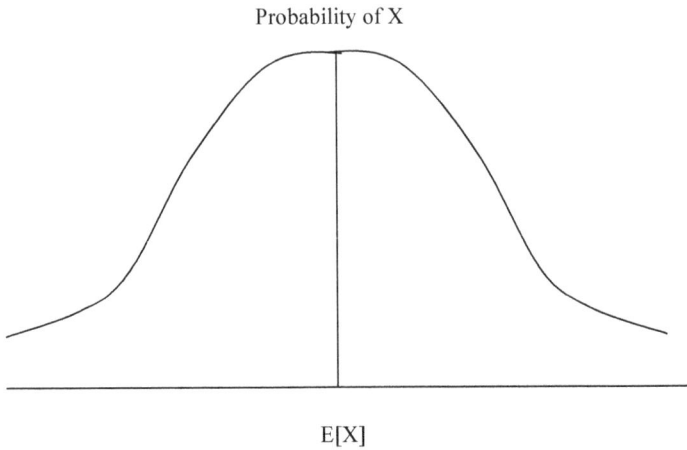

E[X]

The *variance* of a probability distribution is its "measure of dispersion about the mean." The variance is a measure of how wide the distribution is spread. It is usually symbolized by the square of the Greek letter sigma, σ^2, or by Var[X]. The standard deviation is the square root of the variance, and is symbolized by s. For the normal distribution, σ is the distance between the expected value and the inflection point, the point where the curvature of the probability function changes. For most distributions, the larger the variance, the smaller the probability associated with the expected value.

Probability distributions can be categorized into two types: discrete distributions and continuous distributions. Variables that behave according to the former can only take on certain "discrete" values such as 1, 2, 3, ... Such a distribution, for example, could be generated by the throwing of a die. The continuous distribution is characterized by the variable being capable of taking on any values over the range of the distribution, no matter how many decimal places are included in the values. The normal distribution is a continuous distribution. In either case, the sum of probabilities for all possible outcomes must be one. For the continuous case, this means that the area under the distribution curve, usually termed the *density function*, must equal one [44]. A random variable is defined as one that takes on numerical values according to some probability distribution that is the value depends upon the outcome of some chance event such as the roll of a die, the future state of the economy, or other uncertain event. Probabilities can be assigned to these outcomes.

Allow X to be a random variable that behaves according to the probability distribution indicated in the first three columns of Table 4-2. For this distribution, X takes on the values of Xi, and these values depend upon "state" i. This state could refer to economic conditions such as good, bad, or average economy, or it could refer to some other determining factor. The probabilities associated with state i are given in the table. Note that the sum of the probabilities for all of the states must be one as shown.

Table 4-2: Hypothetical Probability Distribution

i	Prob i	X_i	X_i * Prob i	$(X_i - E[X_i])^2$ * Prob i
1	.2	10	2	20
2	.6	20	12	0
3	.2	30	6	20
	1.0		E[X]=20	$\sigma^2= 40$
				$\sigma = 6.32$

The formulas for the expected value of X, and its variance, are given by equations (4-13) and (4-14), respectively [45]. The expected value, sometimes called the *mean*, is calculated by multiplying each value for Xi by its probability, and then summing across states. These calculations are shown in the third column of Table 4-2.

[44] Using integral calculus, if f(x) gives the probability of obtaining x, f(x) is the density function. If the range of x is given 1 ≤ x ≤ h, $\int^h f(x)dx = 1$. For the discrete case, $\sum f(x) = 1$.

[45] Equations (1) and (2) are applicable for discrete distributions. For continuous distributions, the expected value is given by E[X]= $\int^h xf(x)dx$, where f(x) is the density function for x, and 1 ≤ x ≤ h. Also, Var[X]= $\int^h (x-E[X])^2 f(x)dx$.

$$E[X] = \sum_{i=1}^{n} X_i * \text{Prob } i \tag{4-13}$$

$$Var[X] = \sum_{i=1}^{n} (X_i - E[X])^2 * \text{Prob } i \tag{4-14}$$

$$= E[(X - E[X])^2]$$

The variance of X, often symbolized by σX^2, is also an expected value, i.e. the expected value of the square of the deviation of X from its mean. Calculations for the variance are shown in column four of the table. Of course, the standard deviation of X, symbolized by s, is just the square root of the variance.

$$\overline{X} = \sum_{t=1}^{n} X_t /n \tag{4-15}$$

$$\sigma_X^2 = \sum_{t=1}^{n} (X_t - \overline{X})^2 /(n-1) \tag{4-16}$$

Suppose that historical or other data is available for X. This sample data can be used to estimate E[X] and Var[X] even if no probability information is available concerning the possible future for X. To estimate these parameters, it is necessary to assume that the future will reflect the past observations available, and that the probability distribution will reflect the relative frequency of the observed values for X. The estimates computed from this data are termed *sample estimates*, and are given by equations (4-15) and (4-16), where there are n historical observations of the values for X. The sample estimate for the expected value is termed the *sample mean*, and is symbolized as . The sample variance is also symbolized by $\sigma^X 2$.

A third statistic of great importance to risk analysis is the covariance of one random variable with another. Covariance is also an expected value, the expected cross-product of the deviation of one random variable form its mean with the deviation of the other random variable from its mean. The purpose is to measure the co-movement of one random variable with another, i.e. to measure the extent that they increase coincidentally with each other, or move inversely. The formula for the covariance of X with Y, symbolized by cov[X,Y], or σX,Y, is given by equation (4-17). [46]

$$\text{cov}[X,Y] = \sum_{i=1}^{n} (X_i - E[X])(Y_i - E[Y]) * \text{Prob } i \qquad (4\text{-}17)$$

Table 4-3 gives an example of the calculation of cov[X,Y]. Notice that while variance, being the sum of squared terms, must always be positive, covariance can be either positive or negative. It is negative if the random variables move inversely with each other. The probability distribution that describes two random variables that are jointly related in some way is termed a *joint probability distribution*. Independent random variables, however, are those unrelated to each other in the sense that their covariance is zero.

The sample estimate for a covariance can also be calculated from paired historical observations of X and Y. The estimate is symbolized by sX,Y, and it is given by equation (4-18).

$$\sigma_{X,Y} = \sum_{i=1}^{n} (X_i - E[X])(Y_i - E[Y])/(n-1) \qquad (4\text{-}18)$$

Table 4-3: Hypothetical Joint Probability Distribution

i	X_i	Y_i	Prob i	(X-E[X])(Y-E[Y]) * Prob I
1	10	25	.2	-10
2	20	20	.6	0
3	30	15	.2	-10
	E[X]=20	E[Y]=20		$\sigma_{X,Y}$ = -20

[46] For continuous distributions where f(x,y) is the joint probability distribution, cov[X,Y] = ∫∫ (X-E[X])(Y-E[Y])f(x,y)dxdy.

Review Questions:

(1) Suppose a normal distribution has an expected value of D. if the probability of obtaining a value greater than D+d is ε, what is the probability of obtaining a value less than D-d? What is the probability of obtaining a value between D and D+d?

(2) Given the data below, calculate E[X], E[Y], σx^2 and $\sigma x,y$. If the probability information were not given, but the observations represented sample data, how would the parameters of the distribution be estimated?

State	X_i	Y_i	Prob i
1	10	15	.2
2	20	20	.6
3	30	25	.2

Appendix B

The value π, i.e. the Markowitz risk premium, also has an additional interpretation that applies to the case when the initial wealth is W0 rather than W*. If the individual starts at initial wealth W0 (rather than W*), and undertakes the 50%–50% gamble for either +A or –B, then given (4-10), π becomes the expected payoff for the gamble. [47]

W* becomes the expected resulting wealth that is necessary to induce indifference between taking the gamble or not. The individual is indifferent between either staying at the initial wealth W0 with certainty, or accepting the gamble with resulting expected wealth of W* > W0.

In the above analysis, π can therefore be interpreted as either (i) the expected value of the actuarially non-neutral gamble if W0 is the initial wealth, or π can be interpreted as (ii) the Markowitz risk premium for the actuarially neutral gamble if W* is the initial wealth. It is shown below that both interpretations (i) and (ii) are useful for exposition depending upon the context of the problem examined.

---

[47] Note that $E(W) = (\frac{1}{2})(W_0+A) + (\frac{1}{2})(W_0-B) = W_0 + (A-B)/2 = W_0 + \pi$ where (4-10) defines π.

Chapter V

---— ❈ —---

KANT'S CATEGORICAL IMPERATIVE
AND MORAL MAXIMS

Chapter Abstract: *The Enlightenment philosophy of Kant is reviewed along with his use of the categorical imperative. As required in Kantian philosophy, this imperative is used to derive a number of suggested practical moral maxims that are relevant for managerial leadership and firm efficiency. The role of reflective thought in establishing and maintaining these maxims is emphasized. The categorization of these maxims into associated perfect and imperfect duties is reviewed so that absolute prohibitions can be understood as distinctly different from duties with practical limitations.*

1. Enlightenment Philosophy

In Chapter III, we reviewed the Greek-philosophic foundation of intuitionism. In this Platonic-Socratic approach, the individual uses rational inquiry to discern the transcendent moral-truths that become applicable as axiomatic guides for behavior. Kant used and extended this ancient Greek vision. He argued, however, that individuals should bring their intuitive axioms to the filter of democracy where discussion can separate the wheat from the chaff, the good from the not-so-good, and the practical from the impractical ideas. Kant suggested, however, a starting guide termed the *categorical imperative*. This guide is examined here along with a series of possible moral maxims of practical importance to management.

This Kantian approach is best viewed as a culmination of an age of discovery and progress. The historical period termed the "European Enlightenment," or as it is often called the "Age of Reason," is a seventeenth and eighteenth century phenomenon that affected every aspect of European life. It included significant scientific discoveries:

- Galileo (1564-1642) discovered some principles of gravitation, and also by applying the telescope to observations of the solar system, he discovered the moons of Jupiter and the rings of Saturn,

- Copernicus (1473-1543) established that the sun is at the center of the solar system,

- Newton (1642-1727), established the principles of light composition, the elliptical orbits of the planets around the sun as based upon the principles of gravitation, the principle of the conservation of energy, and principles of motion.

- During this historical period the first major modern advances in philosophy also occurred, the first advances since the Scholastic Era.

- Descartes (1596-1650) not only reestablished physics with a mathematical foundation (as with some ancient Greek physicists such as Archimedes), but also articulated the methods for how we establish knowledge and judge what is real.

- Rousseau (1712-1718) explored the *social contract* as the basis for establishing liberty and equality.

- Hume (1711-1776), the ultimate empiricist, exposed the limitations of reason for making the judgments we do make.

This enlightenment period is often contrasted with the European "Middle Ages" that supposedly exhibited superstition and irrationality. Immanuel Kant was one of the last, and the greatest of the enlightenment philosophers. It is this movement, or age, that established the foundations of modern Western philosophy, especially in ethics.

The German philosopher Immanuel Kant's (1721 – 1804) influence on this Enlightenment era of Western civilization can hardly be overestimated. As such, he is one of the major figures in history. He sought to restore ethics to a non-religious foundation as in the Greek philosophy of Plato and Aristotle. Given the religious conflicts and wars in Europe that occurred in the two centuries prior to Kant, he saw this non-religious foundation as necessary for human advancement particularly in the context of the democratic political movements of his era. It should be noted that Kant was a deeply religious man who did not seek to force his religious notions on others [48].

Kant's moral philosophy is spread among several significant works which include *Critique of Pure Reason* (1781, 1787), *Fundamental Principles of the Metaphysics of Morals* (1785), *Critique of Practical Reason* (1788), *Religion Within the Limits of Reason Alone* (1793), and several others. [These writings are rather ponderous and hence difficult, but significant selections can be found in *The Basic Writings of Kant* (2001), edited by Allen Wood. Kant's writings are so often referred to in philosophy that, as in the works of Plato, there is a standard reference methodology, one that is used here.]

Perhaps the basic theme of the enlightenment was declared by Kant in *Answer to the Question: What is Enlightenment?* (1784, 8:36 and 8:37):

Enlightenment is man's exit from his self-incurred minority. Minority is the incapacity to use one's intelligence without the guidance of another. Such minority is self-incurred if it is not caused by lack of intelligence, but by lack of determination and courage to use one's intelligence without being guided by another. Have the courage to use your own intelligence! is therefore the motto of the enlightenment.

All that is required for this enlightenment is freedom; and particularly the least harmful of all that may be called freedom, namely, the freedom for man to make public use of his reason in all matters. (Underline added.)

The development of and use of this "intelligence" is the purpose of our education, particularly of higher education. We seek here to partly show how this "intelligence" should be used in business as it pertains to ethics. We state "partly show"

---

[48] The "30 Years War," 1618 – 1648, was fought largely in Germany and involved most of the European powers. It was initiated by religious conflict (Protestant versus Catholic), and involved the destruction of entire regions.

because we recognize the considerable breadth and depth of this task, and that our efforts can only be partially successful in even exploring this breadth, let alone exploring the depth of each subject within ethics. Nonetheless, we suspect that the student who is successful in exploring this text on ethics will conclude that considerable progress is made through understanding the material presented, especially the material concerning Kant's philosophy, and that of his modern extenders, John Rawls (1921-2005) and Hanna Arendt (1906-1975).

As stated above, the "Enlightenment" formed the basis of modern Western philosophy. The leading doctrines of the Enlightenment age are[49]:

1) *Reason is mankind's central capacity. It enables people to think and act accordingly.*

This places the emphasis on the individual, not the society. People are not seen as mere contributors to society. This particular view is explored in detail in a latter chapter.

2) *People are by nature rational and good, although notions of evil, such as those in religion, are accepted as possible. Kant argued that it must be possible for evil to be overcome by thinking people.*

As we shall explore in a latter chapter, the philosopher Hanna Arendt argues that to prevent evil, people must exhibit the "noble nature" of a willingness to argue rationally, and with logical reflection, in public in order to prevent evil from permeating society. This is especially true when we consider simple bureaucratic applications of codes of conduct that are applied without rational reflection.

3) *Both individuals and humanity can progress.*

According to enlightenment philosophy, society can progress only through the progress of individuals. This contradicts fascistic or communistic philosophy where people's political consciousness must be manipulated by an elite group of leaders.

[49] This review is based upon M.J. Inwood (1995, p. 236-237).

4) All people are equal as to their rationality, and therefore must be viewed as equal before the law.

This certainly contradicts any elitist approach to philosophy. It is necessary that all people be considered as rational as a pre-condition for a democratic approach to governance.

5) Other religions and ways of life must be tolerated.

The "30 years war" proceeded the enlightenment period in Europe. This violence prone period saw religious wars sweep across the continent with almost one-third of Europeans being killed. It is not surprising that enlightenment philosophers would attempt to eliminate this strife by an appeal to non-religious reason.

6) Beliefs must be accepted only on the basis of reason, not on the basis of authority.

The essence of this philosophy is that reasoned discourse, as argued by individuals in public life, is necessary for democracy, which is in turn necessary to prevent the violent religious conflicts that preceded this period.

7) The purpose of education is to disseminate knowledge, not to mould feelings or character.

The Enlightenment exhibited an explosion of scientific, political and philosophical knowledge. It was contrary to any overly narrow religious education that is based solely upon the molding of character. Ethics, in particular, came to be based on logic, not any appeal to religious or other authority. [50]

Reasoned reflection about the moral problems we face is a fundamental duty in the Enlightenment vision. Reasoned reflection is the very basis of the Greek origins of Western ethical philosophy. In this sense, Kant's philosophy builds upon the Socratic-Platonic foundation. It is argued below that Kant's *categorical imperative*, however, provide a focus from which reason can deduce practical *maxims* for which we have a *duty* to follow. It is important to note

---

[50] One should reflect on Galileo's facing the Roman Catholic Church's "Inquisition" in 1633 for arguing that the sun, rather than the earth, is at the center of the solar system of planetary orbits. He was restricted in publishing his scientific findings, and also was restricted in his movements as a penalty for his scientific claims.

that all of our practical *maxims and duties* must be derived from these broader axiomatic principles, i.e. the *categorical imperative* forms the foundation from which our practical duties stem.

2. The Categorical Imperative and Its Three Formulae

Kant's three versions of the "categorical imperative" do not stem from any abstract laws of nature. They would not exist without the imposition of the reasoning man. They do not transcend our experience as in Socratic philosophy, nor are they based upon our experience as David Hume argued. [51] They are person centered and proceed from the reasonable (rational) free will. [52] These imperatives appear to us as obviously true. They are therefore axiomatic, so we can derive practical maxims from them. They need no prior argument to establish them. They stand alone in forming the premises for our supporting arguments in favor of our derived practical *maxims*.

Kant argued that the very notion of morality requires free will, and this requires individuals who are autonomous in their actions. Unlike the Plato-Socratic approach, or that of Aristotle or of Christian ethics (all *perfectionist*), Kant did not attempt to objectively establish notions of *good* in human characteristics, actions or results. He argued that fundamental moral principles as they apply to society must be adopted by a democratic plurality, but this plurality should only be adopted after associated rational thought and discussion.

Kant argued that from rational free will, a "supreme practical principle," called the *categorical imperative,* follows, namely that the moral maxims we decide to live by must be universal; they must apply to all. This rational law is often termed the *formula for universal law*, and is actually only one of three versions of Kant's *categorical imperative*. The second version is often termed *the formula for the end in itself: treat people as an end in themselves, not as a means.* This requires that we allow others to pursue their ends as long as they do not impinge the freedom of others to pursue their interests. Engaging others via deception, as an example, is always in violation.

---

[51] Hume's rejection of Kantian rationality is reviewed below.

[52] By "rational" Kant meant logical, i.e., not self contradictory, but with logical deductions.

The third version of the *categorical imperative* concerns what Kant termed the pursuit of a *kingdom of ends*, an end result that motivates the pursuit of moral imperatives. We explore this motivation in much more detail below. Kant argued that his three categorical imperatives are really different versions of the same imperative, i.e., that each follows from the other two.

The second version of the *categorical imperative* requires that we act so as to allow others to act in their own interests; we do not use others only as tools, but rather as agents and in such a way as to allow them to pursue their own ends. If we follow these versions of the *categorical imperative* in deciding the principles of morality as derived through plurality of agreement, then these principles can form a system of justice. Within this system, each person acts as a contributing legislator, and is bound by the resulting democratically agreed-upon law. [See O'Neill (2000) and Sullivan (1994) for reviews of Kant's ethics.]

As already explained, Kant presents three versions of the *categorical imperatives*. [Below, we use Sullivan's (1994, p. 29) interpretations from the original language of these *imperatives*.] Kant envisioned these versions, presented below as three "formulas," as entirely consistent with each other, and in fact he envisioned each as logically necessitated by the others. It is important to keep in mind that these *formulas* are axiomatic guides for the derivation of our applicable and practical maxims:

Formula 1 – the formula of autonomy or of universal law: "I ought never to act in such a way that I could not also will that my maxim should be a universal law." [Kant (1785), 402]

Formula 2 – the formula for the respect for the dignity of persons: "Act so that you treat humanity, whether in your own person or in that of any other, always as an end and never as a means only." [Kant (1785), 429]

Formula 3 – the formula of legislation for a moral community: "All maxims that proceed from our own making of law ought to harmonize with a possible kingdom of ends." [Kant (1785), 436]

Chapter II briefly mentioned all three of these formulas. We complete this exploration below, however, particularly with respect to notions of "moral community" and "harmonize." First we briefly explain how the third formula is envisioned by Kant as providing the motivation for the first two. This notion of "motivation" is very important to our ethical exploration.

Kant's first formula, the *imperative of universal law*, prohibits us from behaving by personal maxims that are applicable only to us, and that are designed only for our convenience. For example, if our business temporarily suffered from financial distress, and we decided that it would be acceptable to commit some fraudulent act to ameliorate our problem, we would violate the *imperative of universal law*. We could never will this temporarily fraudulent behavior to be universal. That would be equivalent to willing that the foundation of trust upon which our business relations are built be universally destroyed. A *maxim* of "commit fraud only when we temporarily suffer from financial distress" is unacceptable in Kant's ethic.

In a similar way, Kant's *formula for the respect for the dignity of persons* would also be violated by the *maxim* of fraud described in the above paragraph. Fraud is essentially a lie. It deceives others into serving our own ends, while not allowing others to pursue their personal ends. This example illustrates the consistency of the first two *formulas*. Indeed, Kant argued that one *formula* logically follows from, and is necessitated by the other.

The motivation for pursuit of the first two *formulas* lies in the third *formula,* the *formula of legislation for a moral community*. Before examining this motivation, we should explore the notions developed in the Socratic dialogue *Gorgias* [See Plato (1989).] In that *dialogue*, Socrates develops two principles:

- "No man does evil voluntarily."
- "It is better to suffer evil than to commit evil."

With respect to the first of these propositions, Socrates states that to know what is good, and to choose what is evil is an absurdity. No person knowingly and willingly selects evil; they select evil only in spite of the fact that it is evil, not knowingly and voluntarily because it is evil. Evil is merely the necessary result of ignorance. This is true because willingly committing evil is self destructive of the reasoning individual, and no one rationally selects self destruction, at least according to Plato and Socrates. (Of course, this assumes that we are reasoning individuals.) Note that this preserves the notion of *free will* in that people could still select to perform evil actions, but they would do so only out of ignorance.

Reasoned free will is what gives meaning to life, according to Socrates, Plato, and certainly also Kant. By selecting evil, a person therefore destroys that which gives meaning to life. Kant, however, wants to extend this Greek philosophical argument. Kant argues that we seek a *kingdom of ends*, what in Greek philosophy is termed *the good.* **By kingdom, Kant means "the union of different rational beings in a system by common laws" or maxims.** (1785, 4.433) Through the first two *formulas,* duties are derived and motivated by the pursuit of this *kingdom of ends*. These duties are actually derived from the practical *ethical maxims* formed from the *categorical imperative*. **By *harmony*, Kant means that these rational beings pursue consistent and coordinated duties aimed ultimately at pursuing this *kingdom of ends*.** Moral actions are therefore those that are motivated by the pursuit of this ultimate good. They cannot be those that serve only the self at the expense of others in this "union of rational beings." (1785, 4.430) Indeed, in the *Foundations* (1797), Kant argued that examination of motivation is the only basis for judging the morality of some action, and *Formula 3* provides the only justifiable motivation. Other possible motivations are self-centered on the individual actor, and hence are inherently selfish.

To illustrate this motivating notion of pursuing a *kingdom of ends*, consider your childhood conduct among your circle of young friends. You probably argued and persuaded your friends towards establishing fairness in the games you played, or in the division of desserts you enjoyed, or in other behavior. Your motivating thought was not directly "What advantage can I obtain from this notion of fairness?" but rather "How can we obtain harmony among our group?" You sought a *kingdom of ends* in harmonious cooperation. You tried to persuade your friends to seek the same. You did so because of your respect for your friends. This ethical motivation is the ethical motivation according to Kant, and is expressed in *formula 3.* To state that we "respect the dignity of others" implies that we ought to "pursue" notions of the "kingdom of ends."

One should realize the linkage between *formula 1* and *formula 3*. The *universality principle* prohibits us from establishing maxims that are purely self serving. Our maxims therefore must be aimed at, or motivated by, the pursuit of the *kingdom of ends*. For example, consider the case of the temporary lying promise reviewed above. A maxim that allows the temporary lying promise under certain exigencies not only violates the *formula 1*, the *universality principle*, and *formula 2*, *respect for the dignity of persons*, but also *formula 3*, the *kingdom of ends*. A personal maxim that allows us the self-serving temporary lying promise is hardly in pursuit of the harmonious society. We see, then, that Kant's three formulas are consistent with each other, and actually each is required by the other two.

One easily perceives the parallel between religious judgments of proper motivation and Kant's *pursuit of the kingdom of ends*. Religion argues that we should pursue right and not wrong because we seek a final individual *nirvana, or heaven,* or *paradise*, or similar state after death. We see this as a selfish pursuit, but religious explanations of the alternative (*hell*) are so drastically horrible that we are frightened into pursuing this ultimate end. Kant changes this motivation to a current-world social end, one that is not self centered. It is obvious that when one is only concerned with "after death," then pursuit of current world harmony is decreased in importance.

Kant's *kingdom of ends* refers, of course, to a harmonious overall society, one where reasoning people pursue maxims which they form democratically and therefore find acceptable, and which are derived from the other two formulas of the categorical imperative. This *kingdom of ends* cannot be restricted to a single business, but rather applies to society as a whole. Nonetheless, management can act in pursuit of this final social end when forming and acting on its derived maxims. This is the kernel of the argument presented here concerning Kantian propositions for management and leadership.

Note that Chapter II addressed management's obvious need to conform to society's norms (laws), and Chapter II also opened the exploration of behavioral maxims for ethical situations that are outside of society's legal constraints. We previously called the approach applicable for these situations "intuitionism." Following the Socratic method, the intuitionist derives innate axioms of moral behavior. Kant's categorical imperative merely attempts to assert the most fundamental of these innate axioms. Our management maxims for our particular business can, and should, be derived from these imperatives (or formulas). The *kingdom of ends* we seek is broadly social, but since we view our business relations as an important part of this society, we seek a management ethic that produces harmony with this ultimate goal for our business organization.

Certainly one can argue that pursuit of this *kingdom of ends* is not practical, especially within a business. What else, however, could motivate managers: greed, gluttony, sexual addiction, … ? These pursuits are also not practical in that they can never be ultimately satisfying, but only transitory in satisfaction, if even that. These pursuits will also not lead to any successful business organization. Pursuit of *harmony*, however, has the potential of leading to success in business, even if perfection in that pursuit is not ultimately achievable.

As explained in Chapter II, management acts as the legal agent of the firm's owners. As such, they have a legal and ethical obligation to serve the interests of the goals of the owners, but always within other legal and ethical constraints. As management, we seek to serve these interests because they are consistent with Kant's categorical imperative, particularly with the *formula for the respect for the dignity of persons:* the owners employ management to serve the owners' ends provided we allow other stakeholders to pursue their own ends. Shareholder wealth maximization (SWM) is not unethical when properly pursued in this way.

When managers apply a consistent set of maxims, derived from Kant's *categorical imperative*, they can produce a reasonably harmonious organization that satisfies the most basic interests of stakeholders. We mean this in the Socratic sense that people do not willingly seek evil. In general, people do respond positively to the "pursuit of the good," although their egos often point them in contrary directions. [53]
It is our belief that stakeholders will respond favorably to this *harmonious management ethic*, and this motivates our exploration of Kant. It is important to note, however, that although this *harmonious management ethic* may be a necessary condition for SWM, pursuit of this goal is not the motive for behaving according to this ethic. SWM may be the goal of the firm, but the motive for management behaving ethically should be the pursuit of the *kingdom of ends.* This is an essential distinction.

[53] This is essentially Chambers and Lacey's (1996) argument that pursuit of SWM serves society's sense of ethics because capital and product markets force firms to conform to society's ethical preferences. This argument is explored in some detail in a latter chapter.

We explore below some of the practical *maxims and duties* suggested by Kant, and we also derive some of our own maxims for business decisions. We shall see that the three *formulas of* the *categorical imperative* provide very practical tools for business leadership and decisions. They also ultimately form an ethical system that can be considered a productive factor-input to the firm, and as such, a necessary mechanism for the pursuit of organizational goals.

3. The Bankruptcy Declaration Example

Kant's formulas for the *categorical imperative* can be guides for the manager in forming practical maxims and duties. For example, among the practical problems to which Kant applies the imperative, he explores the possibility of lying to obtain a loan. This is found to violate the imperative because it utilizes another to achieve a personal end, and in the process, deprives the first party of the pursuit of their own ends.

A more seminal problem for hypothetical exploration of ethical dilemmas would have been (provided bankruptcy laws existed during the 18th century of Kant) "When ought one to utilize a bankruptcy declaration?" The stakeholder tradeoffs implicit in the timing of the declaration, and the reorganization plan itself, make these decisions more difficult for application of Kant's imperative. For example, under conditions of financial distress, waiting to declare bankruptcy may improve the prospects for shareholder wealth recovery, prospects that may currently be dismal, but only at a cost of deterioration of the value of the assets available for recourse to the debt holder if eventual liquidation is necessary. In addition, worker interests could also be at stake since any reorganization plan, or court established control of management, affects their interests. The categorical imperative does not provide any direct guide without considerable extension.

To explore these problems in more detail, consider a firm with a debt payment of $100 due in one year, the debt being contracted with debt holders who are fully knowledgeable concerning the riskiness of payment. The current liquidation value of the assets is $100. If the firm continues in business, however, it faces a two-state future as described by Table 5-1. Income will be earned over the next period and this is capitalized into the value of assets as shown. In addition, if the firm decides to continue in operation, it must select under which scenario it will operate, A or B. (We assume a choice of marketing plan or capital investment determines the A or B scenario.)

Tables 5-1a, 5-1b, and 5-1c give the values of the firm's assets, debt payments and equity value [the value of assets – the value of liabilities] under scenarios A and B in the two-state world.

Table 5-1a: Value of Firm's Assets in Two State Future

State	Scenario A	Scenario B	Probability
1	$100	$150	½
2	$ 90	0	½

Table 5-1b: Value of Firm's Debt Payment in Two State Future

State	Scenario A	Scenario B	Probability
1	$100	$100	½
2	$ 90	0	½

Table 5-1c: Value of Firm's Equity in Two State Future

State	Scenario A	Scenario B	Probability
1	0	$50	½
2	0	0	½

If the firm does not continue its operations, employees suffer and there is no residual value for the equity holders; the debt holders receive all the value of the firm's assets. If the firm continues under Scenario A, then the firm must be liquidated to pay the debt holders either in full ($100) or in partial default ($90) depending upon the uncertain future state of the world. The expected payoff for the debt holders is $95; debt holders would prefer liquidation now rather than having the business continue since current liquidation yields full payment of $100 with certainty.

If the firm continues under Scenario B, the equity owners have a 50% chance of retaining wealth of $50 (in State 1), but also a 50% chance of having no residual value to the equity. They would prefer that the firm continue under B since it allows the only possibility for equity having any worth. The employees would also prefer B since the firm would be ongoing. The debt holders have only a 50% chance of receiving $100 under B, their expected payoff is only $50, i.e., [½($100) + ½($0) = $50].

Of the three possible courses of action reviewed above, the debt holders prefer current liquidation to continuing operations. The equity holders prefer continuation under Scenario B, the worst course of action for the debt holders. Provided the debt holders entered the agreement knowing the uncertainties involved, and the terms of the debt were fully negotiated and arranged to reflect the risks, then Kant's *categorical imperative* offers no direct solution, but does offer a derived solution of democratic discourse based upon rational reflection.

John Rawls' political philosophy tries to provide a framework that establishes the conditions under which democratically established law is justified as the necessary extension of Kant's categorical imperative. We review this Rawlsian material in detail in a latter chapter. It is sufficient to claim here that given these conditions, this law can be described as providing "justice as fairness," and has the potential to provide the moral imperatives necessary to resolve these complex business problems, such as the scenario problem above.

Society's current notion of the optimal solution to the bankruptcy declaration problem is presented by SWM as constrained by law and negotiated debt-indenture agreements.[54] SWM dictates that the firm continues its operations under scenario B. Our limited liability law allows the $0 payment to debt holders under state 2, scenario B, and this is judged fair provided the debt holders are fully knowledgeable about the risks of payment when they purchase the debt[55]. In a free market for the debt claims, the original terms of the debt, that is the price or interest rate agreed to, would reflect the risks of payment. Furthermore, our bankruptcy law favors this solution in that it purposely favors firm continuance whenever possible, thereby

---

[54] Debt indentures are the legal details that accompany any debt contract (or bond) that restrict the actions of the borrower, and also specify the monitoring activities that the lender is allowed to engage in. For example, debt indentures often restrict the production activities that the borrower can engage in, where approval of these activities must be granted by a legal representative (legal agent) of the lender. Violation of these debt indentures mean the lender can take immediate recourse, frequently associated with a court action.

[55] Limited liability in corporate law means that debt holders cannot sue the shareholders for personal liability in order to recover their claim. The liability of shareholders is limited to the value of the firm's assets, and does not extend to the personal assets of the shareholders. Nonetheless, debt holders with diversified portfolios of different companies' bonds, would receive, on average, a payoff that reflects the riskiness of the portfolio of claims.

allowing continuation of employment. This is a solution reached after considerable democratic debate that is imbedded in our bankruptcy law.

The law does not allow, however, what is termed "risk shifting," it prohibits the firm from declaring (in its *intended use of proceeds* section of the debt prospectus) that it will use the debt to proceed under scenario A (the scenario more favorable for debt holders) and then shift to B (a less favorable scenario for debt holders). The firm must divulge its intentions *a priori*. Violation of this disclosure requirement violates the categorical imperative in that it constitutes a case of lying. These rules of fairness built into the legal arrangements for debt and bankruptcy provide a clear notion of Rawls' *justice as fairness* as explored below. These rules are examples of practical moral maxims derived from democratic reasoned discourse.

4. Conclusion Concerning the Use of the Categorical Imperative

At this point, it is important to realize that the crucial difference between the intuitionist approach, as previously reviewed in Chapter II, and the Kantian approach lies in the categorization of applicable axioms. The intuitionist asserts axioms from natural law, as described by logical inquiry. These laws cannot be justified by use of other axioms. (By their nature, axioms are self-evident.) Kant's assertion that man is an end in himself, however, allows logical derivation of other *maxims* through democratic discourse. Kant differentiates the moral imperatives man might establish from other will-derived intuitionist maxims that might serve personal happiness. In particular, in Kant moral *maxims* must be followed because of the pursuit of the *kingdom of ends*, not because of any other motivations whether intuitionist or otherwise. One should not lie, not out of fear of discovery and ruination of reputation, or out of fear of the consequences in some afterlife, but because of the pursuit of social harmony.

Also, if one poses a moral *maxim*, one should desire that it be universally followed. Hence, a maxim such as "I should visit my aunt!" cannot be categorized as an absolute moral imperative due to its narrowness. This categorization is not frivolous, but rather lends itself to a high degree of seriousness when we consider moral pursuits. If I argue that some maxim should be universal, and others pose their versions of universal maxims, then whatever we agree to through democratic discourse should be considered by all as universally binding.

We shall see in latter chapters, however, John Rawls extends Kant by laying the foundation for democratically establishing *fairness* rules as the basis for other derivative moral *maxims*, derivative in the sense of extending from the *categorical imperative*. This examination of *fairness* applies to our social contract, and therefore laws. Violations of *fairness* can then be judged by their degree of violation. This is the subject of a latter exploration especially in the context of managers acting as agents of business owners.

5. Maxims for Achieving the Harmonious Organization

Kant's *categorical imperative* in the form of *formula 2 – the formula for the respect for the dignity of persons*–is the fundamental proposition concerning correct conduct, and as such, its application is necessary for achieving an harmonious organization. Harmony, or its lack, is one necessary factor that affects the economic efficiency of the organization, but economic efficiency, although very important even from a moral standpoint, should only be considered as a side benefit of this Kantian ethical behavior. An argument in support of the essential importance of harmony is presented here, but only after we review several potential maxims.

The following notion of *harmony* is essential to the ethical system presented here.

By harmony we mean the achievement of a high degree of cooperation among management and employees so that clarity in managerial pursuit of derived moral maxims is accomplished.

This *clarity* can be achieved only after management fully understands that the three *formulas of the categorical imperative* are:

- worthy of pursuit,

- that the behavioral maxims utilized by the firm are derived from the categorical imperatives, and

- that the pursuit of these maxims is consistent with the *kingdom of ends*.

Indeed, it is argued below that managerial leadership in pursuit of this *harmony* is in part necessary for SWM.

Achievement of harmony in the organization requires two general categories of managerial actions:

i. Respect for the dignity of others as thinking individuals.

Today's business organizations seldom utilize individuals solely for their physical labor. Creative input from employees is generally sought and valued. It is efficient and productive to seek and respect the creative and thoughtful input of employees as thinking individuals.

ii. Reflective thought about the ethical and other problems faced by the organization.

This is a necessary requirement for any agent as manager, or even owner-manager of a business organization. This requires mental effort, a thoughtful analysis, in seeking necessary information that is relevant to any business problem, and this includes ethical aspects of business problems.

It is argued below that the second of these general categories of actions is necessary to avoid the breakdown in the organization that is generally associated with the firm becoming overly bureaucratic in its decision making, particularly bureaucratic in application of "codes of conduct." This is an especially difficult modern problem, and it will be explored in some detail below. [56] The first of the actions listed above is explored in much more detail below.

In the *Foundations of the Metaphysics of Morals* (1785), Immanuel Kant reviewed some maxims against particular actions, these maxims being derived from his *categorical imperative*. We review some of these here. [57] We also develop other *maxims* applicable to business situations where these *maxims* are consistent with the *categorical imperative*. The limitations of behavior posed by these maxims are certainly required for maintaining an harmonious organization. They are certainly consistent with the motive of respect for the reasoning individual as a moral agent, and they should form the basis for much reflective thought about the ethical conundrums faced by management.

Previously we partially examined the first of these maxims, *the maxim against the lying promise*. We extend this examination here. It is important to note that

[56] The Brickley, Smith and Zimmerman (2007, Chapter 22) text reviews the application of these codes to business.
[57] The material reviewed here relies on Sullivan (1994).

in all of Kant's ethical philosophy, it is the agent's aim in acting on the particular maxim that forms the ethical content. The motive for action is fundamentally important in the ethics of Kant.

Maxim 1: *We ought not to make lying promises.* This maxim is properly illustrated by the following question:

Question: "When in distress, may I make a promise with the intention of not keeping it?"

The motives for the *lying promise* might be to avoid financial, physical, or psychological distress, or to achieve some pleasure or avoid some inconvenience. In all cases, the lying promise violates the *categorical imperative*. People, and business managers, who make lying promises in pursuit of personal gain or advantage, violate the *imperative.* They lack respect for the reasoning individuals they interact with. They are trying to manipulate others into pursuit of the ends associated with the lie, but in the process, they frustrate the pursuits of those manipulated. Harmonious relations are destroyed by the promise. Any sense of team work is violated, and the potential for future team cooperation is upset. One can never envision a society or business organization that could function efficiently if lying promises were common, and therefore the maxim prohibiting them satisfies Kant's demand for the *categorical imperative* as expressed in all three of its *formulas.*

Maxim 2: *Within practical limitations, we ought to help others pursue their own ends where and when we can.* This maxim is properly illustrated by the following question:

Question: "My life is flourishing. I do not directly or immediately need the help of others. Shall I neither beneficently contribute to the welfare of others, nor expect their help in return?"

When making decision about our social and business relations, it is obvious that we must take into account that all people are dependent and vulnerable, and most have continuous needs. When we are satisfied that our needs are met, we might avoid helping others pursue their own ends. We know, however, that this independent state cannot be permanent. We are social beings who are, by nature, not self sufficient. We all need the help of others to promote our natural welfare and happiness. We cannot totally renounce this help, and we must cultivate it. We cannot reasonably make the universal claim that everyone can remain independent of the beneficence of others. We must, therefore adopt *Maxim 2* as a positive obligation that is necessary for the harmonious organization. It is certainly derivative of *formulas 1 and 3* of the *categorical imperative*. It can also be effectively argued that it is logically derivative of, or at lease consistent with, *formula 3*.

Maxim 3: *We ought to behave as though all our actions are publicly known, even when some actions must be kept private.* This *maxim* is properly illustrated by the following question:

Question: "A company intends to close a particular branch in the near-term future, but for competitive reasons, it cannot disclose its plans. When workers enquire, should management deceive them about the future in order to protect this confidence?"

To be competitive, business must frequently keep various secrets. Nonetheless, *formula 2* prohibits us from deception for the purpose of motivating others to pursue our ends. When enquiries are made, simple declarations such as "I cannot divulge that information!" are sufficient to be consistent with *formula 2* provided we clearly do not mislead others in any way. This situation has the potential of illustrating the claim of "I have obeyed the code" of not divulging the information. If one merely states the words "I cannot divulge," but via facial expression or body language, one violates the spirit of the code, then this also violates the maxim.

Maxim 4: *Whenever we use others to promote our own welfare, we ought not to humiliate them, or fail to recognize that they have a dignity equal to our own.* This maxim is properly illustrated by the following question:

Question: "When we observe others underperforming, should we use humiliation to motivate them?"

Nobody seeks an end of humiliation for themselves. If we humiliate somebody, we violate Kant's categorical imperative as stated in *formulas 2 and 3*. We disrupt harmony by breeding frustration within the humiliated individual, and also, it should be argued, we show a lack of self respect for ourselves due to our own frustration. We should, however, be able to manage that frustration. Managers should be able to present cogent arguments, effectively assign responsibilities, evaluate and reward employees by *fair* systems in order to achieve the motivation desired. Humiliating behavior is a disease that destroys the harmonious organization.

Respect for the reasoning individual is always superior for motivating people. Frustration with the performance of others will always be with us. Our task is to overcome this psychological problem without giving in to humiliating behavior.

Maxim 5: We must recognize the dignity of others even when we personally dislike them or feel indifferent towards them. This *maxim* is properly illustrated by the following question:

Question: "Should we limit contact with another employee merely because of some past personal dispute?"

If we are to allow others to pursue their own ends, we must not avoid them because we do not feel comfortable interacting with them. This certainly would disrupt harmony within the organization. It would show a lack of respect for the other reasoning individual. This behavior would directly violate *formulas 2 and 3*, but it would also violate *formula 1, the universality principle.* Are we to say that people should select only those we like as deserving of respect? This principle could hardly be a universal maxim. If it were, *respect for the dignity of other persons* would be a rare characteristic.

As with *maxim 4*, we must strive to overcome the psychological problems that interfere with the efficient and harmonious organization. *Maxim 5* requires efforts similar to those required by *Maxim 4*. Frustration with or repulsion from people we do not like requires effort to overcome.

Maxim 6: We must recognize the dignity of others even when they are not considered longer-term members of the organization. This maxim is properly illustrated by the following question:

Question: Should we apply the maxims above to someone we are about to terminate from the organization for poor performance?

Respect should be shown to all, even those about to be separated from the organization. We must allow all to maintain their rightful self-respect and dignity. We expect to be treated with respect, and we should offer it in return. Management should lead the organization to establish this culture, and show that it is manifested in all its relations. This is required of all three formulations of the *categorical imperative*.

Consider the *maxims* presented above, and ask "What are the characteristics of an organization that does not pursue these *maxims*?" The student should be able to draw the conclusion that the characteristics would be:

(1) A lack of trust among stakeholders.

Violation of any of the *six maxims* presented above would lead to this lack of trust.

(2) A lack of beneficent cooperation among management and employees.

Maxim 2 particularly pertains to this conclusion.

(3) A general lack of truthfulness.

Maxim 1 particularly pertains to this conclusion.

(4) A psychological state of inferiority among employees with associated fear of contact with superiors.

Maxims 4 and 5 apply to this conclusion.

Is it possible that a firm exhibiting these characteristics could adequately pursue SWM, or any other worthy goal? It is for this reason that managerial leadership in pursuit of these, and/or other maxims consistent with Kant's *categorical imperatives* must enable them to pervade the organization. Indeed, this is the essence of leadership in managerial ethics. As such, leadership towards inculcating these maxims into the organization is a necessary condition for effective management. We state it is necessary, but it may not be sufficient for effective management since other characteristics such as strategic creativity and proper analysis of the risks the firm faces are also required. Nonetheless, this leadership is necessary for effective pursuit of SWM, or any other worthy goal.

6. Positive and Negative Duties

Kantian analysis distinguishes between positive and negative duties generated by our derived moral maxims. The following indicates the differences:

- Negative duties (often termed perfect duties) are absolute prohibitions against actions that violate a moral maxim. For example, there is an absolute prohibition against the lying promise, or fraud.

- Positive duties (often termed imperfect duties) are requirements for actions that fulfill some moral maxim, but that have practical limitations. Charity, for example, must have practical limitations or the individual would not be capable of functioning in the everyday real world.

Maxim 2 reviewed above requires a positive duty of beneficence. It must have a practical limitation for managers and employees or they might not be able to function in their other business duties. Where should the line be drawn between what is practical and what is not? This is not easily answered, but requires reflective thought, and is certainly unique to the situation at hand.

Maxims 1, 3-6, however, all provide examples of absolute prohibitions (negative duties).

7. Some Additional Maxims and Agency Obligations

We suggest two addition maxims that are particularly applicable to business.

Maxim 7: *We must recognize all agency obligations without obfuscation. This requires the following:*

a. *We recognize and communicate all conflicts of interest we might have to all relevant parties, and we must do so prior to relevant decisions.*

b. *We must recognize and pursue all of our business-functional obligations without evasion.*

The first of these obligations (a) appears so obvious that further elucidation should not be necessary. The second obligation (b), however, is often not so obvious. To elucidate, consider the following question: When psychological stress is placed upon managers to grant compensation increases or promotions, should managers argue that a "happy" employee is of prime importance and hence grant the request, or should they negotiate (however fairly) as the owners' representative? The answer to this should be obvious. Managers represent (are agents of) the owners, and must fairly negotiate with other stakeholders including employees.

Perhaps a more important question to consider that addresses question (b) above concerns the primary financial reporting problem: Should management obscure accounting-financial reports so as the make management's performance appear better? This need not necessarily be deceptive accounting, but just not the best or most revelatory. The purpose of accounting is to provide information to the owners and to financial markets (other than the tax reporting purpose). This is a primary functional obligation of management. In addition, to not present the most accurate and complete accounting information, even if it must be revealed in footnotes, would violate the conflict of interest requirement of (a) above. It is also ultimately deceptive. It violates the *formula for universality*, and the *formula for the kingdom of ends*.

Managers who argue that they are balancing the interests of stakeholders are generally violating *maxim 7*. They are obfuscating their agency obligations, and we suspect, they are frequently just using the stakeholder balance argument to hide their own self-serving actions.

We also suggest an eighth maxim that stems directly from the *three formulas*, and is also central to assuring a high degree of efficiency for any business.

Maxim 8: *Management must provide transparent and systematic evaluation and reward methodologies that reflect the assigned responsibilities of employees.*

The firm's evaluation and reward system is frequently termed its *control system*. If employees are to be free to pursue their own ends, they must know the linkage between performance, evaluation and reward for their performance. Transparent procedures for evaluation are therefore necessary, and are usually provided through employee manuals. In addition, these kinds of control systems are necessary to stimulate firm performance, and hence they are in the interests of shareholder wealth.

Other firm maxims could specifically address issues in marketing, particularly vague or misleading promotions such as bait and switch, or employee promotion policies. Additional maxims might be required in order to isolate particular egregious practices, even if they appear redundant. Redundancy can aid in clarity and commitment. An important point to remember, however, is that all of these maxims must be accompanied by reflective logical thought. They must be accepted by all relevant agents. Managers and other relevant stakeholders must believe that they are important to the proper functioning of the firm.

The set of maxims presented above do not directly concern two of the more common psychological problems found in business, the problem of *cognitive dissonance* and the problem of *fight or flee.* The first of these concerns the inability to accept what is obviously true as based upon objective new evidence. People often form hard opinions based upon old evidence, and become difficult with others when new contrary evidence is presented. There is no purpose in declaring a maxim that people must not suffer from this psychological problem since it is a human trait. Nonetheless, systems should be in place to help managers and employees to overcome *cognitive dissonance* since the very existence of this problem, along with the psychological distress suffered, can lead employees to violate ethical maxims which they would otherwise not violate. These systems can consist of frequent reviews of new data as it becomes available, so that there is little surprise when new evidence contradicts previously held beliefs. Once people become used to reexamination of evidence and the reformulation of belief, cognitive dissonance problems become more manageable.

The *flight or flee syndrome,* particularly when associated with evaluation of performance and associated rewards, also pose difficult psychological problems. It is generally overcome by installing systems of frequent routine evaluation that the employee learns are not threatening. Nonetheless, the problem exists, and can lead to humiliating behavior, or even secretive behavior. These are human psychological problems that must be understood by management. The systems used to deal with these problems must themselves be consistent with the *maxims* presented above.

Review Questions:

(1) In the *Oxford Companion to Philosophy* (1995), or the *Cambridge Dictionary of Philosophy* (2006), or the *Concise Rutledge Encyclopedia of Philosophy* (2000), find the reviews of each Philosopher listed above. List and briefly explain their most significant contributions?

(2) What does it mean to" make public use of (your) reason?" How did this notion contribute to the democratic movements of the 18th Century? (Consider the Continental Congress and Constitutional Conventions that met in Philadelphia in the late 18th Century. List a few philosophical contributions made by the delegates at these conventions?) How did the "doctrines" briefly reviewed above contribute to this movement?

(3) What is the role of ethical education if it is "not to mould feelings or character?"

(4) Are all people "rational and good?" Consider the evil of the 20th Century. How did rational thought overcome this evil?

(5) Can religion form the basis of rational belief? If so, can one argue that these beliefs are true without reference to their religious foundation? How are the answers to these questions germane to our democracy?

(6) Explain what Socrates meant in arguing "No man does evil voluntarily!" and that "It is better to suffer evil than to commit it!"?

(7) Define Kant's notions of "kingdom," and also "harmony?"

(8) If we explore "what gives meaning to life," is it more than "reasoned free will?" What other fundamental aspects of life give it meaning for you? Consider adventure, gender interaction and natural preservation as possibilities. How might these aspects affect your notions of ethics?

(9) Define "axiomatic" as it is used above? Can there be any other axiomatic basis for universal maxims than *formula 2?*

(10) Other than *formula 3*, what basis for the motivation of ethical actions exists? How would Socrates answer this question?

(11) Is it possible to have a set of ethical *maxims* that are not generated by the *categorical imperative* of Kant, and have these *maxims* effective for the organization? Explore some alternative set?

(12) Are the characteristics of trust, beneficent cooperation among management and employees, truthfulness, lack of employee fear of contact with management all necessary for an effective management? Review some actual business-decision problems from other business subject areas, such as finance or human resource management, and explain how these characteristics are necessary for optimal solutions to these problems?

(13) For two of the *maxims* presented above, draw another alternative illustrative question similar to the one posed above? Present an analysis that answers each of these alternative questions?

(14) Form a new *maxim* related to some category of business problem, and pose an illustrative question with an associated analysis and answer?

(15) Review and explain the importance of the terms "harmony" and "clarity" in the context of the Kantian system of ethics explored above?

(16) For *Maxim 2*, list and review some of the "practical limitations" that restrict our obligation of helping others pursue their own ends? (Hint: Will you occupy your entire day helping others? Why not?)

(17) Fully explain Table 5-1 as an illustration of a democratic solution to an ethical problem?

Chapter VI

———— ❦ ————

ETHICAL VIRTUES AND IMPLEMENTATION
OF THE KANTIAN MODEL

Chapter Abstract: This chapter takes a Rawlsian approach to distinguishing between personal moral virtues, and moral managerial decisions. It examines the question, "Might virtuous managers still make unethical decisions?" In addition, the set of virtues required of management to implement a Kantian program of harmony is reviewed, and an explanation of how this program establishes constraints on the pursuit of shareholder wealth is presented.

1. Introduction

This chapter reviews some of the generally accepted notions concerning the personal attributes worthy of cultivation by the manager who aspires to moral action. As such, this chapter provides a very brief introduction to *virtue ethics*, an introduction necessary to support various useful arguments that complement our Kantian framework. In addition, we carefully separate the personal moral traits we expect of managers from the required characteristics of moral decisions. We show that having these personal moral traits does not assure that moral decisions are made, if for no other reason than the manager may not fully recognize the ethical complexities involved in some decisions. Sharpening the manager's ability to recognize these complexities is a paramount motive for examining the necessary requirements for decisions to be judged as ethical. Managers who have these moral traits are more likely to make decisions that meet requirements for being ethical. We do recognize, however, that while some initial minimum level of moral virtue is necessary, an organization can develop these personal moral traits among its managers by establishing an environment of frequent rational reflection about the purpose of the moral code it establishes.

Later in this chapter, we also explore the set of managerial moral traits that may be necessary to implement any Kantian program of *clarity* and *harmony*. We remind the reader that *clarity* means a full understanding of the *moral maxims* the firm establishes as appropriate. *Harmony* means the pursuit of these *maxims* by relevant stakeholders. We argue that a particular mix of personal attributes, identified as virtues, is required to effectively implement any Kantian program.

This chapter also attempts to link the personal moral traits examined here to the requirements for actual moral decisions. In particular, in Chapter VII we link these personal characteristics to the requirements for *fair negotiations*, a frequently encountered managerial problem. Business negotiations are a broad category of managerial actions that involve moral complexities, and therefore provide a particularly rich area for exploration of ethics. The idea of *fairness in negotiations* is essentially an extension of Rawlsian analysis.

2. Personal Moral Characteristics

The philosophy of *virtue ethics* argues that moral virtues are more basic than other moral concepts; that these virtues are fundamental in that the other moral concepts, such as the Kantian derived *moral maxims*, are reducible to underlying claims about people having these virtues. These virtues therefore provide a foundation for an ethical philosophy. The focus here is on character rather than behavior; that the latter follows from the former. To the extent that behavior is judged as moral, it is because the characteristics of the virtuous dictate that it be so judged. Note that we do not argue that this is the correct philosophy. It is just as rational (perhaps more so) to argue that the ethical defines the necessary predispositions we term virtues. The philosophy of virtue ethics is not a Kantian view. We merely cite *virtue ethics* as a school of thought worthy of consideration and investigation. We shall also show the subject's relevance to our Kantian approach to management.

Aristotle conceived *moral virtue as a disposition to choose morally under the guidance of reason,* and defined this *disposition as that necessary for a flourishing life*. The *Aristotelian* model is depicted in Figure 6-1. The essential idea of this model is that a *flourishing life* is understood as one that meets the standards of one's culture and tradition. In this sense, virtue ethics can be said to suffer culturally relevant bias. In our culture, these virtues would certainly include *benevolence, veracity*, and *fidelity*. We could, however, follow our Kantian motivation provided by the *third formula of the categorical imperative*, that is the *pursuit of harmony* within the organization and society, and identify this *pursuit* with the *flourishing life*, both for the organization and the individual. This is a tenuous (or lose) identification, but nonetheless an obvious one. We can use this identity to link the virtue ethics approach with the Kantian approach of reason as based on the *categorical imperative*.

Figure 6-1: Aristotle's View

Definition of *virtue*: A *disposition* for certain choices.

↓

These certain choices are required for a *flourishing life.*

↓

A *flourishing life* is a culturally dependent notion.

↓

Example from American culture:

Benevolence, veracity and fidelity lead to harmony.

It is important to note that these personal virtues are not viewed as *duties*, nor are they dictated by Kantian *moral maxims*, but according to this Aristotelian based philosophy, they are self-centered and designed to pursue the good life of the individual. Kantians argue, however, that these commonly cited virtues are incorporated in Kantian philosophy as duties required for the pursuit of the *kingdom of ends*, a social-centered goal of *harmony*. As a result, we see both divergence and synthesis in the two visions as depicted by Figures 6-2 and 6-3.

The so called *cardinal virtues* of ancient philosophy include *temperance, justice, courage, and practical wisdom.* In addition, Aristotle's *Golden Mean* doctrine asks that people follow a non-extreme temperance of avoiding polarity, of developing characteristics of moderation. One cannot reasonably argue that these *cardinal virtues* are unworthy of pursuit. Indeed, these dispositions might even lead to what we might ex-post judge as moral decisions. This divergence between the Aristotelian and Kantian views, however, is important for practical decision making. Having a *disposition for moral choices* is not the same as having the ability to reason through ethical conundrums so as to recognize the duty required. Ethical reasoning involves both the necessary *dispositions* to make the moral choice, and the ability to logically reason the required choice.

Figure 6-2: Divergence Between Kantian and Aristotelian Models

Aristotelian model: Moral choices stem from personal characteristics (virtues or dispositions), which should be developed as required for culturally determined *flourishing life*.

$\neq$

Kantian model: Moral choices stem from *duties* that stem from our *moral maxims* that in turn are consistent with Kant's *categorical imperative*.

$\downarrow$

Divergence: Kantian *duties* are logically derived. Aristotelian *virtues* are developed.

Figure 6-3: Aristotelian and Kantian Synthesis

Kantian motivation: Moral choices pursue *kingdom of ends (harmony)*.

$+$

Aristotelian motivation: Moral choices pursue *flourishing life*.

$\downarrow$

Synthesis: Identify culturally relevant *flourishing life*

with Kant's *kingdom of ends* (harmony).

As a substantive example of this divergence, consider those we often consider as *criminals*. By definition, they commit criminal acts. Nevertheless, they might, and they often do, demonstrate a variety of what we judge as *virtues*:

- physical courage in that they are willing to place their lives in danger,

- benevolence in that they are frequently charitable towards their compatriots,

- fidelity in that they are loyal to their compatriots. [58]

We might also consider certain *warrior cultures* that try to develop dispositions of veracity, fidelity, courage and benevolence among individuals. However much we might admire these virtues, we should recognize that there is no reason to believe that one who exhibits warrior virtues can reason solutions to moral conundrums.

The attributes explored below, which are utilized in Chapter VII to examine notions of *fairness,* are based on those listed by Rawls (1951) as required for the moral judge. This list is extended here to those required of the ethical manager. This is logical in that both judge and manager are essentially decision makers who face ethical conundrums while representing the interests of others. The judge represents society and its laws. The business manager represents the owners and society through the law in that he or she must certainly conform to all prior legal and ethical agreements.

Both manager and judge must make decisions that conform to society's ethical standards. To this end, we extend our examination of the requirements to ethical managerial decisions. This list of attributes follows Rawls (1951, 1958), and shows that ethical judgments and ethical managerial decisions are very similar in all respects.

3. Sympathy as Motivation and the Primary Moral Trait
McDowell (1985) and Nagel (1986) argue that the moral sense of individuals must be developed, that this sense is not entirely natural. In particular, sympathy for the moral pain of others must be developed as a motive for origination of

[58] The criminal Al Capone demonstrated these characteristics, along with a disposition to murder his opponents. Adolf Hitler also demonstrated these dispositions along with a certain austerity in his life style. He was also a mass murderer.

moral intuition. Otherwise, the moral implications implicit in ethical conundrums may not be perceived or understood. This *sympathy*, they argue, is therefore a criterion for pursuit of the ethical, and must be listed as the *primary moral trait*.

This notion of *sympathy* is also central to both Hume's (1751) and Smith's (1759) constructions of ethical philosophy. Hume argued that this *sympathy* provides a psychological motivation of why the wellbeing or misery of one person is of concern to others; that morality is only a matter of feelings as they are informed by the instincts of sympathy, and modified by the socially contracted rules of justice.

Smith also uses this notion of *sympathy* as a psychological emotion experienced by the impartial observer after viewing the difficulties of others. This requires a sort of mental substitution of oneself into the position of others who experience pain. We can conclude that as a result of this mental substitution process, one is then capable of participating in a Kantian discourse that potentially can develop generally acceptable *moral maxims*, as we reviewed in the previous chapter. We can also argue, however, that this notion of *sympathy*, as discussed above, is a necessary trait for any manager who expects to successfully apply any set of *moral maxims* similar to the set previously reviewed.

We should also view this *sympathy for the misery of others* as one precondition for making ethical decisions. Some other preconditions explored below include intellectual capabilities, a predisposition for applying effort in probing the complexities of potential ethical problems, and a predisposition for exploring possible acceptable solutions. We previously examined Kant's pursuit of the *kingdom of ends* as the proper ethical motivation, but we must also understand that *sympathy for the pain of others* is a trait that feeds this motivation. Harmonious organizational pursuit of these *maxims* is the characteristic of this *kingdom of ends*. This *harmony* will not exist if our applications of moral maxims leave others suffering. We conclude, then, that this notion of *sympathy* is required not only for the resolution of our moral maxims, but also for their effective administration. This *sympathy* therefore provides the motive for the pursuit of Kant's *kingdom of ends*.

Figure 6-4: Views of *Sympathy*

Hume's view of *sympathy*: An instinct for the well being of others.

+

Smith's view of *sympathy*: A Disposition to imagine ourselves in the position of others who suffer, and also to imagine that suffering.

↓

Sympathy as a necessary *virtue*: (1) Required for the Kantian discourse that is necessary to derive our *moral maxims*. (2) Leads to the expectation that one will apply our moral maxims. (3) Feeds our motivation to pursue the *kingdom of ends*.

4. Additional Characteristics of Moral Business Managers

Like Kant, late 20th century philosopher John Rawls (1951, 1958, 1980 and 2001) utilizes freedom and rationality for his ethical (some claim ethical-political) philosophy as the basis for a system of justice, which he shows may result from properly constrained democratic processes. By this system, Kantian notions of the *categorical imperative* are transformed into "justice as fairness," within which the notion of the ethical is embedded. [59] In this way, Rawls extends Kant's person-centered enlightenment philosophy.

One can view Rawls' analysis as first stating the requirements one should meet in order to be in a position to morally make a decision. Once these initial requirements are met, the moral judge's decision must further meet some additional requirements of rational reflection in order to have the potential to be ethical. These requirements are listed below. To a considerable extent, they provide a list of personal attributes, other than sympathy, necessary for implementation of the Kantian *moral maxims*.

The foundation of Rawls' system lies in the twin notions of *competent moral judges* and *considered moral judgments*. The class of *competent moral judges* fits the five characteristics listed here. For the reasons cited above, they also apply to the moral business manager.

---

[59] Rawls (1989) delimits applicable procedures for applying the categorical imperative through democratic discourse, and does so following Kant's examples.

I. The average intelligence requirement: The moral business manager must have a requisite degree of intelligence, average intelligence being sufficient.

We saw in Chapter V that Kant argued that a minimum degree of intelligence was required for participating in society's democratic debate aimed at establishing its ethical maxims. It was very important to Kant that average intelligence be sufficient; otherwise we could never expect society to agree to any set of ethical norms. If we must rely on intellectual elites to establish and apply moral maxims that conform to the *categorical imperative,* then the prospects for a moral society would indeed be slim.

For similar reasons, average intelligence is all we claim is required for the ethical business manager who must apply the maxims society establishes. To demand a higher degree of intelligence would hardly be realistic given the large number of business managers necessary for any functioning modern society.

More important than the reasons cited above, however, is the argument that an understanding of the moral maxims we draw from the *categorical imperative*, maxims similar to those enumerated in Chapter 5, do not require above average intelligence. We should be optimistic about the ability of business managers to apply them.

II. The knowledge requirement: A willingness to acquire the requisite knowledge of the consequences of our actions is required of the business manager, and also a willingness to acquire the knowledge of the facts of the problem at hand.

This requirement for factual knowledge, and also of the likely consequences of managerial actions, goes beyond the narrowly defined logic requirement for analyzing ethical dilemmas. The moral manager must never "shoot from the hip." This characteristic essentially requires a willingness to put forth the effort to acquire the necessary factual knowledge, and then requires a willingness to analyze it. The effort required for the acquisition of the relevant knowledge of the facts, and to reflect upon those facts, and also the consequences of our actions, even actions that have no obvious ethical implication, is itself an ethical obligation. The business manager represents the business owners. Effective managerial decisions require knowledge of both the facts and the consequences of actions.

This concerns all business problems. Laziness in fulfilling one's business obligations certainly is unethical.[60]

Moreover, laziness in obtaining knowledge concerning any moral conundrum is particularly unethical. Laziness in reflective thought concerning the logical consequences of the possible outcomes of managerial decisions would be particularly callous. This sort of laziness would certainly exhibit a lack of empathy for the possible suffering of those who might be affected by our decisions.

III. The logic requirement: A desire to use inductive logic is required of the business manager, as well as a desire to explore all options for decisions.

This attribute follows from II. It is obvious that logical exploration of decision-options is required for modern business. How else can the consequences of our actions be explored? Furthermore, we have a pro-active obligation to not bring our prejudices or preconceived notions to our examinations. Our pro-active obligation is to logically explore our options, to find new ones if possible, and to use our imagination and creativity in this exploration. This is frequently the essence of the mental activities we are obliged to devote to our managerial decisions.

Under characteristic I, we cite that average intelligence is required for our ethical judgments. Logical and imaginative efforts, however, can certainly utilize above average intelligence if available. This is the role of the personal characteristic of above average intelligence. This is not ethically required unless available to the business manager. We must keep in mind, however, that utilizing and listening to those who offer particularly creative analyses, perhaps from those below in the managerial hierarchy, is associated with this characteristic. This information must be considered. If above average intelligence is available in others, then it must be utilized fully. This is an agency obligation management owes to owners and other stakeholders.

IV. The open mindedness requirement: The business manager must have a willingness to reconsider judgments in light of new evidence. In addition,

---

[60] As an example of a managerial problem with perhaps no apparent ethical implication, consider the obligation for managers to economize on costs. This is an obligation managers have towards owners, and perhaps other stakeholders. This surely requires effort to explore options, and to apply costs savings procedures, and this is an obvious ethical obligation of management.

knowledge of his or her own predilections, and a desire to consider all con-flicting interests, is required.

Ideology, prejudice and bias, can have no role in effective managerial decisions. Knowledge of self, and any biases one might have, is a necessary first step for overcoming those predilections. New evidence pertaining to managerial problems is frequently encountered, and we must utilize it in reexamination, and possibly in reformation of our decisions. This attribute is really an extension of II above.

Consideration of all conflicting interests, however, does not mean managerial discretion in balancing stakeholder interests. Knowledge of the conflicting inter-ests of all stakeholders is required. The manager represents the owners of the firm, but must fulfill all legal and contractual obligations to other stakeholders whether explicit or implicit. Sometimes these interests can be conflicting. For these problems, ethical judgments can be difficult but unavoidable. Open mind-edness, logic, and application of the maxims explored in Chapter V, must all be brought to bear.

V. The fair-minded requirement: The managerial decision maker should be unaffected by the foreseeable consequences of the decision at hand, i.e. there are no inherent conflicts of interest.

This fair-minded characteristic is generally assumed of moral managers, but it is difficult to realize since almost all decisions have some consequent effect on the manager involved. This attribute requires, however, that the manager has a disposition to try to recognize any inherent conflicts of interest and to do all that is possible to avoid them. For example, the manager of company X who signs contracts with company Y, a company she also owns, cannot be said to be trying to avoid this conflict of interest.

Conditions III, IV and V define "reasonableness" according to Rawls. These attri-butes fit the description of what we should all define as the "reasonable person." We expect all of these attributes to be present in our moral managers.

VI. The noble nature requirement: The moral manager must exhibit the Socratic *noble nature* of speaking out in a social context about the results of his or her reflective thought concerning ethical problems.

We will examine this attribute in much more detail later in this text. We must understand, however, that the other attributes listed above may be of little value if the manager is unwilling to exhibit leadership in speaking to others in the organization about his or her analysis of ethical problems.

Conformity is a desire to not make waves within the organization. It is the opponent of the "noble nature." This noble attribute is necessary to resist the mob psychology that can sweep through organizations while justifying even the most unethical actions. This attribute, however, is also necessary to prevent bureaucratic behavior where non-reflective application of "codes of conduct" are gamed to allow unintended behavior that violates the spirit of the code but not the letter of the code.

The five attributes indicated above are prerequisites for the moral manager, but they do not imply that those who have these characteristics automatically make ethical decisions. These attributes help considerably in the pursuit of the latter. Certainly all of these characteristics are generally appropriate for any claim to leadership. In fact, we as a society expect these characteristics of anyone aspiring to leadership. We must, however, further pursue definitions of the characteristics of these decisions.

It may be useful to briefly repeat the a-priori personal characteristics (developed above) we expect of managers in order for them to be consider moral:

- *They have at least average intelligence.*

- *They have a requisite knowledge of the problem.*

- *They have a disposition to apply inductive logic to find a solution.*

- *They have a disposition to be open minded in considering all conflicting interests and any new relevant information that may be posed.*

- *They are fair-minded in avoiding to the extent possible any conflict of interests in making decisions.*

- *They have the noble nature of voicing their reflective reasoning among interested and affected parties.*

- In addition to these six predispositions, we add a seventh crucial requirement:

- *The sympathy requirement:* The moral managers must have sympathy for the pain and misery of others.

As we will see below, these characteristics do not guarantee that the manager makes ethical decisions, but we cannot expect moral decisions from those who do not have these predispositions. Nonetheless, we must also list certain necessary characteristics of the decisions themselves in order to judge them ex post as to whether they might be ethical. Although this list is presented below, we must keep in mind that even those decisions that meet this list must also meet our *moral maxim* standards as presented in the previous chapter.

5. Moral Managerial Decisions

The individual characteristics listed above are expected of those we would characterize as moral managers, although we certainly might be capable of expanding this list. Nonetheless, these personal characteristics do not guarantee that each individual decision is ethical. We can and must explore the characteristics of the individual decisions so that we can possibly analyze each to discern whether it is an ethical decision even when it is made by someone who fits the attributes of the moral judge or manager. In this section, we list here the characteristics we expect of these individual decisions.

As stated at the beginning of this chapter, virtue ethics links the appropriateness of actions back to what we identify as admirable personal attributes. To a considerable extent, we establish that linkage here. We can, however, also view the various ex post decision-characteristics as evidence of these desired personal attributes. It is important to realize, however, that these decision characteristics only potentially accomplish our task of providing ex post evidence of virtue. For some virtues, evidence is more nebulous rather than substantive. The virtue of sympathy, for example, is difficult to verify. Nonetheless, prior to implementation of any Kantian program, we want our management team to demonstrate as much as possible an ex post record of these moral decisions.

It is also important to note that we seek the virtues, and the associated list of decision characteristics, that implement our Kantian *moral maxims*. Providing a thorough list of decisions that exhibit the characteristics listed below, however, does not assure that our *moral maxims* are implemented, but only that management exhibits the virtues that create a tendency towards this implementation. For example, those who exhibit our list of virtues may still be lacking a full implementation of our maxim to avoid humiliating others. This separation or distance between virtue and implementation of company policy is always an ongoing practical business problem.

Consider our possible characterization of a particular judge as being "great," or particularly judicious. This does not imply, however, that we agree with all of his or her decisions. You might object to some interpretation of the meaning of the law. You might also find some to be unethical. Rawls (1951) listed the characteristics of moral decisions so that we can identify what it is that might be potentially unethical. Likewise, we could characterize managerial decisions by a similar but modified list. The list presented below is a slight modification of Rawls' list that he applied to the *moral judge*.

Our first characteristic follows directly from our *fair-minded virtue*.

I. Conflict of interest requirement: The manager is immune from reasonable foreseeable consequences of the managerial decision, i.e. the manager is personally disinterested.

For investigation of negotiation, the implication of "I" for business ethics is strong: the manager as intuitionist may satisfy the personal characteristics of moral management, but the legal-agency relationship with owners violates requirement "I" so that management's intuitionist decisions could never be considered moral. The view of manager as intuitionist is flawed; affected stakeholder parties, other than the owners, could not accept resulting decisions as ethical. This realization markedly shifts the foundation of business ethics to a firmer position in properly constrained democratic processes and resulting expression in law and negotiation. This foundation of *fair negotiation* is explored in detail below.

II. The effort requirement: The manager obtains the relevant facts, and intellectually explores the relevant options for solutions.

This is the application of the personal characteristic "II" listed above. Decisions must be based on a convincing managerial effort in obtaining the required factual evidence, and in exploring creative and possibly imaginative solutions to the problem at hand. The decisions must be supportable by evidence, and this evidence must support the proposition that options were adequately explored. The supporting objective evidence of option-exploration must be present if any decision is to be judged as ethical.

III. The open opportunity requirement: All affected stakeholders have fair opportunities to provide evidence, and to pose possible solutions.

This is an application of personal characteristic "IV" reviewed above. The argument that stakeholders must have the opportunity to provide relevant input to the decision process does not imply the stakeholder-balance approach to management. Management must consider the evidence and frequently it must decide the optimal solution in the context of negotiation. This might require that some stakeholder groups be disappointed. The psychological stress that can result for management is something that must be suffered in order for ethical decisions to be made and implemented.

Knowledge that this stress might result can lead management to hide their decision either *a priori* or *ex post*. In the *a priori case*, management does not seek the stakeholder input before the decision is made because management knows that the stakeholders might argue their case in an emotional way. If the decision is perceived as not in their favor, then the stakeholder group might apply the technique of causing stress, the very thing management seeks to avoid or limit.

In the *ex-post case*, the decision has been made but hidden from the affected stakeholders. Management might even announce that the decision is one way, while in fact it is the opposite. The whole purpose is to keep the stakeholders satisfied, but this practice is clearly deceptive. In both the *a-priori* and the *ex-post case* the *opportunity requirement* is violated, and the managerial decision is unethical. A record of this sort of perverse behavior should not exist for those we ask to implement our Kantian program.

IV. The logic requirement: The decision is supported by a clear logical structure, one that is supported by evidentiary premises and a logically drawn conclusion. The decision is not based upon mechanical application of principles in an ideological way, but rather it must be a considered, i.e. logical, decision based upon examination of the case.

This is an application of personal characteristic "III" reviewed above. Sometimes we encounter agreements that we deem as "intellectually dishonest." These arguments either do not utilize relevant evidence, or use the evidence in a biased way, or they draw illogical conclusions from the evidence. In any of these cases, the decision is clearly unethical. Using a-priori ideology to bias our analysis is a typical example of violating this requirement. A record of intellectually honest decisions must be expected of those we seek to implement our Kantian program.

Supporting evidence for the personal attributes of intelligence, the noble nature, and sympathy for the pain of others is difficult to discern from individual decisions. We can, however, discern tendencies over a lengthy series of decisions. For example, we can note that some manager has never spoken out against peer pressure, and publicly proclaimed "This is wrong!" Also, we can note that there are no instances in a series of many decisions when this manager indicated concern for the consequent pain of others adversely affected. These examples would provide evidence of diminished capacity to implement our Kantian *maxims*.

6. Personal Moral Attributes as Inputs to Personal Productivity

Consider the virtues reviewed above as factor inputs to the individual manager's productive capacity for developing and implementing the Kantian *moral maxims* developed by the firm, i.e., the *clarity* and *harmony* objectives explored in Chapter V. It helps our exposition if we identify the following *personal attributes or virtues* with the indicated associated symbols:

(1) Intelligence (I), as in an ability to use logic.

(2) A disposition to acquire knowledge relevant for the problems at hand (K).

(3) A disposition to apply logic to resolve the problems at hand (L).

(4) A disposition of open mindedness to consider the arguments of all affected parties (O).

(5) The disposition to be fair-minded in trying to avoid conflicts of interest (F).

(6) The *noble nature* of willingness to voice reflective thought in the relevant social setting (N).

(7) Sympathy for the pain of others (S).

We consider these *virtues* as factor inputs to the personal productive capacity of the individual manager to implement the company's Kantian *moral maxims*. In order to analyze this productive capacity, we need to answer the following interrelated questions:

- What is the degree of substitution of the 7 *virtues* listed above?

- To what extent are any of the 7 *virtues*, or combinations of them, required in fixed proportions?

- To what extent can these virtues be measured on a continuous scale?

The last question above, the measurement question, is very difficult. Virtues are nebulous by nature. We can envision an IQ test for ability to apply logic, and score this ability on a scale where 100 indicates the average, as is generally done for IQ tests. Data can be envisioned in terms of how many data sets we have gathered. Perhaps this data set concerns a constituent stakeholder, and gathering more data means gathering a wider statistical sample for analysis. The other virtues, however, are not so easily measured, but for purposes of our analysis below, we should envision them as measurable as indicated. This aids in reaching some understanding about how they might interact to increase this ethical capacity.

It appears obvious that the first 3 *virtues*, intelligence (I), disposition to acquire the knowledge of the problem at hand (K), and a disposition to apply logic to resolve these problems (L), are all required at some minimum level. As an example, this means that there is no reason to acquire the relevant knowledge without a desire to apply logical analysis to solve the problem. In addition, effective application of knowledge requires a certain minimum level of intelligence. It does not appear that one substitutes for the other, but rather they compliment each other, and are likely used in fixed proportions. More knowledge without logical analysis is probably not productive.

We assume that the disposition to be open minded either exists in the manager or not, i.e. O equals either 0 or O*, where O* indicates a disposition to be open minded, and 0 indicates the null of the opposite. In a similar way, either the manager is fair-minded (avoids conflicts of interest) or not, so that F equals either 0 or F* where F* indicates the state of fair-mindedness. Also, either the manager has the courage of the noble nature to speak in a social context or not, so that N equals either 0 or N*. Lastly, either the manager has sympathy for the pain of others or not, i.e. S equals either 0 or S*. Without this last virtue, knowledge, logic and intelligence are likely to not be useable as moral traits. This is in keeping with Hume's (1751) and Smith's (1759) arguments about the centrality of this *virtue*, and also in keeping with the arguments of McDowell (1985) and Nagel (1986).

It is possible that to some small extent these four virtues (O, F, N and S) could be developed through a professional education program of having managers examine various hypothetical exercises and pose solutions, but probably not to a sufficient extent that the first three, I, K and L, can be developed. Training exercises can show managers the importance of applying logic to find optimal solutions, and the need for gathering sufficient information to make sound decisions. Exercising logical faculties can also help its development.

We therefore express a production relation p for the manager's productive capacity (P) to implement the Kantian *harmony* as given below by (6-1), where the necessary levels O*, F*, N* and S* are maintained.

$$P = p(I, K, L \mid O^*, F^*, N^*, S^*) \qquad\qquad (6\text{-}1)$$

Figures 6-4a and b illustrate the effects of the dispositions to acquire relevant information (K) and to apply logic (L) on the productive capacity of the manager to implement *harmony*. We assume that K and L are continuous possibilities, but they must work in fixed proportions where $K/L = \alpha$. This fixed proportion concept is reasonable since additional disposition to acquire knowledge is unproductive without the disposition to apply logic and use it to solve the problem at hand.

The fixed proportion nature of K and L ($K/L = \alpha$) means that both must expand together or no additional increase in P is obtained. If this proportional expansion occurs, however, then as illustrated by Figure 6-4a and b, diminishing marginal returns to these virtues exists. This is certainly true for increases in information where beyond some point, more information will not aid in obtaining a more ethical result. This is certainly also true of logic where once an ethical solution is reasoned, application of further logical analysis is unproductive.

Figure 6-4a and b: Fixed Proportions Production Functions for K and L: K/L = α

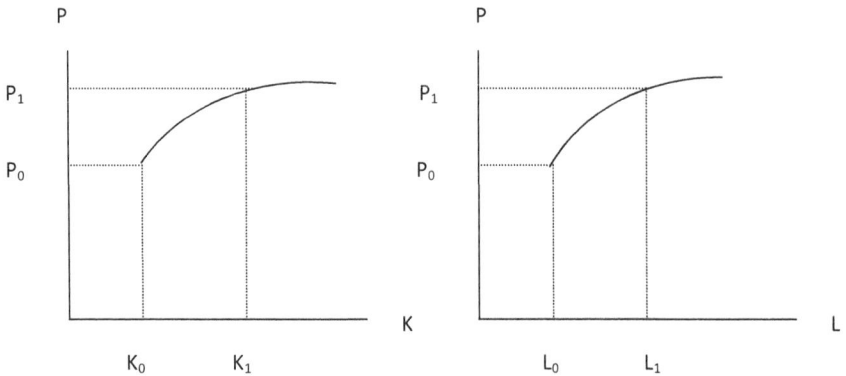

Where K = αL.

This fixed-proportion production relation is further illustrated by the isoquants of Figure 6-5 [61]. As shown, the farther from the origin, the higher the productive capacity, but increasing K without increasing L does not obtain a higher isoquant. One must increase both together, and at the proportion α. This notion is expressed by the ray from the origin of slope α, where this ray is the expansion path for these virtues. One cannot substitute one factor for the other and obtain higher capacity. In addition, in order to have any productive capacity at all, trait levels of O*, F*, N*, and S*, must be achieved.

Of course, the noble nature virtue (N) may not be so discreet in measurement, and the same might be true for the sympathy for the pain of others (S). N might be better envisioned as continuous where some exhibit a significantly greater tendency towards courageously speaking in public about what is unethical, perhaps persuasively so, and they might be willing to do so even when no one else is apparent in reinforcing this moral outrage. Others might merely have the minimum

---

[61] Isoquants are the loci of points of combinations K and L that yield a constant level of production P. In fixed proportions production, there is no tradeoff of K for L in that $\partial P/\partial K|_{L=L^*} = 0$, and $\partial P/\partial L|_{K=K^*} = 0$.

courage necessary to speak when egregious problems occur, and then only when they perceive some others as willing to stand behind them in this argument.

Figure 6-5: Virtues and Capacity: K and L, K/L = α

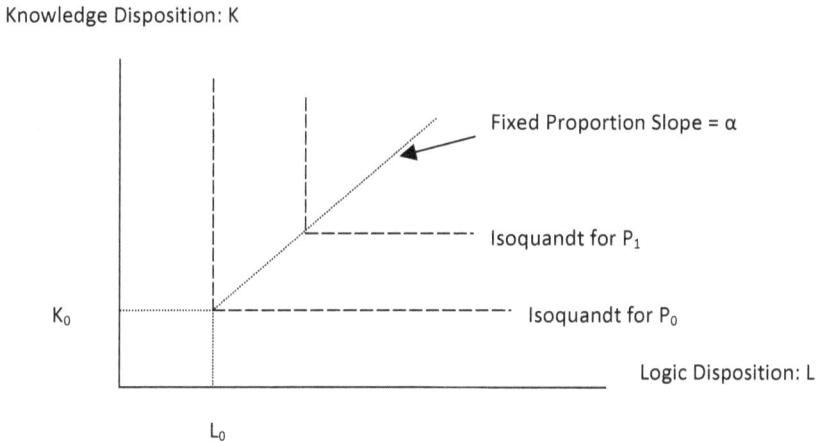

The virtue of *sympathy for the pain of others* might also exhibit a continuous scale. It might also exhibit severe diminishing marginal returns in that we can envision the possibility that this virtue, if highly developed, could inhibit some managers from ever making effective business decisions in that the effort to envision who might be hurt, and by how much, might be paralyzing in costing extreme delays.

Arguments of this sort could also be potentially true with the disposition to seek new knowledge (K), and the open mindedness disposition (O). Seeking continuously higher levels of new knowledge can also be paralyzing, resulting in the manager being ineffective in making decisions. The willingness to hear continually more arguments about the problem at hand can also paralyze the manager in the same way. Both traits can exhibit sharp diminishing marginal returns to effective ethical problem solving in that they can lead to no solution being posed.

7. Personal Productivity as Inputs to the Firm

Ideally, we expect our top level executives to exhibit very high degrees of the virtues we listed above. We hope that this is the case because, as we have argued, these dispositions lend themselves to application of our Kantian moral maxims. Perhaps to obtain top-level managerial positions, these virtues must be exhibited; that the selection process for promotion to the top levels assures these virtues are present. It is obvious, however, that these dispositions are present in mixed combinations for any particular person, that some will exhibit more logic, others more sympathy for the pain of others, etc.

To simplify our presentation, however, consider our list of virtues as existing in some fixed homogeneous combination. In this way, we can graph our combination as in Figure 6-6. Here, we indicate the firm's expectation for management exhibition of virtues. This exhibition is measured against the distance from the CEO, i.e., the farther from the CEO, the lower the level of virtue exhibition we expect to find. We generally believe that the CEO should be the keeper of our moral maxims, the one who propagates our organization's *clarity* and *pursuit of harmony*, and the chief enforcer of these maxims. As argued above, our 7 virtues are factor inputs to this process.

Every manager, top-level, mid-level, or low-level, is individually responsible for developing and demonstrating our list of virtues. This is because they are individually responsible for the *clarity* concerning, and the effectiveness of, *the pursuit of harmony.* It is just that the higher the level of management, the greater the degree of expected responsibility.

Figure 6-6 also indicates (by the dashed line) a minimum acceptable degree of these *virtues* as a function of this distance from the CEO. Note that by showing this dashed line above the solid line (the function that represents the generally accepted industry level), we indicate that the firm depicted has higher standards than the average for the industry.

The personal production function of (6-1) indicates the capacity of the individual manager to contribute to the firm's Kantian *harmony*, i.e., the development and implementation of our moral maxims. We argued in Chapter V that this *harmony* is a factor input to shareholder wealth; that our stakeholders should be convinced of management's commitment to these maxims, and if so, their cooperation will lead to a more productive firm.

Figure 6-6: Management Level and
Virtue Demonstration

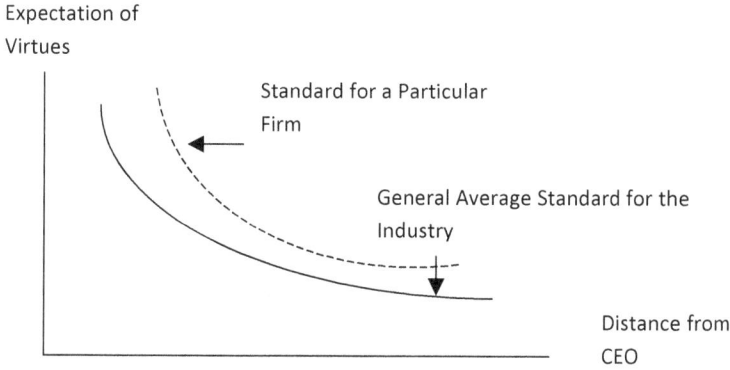

Expectation of
Virtues

Standard for a Particular
Firm

General Average Standard for the
Industry

Distance from
CEO

We indicate the firm's capacity for implementation of its moral maxims as a function of the individual managers' team of collective capacity by function (6-2) where FC is the firm's capacity, and Pj is the capacity of the individual manager j. The firm's mix of P1 to Pn is, however, of particular concern. For example, consider an array of 1 to n-1 managers who all have high levels of productive capacity, but these levels are all resulting from high levels of virtues other than the *noble nature*. The first n-1 managers each have only the minimum level of N necessary to be qualified team members. The n'th manager is, however, the one who does exhibit more of the *noble nature* than the minimum necessary. The fact that this person is the only one with a higher exhibit of this virtue makes him/her potentially very productive in capacity.

$$FC = f(P_1, ..., P_n) \tag{6-2}$$

The point is that the interpersonal virtues can be complimentary and even substitutable among the team members, although not necessarily within each individual. The standard the firm seeks for an individual manager should be high for the *noble nature* if other existing managers have low levels of this attribute. This would generally be true for any attribute lacking in the management pool. The problem is that there is always a tendency for the team to want to replicate themselves, or to replicate what is in effect a mean of their attributes. This can lead to the sort of deficiencies that result in no one speaking out, or no one envisioning the pain that might be caused to some non-team individual as a result of managerial actions, or no one is being willing to hear the views of some important stakeholder group that is affected.

8. Implementing the Kantian Model

So far we have envisioned our Kantian model of *clarity* and *harmony* in the implementation of our moral maxims as constraints on shareholder wealth maximization (SWM). By this idea of constraint we mean that some minimum level of implementation of our moral maxims must be established or unethical results occur. The distrust, lack of truthfulness, lack of communication, and lack of benevolent cooperation among and with management and various stakeholders might even cause serious SWM erosion. Improvement in implementation of our moral maxims beyond this minimum required may, however, enhance SW at least up to some point. We deal with this last point later. For the moment, we envision merely implementing some minimum acceptable level of *clarity* (understanding) and *harmony* (general commitment to pursue these maxims). For the moment, we seek a cost minimizing level of implementing this model.

We remind the reader of the *moral maxims* presented in Chapter V by presenting this brief list:

(1) *Prohibition against lying promises.*

(2) *Practical benevolence towards others.*

(3) *Act as though our actions were publicly known.*

(4) *Respect for the dignity of others within the organization, or within other stakeholder groups, even when we*

    a. personnaly dislike them, or

    b. they are not to be long-term members.

    This implies proper communication and a prohibition against behavior that humiliates others.

(5) *Full recognition of agency obligations without obfuscation and with associated revelation of conflicts of interest to affected stakeholders.*

(6) *Implementation of systematic evaluation and reward methods that reflect responsibility assignments.*

The firm may have other maxims that it establishes as a result of social interaction with stakeholders, discussion and logical reflection. These also would have to be implemented according to some minimum acceptable level. **By minimum acceptable levels, we mean the level necessary for stakeholders to be convinced of the efficacy of the harmony program, that in fact, they are convinced the firm has a commitment to keep each of the established *maxims.*** Once convinced, they will pursue the maxims in the intended way. If we do not achieve this efficacy, the program of *harmony* will fail. We shall explain later how levels beyond this minimum level could be maintained in light of few and minor aberrations of our implementation.

As reviewed above, and as indicated by equation (6-2), the program cannot succeed without a sufficient level of firm capacity (FC), i.e., the mix of moral attributes among management that enable implementation of *clarity* and *harmony in pursuit of the moral maxims*. This means that there is a requisite degree of understanding of the maxims, plus dispositions to acquire knowledge, apply logic, to be open- and fair-minded, to have sympathy for the pain of others, and to have the *noble nature* of speaking ethical concerns in the appropriate social setting. All of this capacity requires that the individual managers have these attributes in various mixes, and that they should be used to complement each other so as to be highly effective. Shareholder wealth considerations require that the initial program's implementation, and the ongoing program design, would minimize costs provided the minimum acceptable level is established. The costs referred to consist of both the costs of implementation, and the expected costs of failure, in establishing *harmony*.

What do we mean by going beyond this minimum acceptable level, as defined above? Perfection in meeting all of the maxims may not be possible at any price. For example, employee manuals may be written so as communicate benefit packages understandably among almost all affected. Someone, however, may be confused, and accuse management of a "lying promise." Perhaps upon ex post review, some section of the manual might be seen as slightly confusing even though it communicated the idea to the vast majority of employees. Improvements might be made, but perfection is not likely achievable.

All of the maxims listed above have practical limitations. It is the general perception among stakeholders concerning implementation that is important, but this general perception may require effort towards periodic improvement. We could apply an economic marginalist solution to the problem, i.e. extend the program until the marginal increment to shareholder wealth is zero. This occurs where the present value of the marginal cost of implementation equals the present value of additional net cash revenue.

This solution is illustrated by Figure 6-7 where the marginal contribution to shareholder wealth (MSW) is shown as a function of firm capacity (FC). The minimum acceptable capacity (our constraint) is indicated by FCM and the optimal, the point where the marginal contribution is 0, is indicated by FCO. This "minimum acceptable" notion stems from the social-ethical norms of the firm's stakeholders, where these constituencies turn away from the firm if their perceptions are that the virtue characteristics of management are deficient as compared to society's standards. The marginal contribution to shareholder wealth contributed by firm capacity is indicated by MSWFC in equation (6-3) and the marginal increase in firm capacity due to the set of virtues P of the individual manager is indicated by MFCP. [62]

The neoclassical economic model requires that the marginal contribution to wealth of the individual's attributes be employed up to the point of equality with the market wage of compensation. At this point $\partial SW/\partial P = 0$. For practical purposes, however, we can state that firm capacity will be somewhere between FCM and FCO. Obtaining the optimal requires changing the managerial makeup in such a way that the association transactions costs might hinder this fine tuning.

Figure 6-8, however, shows a different situation for the minimum firm capacity (FCM). For this possible situation, the minimum required capacity exceeds the point where marginal return to shareholder wealth is zero. Movement from FCO to FCM causes erosion of wealth, but nonetheless, since our program acts as a constraint on wealth maximization, and firm capacity acts as a constraint on

[62] Equation (6-3) can be expressed as $(\partial SW/\partial FC)(\partial FC/\partial P) = (\partial SW/\partial P) = 0$.

our Kantian program, the constraint must be met. We can argue, however, that this is unlikely to occur because the Kantian program is essential to generating shareholder wealth. If it is that crucial to wealth, then as exhibited in Figure 6-7, FCM < FCO is likely, and an optimal will be established.

Figure 6-7: Contribution of Firm Capacity (FC) to Shareholder Wealth (SW)

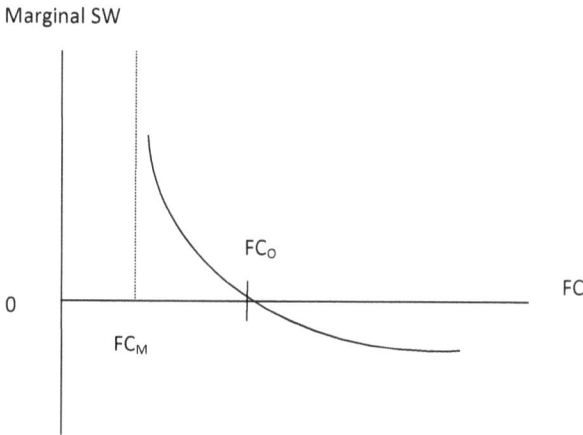

$$(MSW_{FC})(MFC_P) = (MSW_P) = 0 \qquad (6\text{-}3)$$

where MSW is marginal shareholder wealth, MFC is firm capacity for implementation of Kantian program, P is the individual manager's capacity for contributing to the firm's capacity.

From the practical view, the firm might inherent a team of managers employed prior to the implementation of the Kantian program. If this team is viewed as deficient, or insufficient, i.e., if FC < FCM, then personnel changes will be made either through engaging new additional managers, or replacing old ones. This process will occur until FCM ≤ FC ≤ FCO.

Once the appropriate Kantian program is decided (the appropriate mix of maxims to be emphasized), then this should be considered a constraint on the shareholder wealth maximizing goal. The capacity necessary to produce this program is then decided along with the managerial attributes necessary to provide this firm capacity. The cost minimizing combination of managers necessary to achieve this capacity could then be sought. It should be obvious, however, that managerial characteristics other than the attributes examined above are likely to be the determining factors in employing the management team. Their abilities in the traditional areas of finance, production and marketing will be the primary factors. The suggestion in this chapter, however, is that the required attributes necessary for implementation of the Kantian program of *clarity* and *harmonious pursuit of these maxims*, must themselves be considered as constraints that must be met by the management team employed. Some of these managers, however, must exhibit attributes beyond the minimums required; they must be able to lead this program implementation, especially with respect to the *noble nature*.

Figure 6-8: Contribution of Firm Capacity (FC) to Shareholder Wealth (SW)

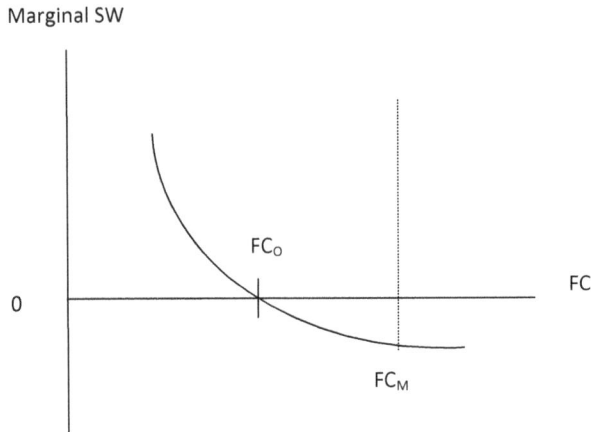

9. Costs, Codes and Catastrophe

The CEO is ultimately responsible for any program of Kantian maxims. Implementation of a program requires the recognition of the associated costs, particularly of the cost of failure, i.e., of *catastrophe*. As we have observed with many business scandals, catastrophic moral failure generally results in serious disruption of the firm, massive wealth and income erosion, and sometimes ultimate liquidation of the firm. (Barings Brothers Bank, Enron and World Com are some examples.) While the motivation for our moral maxims is not "We behave this way so as to preserve wealth!", we nonetheless must recognize the social costs of our maxims, and the consequences of catastrophic failure. Our *kingdom of ends of harmony* should be our motivation for implementing our program. This pursuit is not served by a poor initial design that raises the probability of failure needlessly.

The most significant danger associated with implementation of our program is that for behavioral practice, our maxims may be reduced to a shallowly held *code of conduct* such as explored in the previous chapter. Codes of this sort are easily violated and discarded. Catastrophe is then likely. Our implementation method must therefore be ultimately aimed at avoiding this code problem. Engaging a management team with the capacity traits reviewed above helps considerably to avoid this problem, but implementation must still manage to monitor managers, reinforce positive behavior, remediate destructive behavior, and monitor stakeholder feedback.

The costs of implementing and maintaining the program can be classified into 3 categories as indicated here:

(1) Implementation costs:

> a. The costs of engaging managers with the required capacity-attributes (*virtues*).

(2) This requires finding managers who demonstrate an adequate past record of having the attributes as indicated above.

> b. The costs of any required initial remedial-development program necessary to establish the required capacity and understanding among existing managers.

> c. The direct costs of initial implementation due to the development of policies and procedures, and their communication.

(3) Ongoing costs:

> a. The costs of monitoring which include the time and effort of management to seek stakeholder feedback concerning the program, and also periodic review and improvement of the program. Periodic reviews require periodic restatement and reinforcement of the program so that management is reminded of the importance of the program.

b. Ongoing remedial costs which include the costs associated with correction of personnel, the costs of termination and training of replacements when necessary, and any incentive costs necessary to induce the time and effort required to make the program a success.

(4) Failure costs:

a. The costs of bearing a failed program assuming the firm survives relatively intact, but needs to re-implement a new program.

b. The wealth and incomes lost if the firm fails because of major ethical lapses.

Consider the implementation costs. Finding managers with the required moral-attributes is likely to be more expensive than typical employment searches because verifying the record of attributes is not the usual HR practice. References who can verify these records are more difficult to find than the usual. Yet this record of seriousness with respect to implementation of the Kantian program must be established or the risk of establishing a mechanical *code of conduct* supported by shallow belief, and therefore with considerable risk of non-enforcement, is born. In addition, the costs of remedial programs necessary to convince and educate managers about the program, will also be more expensive if the engagement of managers with a more limited record is practiced.

Given observations in recent years of the costs associated with catastrophic failure, i.e. the shareholder wealth loss, it should be obvious that implementation costs are likely to be far less than failure costs; they are even less than expected failure costs when the probability of failure is low. Although for exploratory reasons we do list our ongoing costs as separate components, these costs should become so intertwined with general management practice that separating these as line items is not possible.

Non-catastrophic failure is more likely to be found in business than catastrophic failure. The former generally occurs through violation of our fifth (conflict of interest) or sixth (implementation of evaluation and reward systems) maxims listed above. For example, as indicated in Chapter II, management is inherently more risk averse than owners because the human capital of management generates most of their wealth, and this human capital is heavily invested in the firm.

Management therefore attempts to avoid any probability of financial distress. Owners, at least for publicly traded firms, are more likely to have their wealth more diversified. They prefer to bear a greater level of firm specific risk given that this generally leads to a higher on-average rate of return. Overly cautious behavior by management leads to stagnant underperformance, so it is a clear violation of management's agency obligations towards owners. This is frequently manifested by excessive liquidity at the expense of investment in real higher-earning assets, and also lowers than optimal leverage, and conglomerate diversification with associated less efficient management.

Effective evaluation and reward systems that are aligned with the assignment of responsibilities and performance are not easy for management to implement and practice. For example, implementation of proper capital-budgeting systems that solicit new product line suggestions, or new marketing suggestions, are necessary for optimal firm growth. There is stress involved, however, in evaluating co-workers. People are seldom saintly. They react to incentives. Faulty evaluation and reward systems is not only inefficient, it is an ethical obligation of management.

In Chapter XI, we review the arguments of Hanna Arendt concerning failure of codes of conduct. It is only necessary here to briefly review some of this argument. Prior to failure, whether catastrophic or otherwise, managers and other stakeholders generally express a lack of belief or commitment to the program. Perhaps this will be manifested by an expression of disbelief of the necessity of, or by a lack of commitment to, one or more of the maxims. This requires the CEO to question whether one or more of the maxims should be logically modified. Easy or quick abandonment of previous commitments pose the problem of contagion.

Arendt argues that a breakdown of the code is generally preceded by a vociferous person who questions the code, and who causes others to have little understanding of the need for, or commitment to, some maxims. This leads to abandonment, and ultimately to moral failure. To prevent this slippery slope, any changes in maxims must be accompanied by considerable reflective thought and open logical debate among management. Adoption and commitment to new maxims must be equally open and clear. Maxims are not to be abandoned due to inconvenience or to serve conflicts of interest. Pursuit of *harmony* is the only ethical motive for change.

In Chapter XI we also review a necessary ex-post evaluation and remediation system required for effective implementation of the Kantian program. When managerial decisions are judged as violating the moral code, the violations must be explained clearly, corrective action explained if necessary and all of this must be viewed as routine and nonthreatening (at least when less severe lapses occur). This continuous corrective system is a necessary part of the frequent reflective reviews that will implement the Kantian system.

Review questions:

(1) What is the essential difference between the philosophy of *virtue ethics* and Kantian ethical philosophy?

(2) How do we reconcile Aristotle's notion of the *flourishing life* to the Kantian motivation provided by the *third formula*?

(3) Are there gangland cultures that exhibit admirable virtues? If so, review these cultures and the virtues developed? Do these cultures exhibit Kantian characteristics in that their moral values are consistent with the *categorical imperative*? Can you envision some business developing a culture that exhibits similar gangland dispositions? How might it conflict with the Kantian *moral maxims* we previously explored?

(4) Explain how *sympathy for the pain of others* aids in Kant's *third formula of the categorical imperative* as the ethical motivation?

(5) Is it possible that a manager who lacks one, or some, or all of the personal traits listed above could still make a moral decision of some serious complexity?

(6) Explain in some detail that addresses each of the traits one by one?

(7) Explain how the *conflict of interest* requirement prevents non-owner stakeholders from viewing managerial decisions as ethical? How does this view emphasize negotiated agreements as solutions to ethical conundrums?

(8) Explain the linkage between characteristics II and III, and then II and IV?

(9) Explain how transaction-cost problems can limit the application of II, III or IV?

(10) What does "fixed proportions" mean in the context of the production function (6-1)?

(11) Explain the minimum levels necessary for O*, F*, N* and S*?

(12) Explain how a team of managers can overcome some individual's virtue deficiency? How is the "noble nature" virtue particularly relevant for this consideration?

(13) Fully explain Figures 6-7 and 6-8? Explain the shapes of these functions and what the comparative graphics illustrate?

(14) Under conditions of uncertainty, why might management allow the probabilities of failure to increase? Why might management allow failure to occur?

Chapter VII

---— ❧ —---

NEGOTIATION AND FAIRNESS

Chapter Abstract: Following Rawls, Kantian principles are extended to establish rules for fair negotiation, rules that prohibit deception, coercion and the like. Using the concept of Pareto optimality, the Edgeworth-box analysis is used to define an optimal result of fair negotiation (a position where all affected parties reach the contract curve), so that the agreement is stable. The implications for firm efficiency and SWM are also reviewed.

1. Ethical Negotiation

Negotiating skill is crucial in business. As reviewed in a previous chapter, the *conflict of interest* requirement for moral decisions makes any management decreed solutions to ethical conundrums suspect among non-owner stakeholders. In addition, decreeing solutions may directly conflict with *formula 2* of Kant's *Categorical Imperative: the formula for the respect for the dignity of persons.* Unless it just occurs by coincidence, we cannot claim we are allowing others the freedom to pursue their own interests if we merely decree actions for them. For this reason, *harmony* is particularly difficult to achieve through reliance on managerial imposed solutions. As reviewed in Chapter V, this Kantian notion of *harmony* requires general clarity concerning the pursuit of moral maxims among the relevant stakeholders, with these maxims being consistent with Kant's *categorical imperative.* This *harmony* requires that management negotiate settlements with non-owner stakeholders. This can be effective in pursuing shareholder-wealth maximization (SWM) provided the negotiations are viewed as *fair* by all parties.

Harmony can only be maintained to the extent that these negotiations are viewed as . It is important to remember that this *harmony*, as defined by Kant's *kingdom of ends,* is required for SWM as also explained previously.

The negotiations referred to above may be either *implicit* or *explicit*. A good example of the former type would be the hiring process where it is typical for an advertisement to be published, one that states most of the requirements of the position. Applicants are solicited who have a general understanding about the employment requirements. Perhaps some similar work experience is specified as required so that training costs are lowered. The wage is communicated, and from the pool of applicants, an offer of employment is made to whoever is considered the best applicant. In this process, it does not appear that the applicants are making any demands in the employment considerations, but implicitly they are when they apply. At this point, they declare that the generally understood requirements are acceptable.

If, however, an insufficient pool of applicants is solicited by the advertisement, then the offers and the advertisement must be changed. The offer must be made more attractive, perhaps through the offered wage, or through some other change in job characteristics. In this way, the employer is *implicitly negotiating* with the labor market even though potential employees are not given the opportunity to sit down with the employer and haggle over terms.

The *fairness* requirement with respect to this negotiation concerns the Kantian issues of deception, or divulgence of sufficient information, or adherence to employment law in that the employer must not violate society's legal norms in the offered employment. [63] If our notions of *fairness* and legalities are not violated, then we presume that the hired employee is pursuing their own ends, and the *categorical imperative* is not violated.

Examples of explicit negotiation are more obvious. They include the employment negotiation where the potential employee and employer do explicitly haggle over all details of the employment contract. All notions of Kantian *fairness* must, of course, apply to these negotiations.

---

[63] An example would be some sort of tie-in agreement such as demanding illegal kickback payments, or other illegal actions.

It should be obvious that all implicit, and many explicit negotiations are actually market negotiations. In fact, it is difficult to envision any market transaction that does not involve either implicit or explicit negotiation. For example, when we walk into a store and see some potential good for purchase, even if it is not a very familiar good purchased many times previously, we still assume certain properties concerning its quality assurance. Indeed, these qualities are often communicated through displays or vender attitudes of familiarity. These are all part of the implicit negotiations of the sort that states, "Keep buying from me and I will assure the quality!"

We shall see, however, that the rules of fair negotiations are more explicit and extensive than we have previously suggested. This chapter uses Rawlsian notions of *fairness*, as well as last Chapter's review of the characteristics of the *virtuous manager*, to derive the *rules of fair negotiation.* By the end of this chapter, we must show how these rules both facilitate and constrain our notions of SWM. Some material presented in Chapter IV will be used as a basis for exploring the notion of *fairness* in negotiation. We can delimit the so called initial conditions required of those who seek to negotiate, and also the rules followed in the negotiation, so that the negotiation itself can be judged as ethical. Thereupon we can judge the resulting agreement as *fair or unfair.*

2. Kantian Notions of Ethical Negotiations

It should be obvious that to be ethical, the negotiation must meet the requirements of Kant's *categorical imperative* as explored in Chapter V and as stated here:

- *Extension of formula 1:* The required characteristics of the negotiators and the rules of the negotiations must apply to all participating parties (the *universality requirement*).

- *Extension of formula 2:* All parties must be allowed to pursue their own ends in that there is no coercion, and all affected parties are equally free to participate (the *respect for the dignity of others requirement*).

- *Extension of formula 3:* Pursuit of the *kingdom of ends* is required in that all participants pursue a final condition of *harmony.*

The meaning of the term *harmony* as used in the context of *fair negotiation* is subtly changed from its definition for *harmony within the organization*, as explored previously. When we examine *harmony* in the organization, we mean a state of all the organization's members cooperating in pursuing the moral maxims established. *Harmony in negotiation,* however, means each negotiating party respects the other's pursuit of their ends even when negotiations occur among external stakeholders such as customers and community interests. Each party should want the other to be successful in improving their condition. This requires that every non-owner stakeholder respects the interests of the owners, who in turn respect the interests of the other stakeholders.

If all three formulas of the *categorical imperative* are met, then we can claim that the resulting agreement has the potential to be ethical, but is not necessarily ethical. To reach this classification, both the negotiators, and the methods of negotiation, must meet certain *a priori* requirements. In particular, the negotiators must meet the traits listed in the previous chapter, and repeated here although in a somewhat rearranged form.

The first three traits are those that we as individuals would require of anybody representing us in some negotiation.

1. *The negotiators must have at least average intelligence, and must have a predisposition to apply inductive logic to reach an agreement.*

If someone is to represent us in negotiation, we would certainly require that they have the intelligence and logical skills to negotiate effectively. That is all we are trying to assure by this characteristic whether it applies to us individually as a negotiator, or to some representative negotiator.

2. *The negotiators must have a requisite knowledge of the issues to be negotiated.*

Effective negotiation without knowledge of the issues at hand is hardly possible.

3. *The negotiators must have a predisposition to be open minded in considering all conflicting interests, and also any new relevant information that may be posed.*

Negotiations can be lengthy and complex, with new data brought to the table at any point. Negotiators must be sufficiently open-minded and flexible to adapt and to analyze any new information.

The latter two traits are those required to assure that the *kingdom of ends* is pursued.

4. *The negotiators must have the noble nature of voicing their reflective ethical reasoning among interested and affected parties.*

The negotiators must not be willing to negotiate for an unethical result. The *categorical imperative* must not be violated. Without the *noble nature* being a characteristic of at least one of the negotiators, it is very possible to reach an agreement that violates our *categorical imperative.*

5. *The negotiators must have sympathy for the pain and misery of others.*

This trait really goes along with #4. It motivates the *noble nature* referred to above.

3. Objectives of Fair Negotiation

The Edgeworth Box Diagram analysis, reviewed in Chapter IV, is particularly applicable to the fairness issue examined here. As a result, Figures 7-1 and 7-2 repeat those presented in Chapter IV. We assume that the two parties to the negotiations, Individuals X and Y, begin with the initial endowments of the two goods, A and B, indicated by *position 1*. This initial position determines the particular indifference curves (constant utility curves) for each individual, IC–X1 and IC–Y1 in Figure 7-1. Any point in the interior of these initial-endowment indifference-curves increases the utility of both individuals and is defined as a *Pareto move*. This illustrates that negotiations that move the individuals from *point 1 to 2*, have the potential of improving the positions of both. The slope of the arrow indicates the *terms of the* trade, i.e. how much of A is traded for B.

The *contract curve*, the loci of points of tangency of the interior indifference curves, are Pareto optimal in that once one of these points is reached, any further negotiated change must leave at least one of the individuals worse off. The objective of our *rules of fair negotiation* is to assure that some point on the contract curve that is interior to IC-X1 and IC-Y1 is achieved. Figure 7-2 illustrates this Pareto optimal point, shown as position 2 where IC-X* and IC-Y* are tangent. Our derived *rules of fair negotiation* do not determine which exact point is achieved; that depends upon the relative negotiating abilities of the individuals. The *rules* can only assure that a *Pareto optimal* position along the contract curve is achieved.

To derive these *rules of fairness*, consider Figure 7-2, and its illustration of moving from *point 1* to *point 3*. This move results in Individual X being worse off, and Individual Y better off, and as such, the move is clearly not a *Pareto move*. There are only 3 possible ways that this move could be negotiated: (1) the negotiations occur with Individual X having an information disadvantage about the ultimate move, (2) there is clear deception on the part of Individual Y that tricks Individual X into believing that the move would make him or her better off, or (3) Individual Y has some coercive power over X and uses it to force the move. Consideration of these three possibilities helps determine the following simple and understandable *rules of fair negotiation*.

4. The Seven Rules of *Fair Negotiations*

In this section, we present seven *rules of fair negotiation* as derived from the arguments presented above. They are:

1. *There is no deception involved in the negotiation.*

It is clear that the rule prohibiting "deception" is required of Kant's *formula 2* of the *Categorical Imperative*. Deception is essentially a lying promise. It may be a "bait and switch scheme," or a purposeful reneging on the agreement to trade. In any case, it certainly will violate Kantian *moral maxims*. It therefore must form one of our *rules of* fairness.

2. *The counter parties are not disadvantaged due to any inequality of information access.*

The rule for information access equality is also essential for fair negotiations. This rule is often difficult to meet in practice. Even if all negotiating parties have equal access to the same information, some might still interpret the information in a biased manner. The rule, if followed, can only assure equal access, not equal use. We can say, however, that this rule is required by all three formulas for the *categorical imperative*. It is certainly required by the *universality* constraint. No individual would willingly accept an information disadvantage in negotiation. They therefore must accept a *moral maxim* that all be equal in information. This rule is obviously also required by the *formula for the respect for the dignity of others*. We cannot keep to this formula while knowingly having important information that our negotiating counterparty does not have. Also, those who are serious in their motivation of pursuit of the *kingdom of ends* will reason that this pursuit is not possible from negotiations that do not begin with a level informational playing field.

3. *The counter parties are equal in power to negotiate so that no exploitation is possible.*

Power is the ability to control outcomes. With respect to negotiation, the only ethical outcome worthy of managerial power is *fairness*. Coercion in negotiation is important to avoid given our *fairness* concept.

Consider negotiations between parties 1 and 2, and allow them to negotiate over the distributions of good A. Party 2, however, knows that party 1 could deprive them of another good B depending upon the results of the negotiation, yet B is not a part of the negotiations. These two parties are therefore not equal to negotiate if B is valued by party 2.

For example, consider the case of the employee who has considerable employment years at some company. Allow the employee to have one more year until retirement. If the employee is fired before retirement, however, then all retirement benefits are lost. Can that employee negotiate effectively over his/her work schedule? Not unless the employee is assured of no undue threat (above the norm) of being fired. To be equal in negotiation, management would need to assure the employee that there is, and there will continue to be, no coercion used. The employee must be assured that within any constraints established (constraints such as "you must work 40 hours per week, and as with all other employees, some hours must be worked at night, or on weekends, etc."), they will be treated fairly in comparison with other workers, or within a clearly established seniority system.

In business negotiations, sensitivity to coercive power is a requirement of management. Managers might actually have coercive power, or just be perceived as having this power. In either case, a fair outcome may not result. To be *fair*, all negotiating parties who do have coercive power must assure their counter parties that this power will not be used. More will be expressed about this below.

4. *The counter parties are free to negotiate; there are no legal or other encumbrances on their authority to bargain and reach an agreement.*

In addition, all parties must be aware of any legal restrictions on others to negotiate. The negotiator cannot negotiate away property rights that are not fully owned or controlled.

5. *Every party that is affected by the negotiation is equally represented in the negotiation. There are no externalities resulting from the agreement.*

The fifth rule is very important, and it is related to the fourth rule. It is certainly not fair that two parties negotiate a negative externality imposed on a third party such as "Let you and I agree to dump our garbage on the property of our neighbor." At least, we cannot negotiate this without the neighbor fully participating in the negotiation. All parties affected must have the opportunity to participate equally in the negotiation. Without this rule, we could hardly state that any of the three formulas of the *categorical imperative* would be followed.

6. *The counter parties communicate and explore various options for negotiations.*

Negotiators need to communicate possible *Pareto movements* in order to actually reach an agreement. This really follows from the logic requirement for negotiations. Logic dictates that the negotiators communicate various possible solutions. This requirement, however, also eliminates laziness on the part of negotiators, i.e., they could be logical but lazy, and as a result, no Pareto movement occurs although some are possible.

It is important to realize that these six *rules of fairness* do not assure that *Pareto movements* occur. A typical problem occurs when one or both of the counter parties stick to preconceived notions of fair-terms *of trade*, but the preconceived notion would not yield a *Pareto movement*. Consider a man walking through a farmer's market looking to purchase an apple. This shopper has preconceived notions as to a *fair price* for the apple, and this price is based upon previous purchases over previous days. Either the demand or the supply, or both, have changed however, and the market-clearing price has risen. If the shopper has sufficient time to explore among the various dealers, he may be able to reform his notion of what a *fair price* is, and perhaps be able to make a deal with one of the merchants, but this involves time and effort, or using different phraseology, *transaction costs*. These costs can prevent a *Pareto movement* in that without the preconceived notion of the mistaken price, the shopper may be willing to purchase at the higher market-clearing price, and consider himself better off. [64]

Consider, however, another sort of negotiation, one involving a union agent and an agent representing the firm's owners. Both begin with mistaken ideas about other wage settlements that are widely divergent. Given time and effort, they could explore previous and recent wage settlements, and perhaps reach some notion as to an agreeable wage. *Fairness* demands that these agents explore this information even though transactions costs are involved.

Transaction costs can inhibit a wide variety of bargaining. For this reason, we assert a seventh rule of fairness.

7. *The negotiating counter parties must not impose unnecessary transactions costs as a bargaining tool for the purpose of obtaining coercive power.*

One can argue that this *rule* is redundant in that the combination of the first six rules implicitly contains the seventh. It is important, however, to indicate the importance of *transactions costs* for inhibiting *Pareto movements*, and so it is perhaps worthwhile to isolate this *rule*. A negotiator can try for advantage by delaying the negotiations, or in various ways making the negotiations uncomfortable. The belief is that by perpetrating these delays and inconveniences, the counter party is worn down, and is willing to accept less advantageous terms. *Fair negotiations*, however, require that all counter parties attempt to limit and reduce the transactions costs associated with the negotiations, and do so for all parties. In fact, negotiations can be very complex and occur in stages. The first stage is often over the conditions utilized for latter stages. It is at this initial stage that negotiators are required to help facilitate a low transactions cost *Pareto movement*.

A perfect example of transactions costs being exploited to obtain unfair advantage are frequently observed in legal tort suits. Lawyers often demand very lengthy,

[64] This can be considered a violation of rule #2, but it is important to fully consider the consequences of this problem in terms of the transactions costs involved.

cumbersome and expensive in time and legal fees, depositions that are primarily just delaying tactics. These tactics are really adversarial in nature, and are not aimed at having both parties better off, but rather at having one party win while the other loses. For these legal cases, transactions costs are used as a weapon, and violate the *rules of fair negotiations*, except we should realize that these rules are not meant to apply to adversarial proceedings. We might, however, explore applying some rules of fairness to the system of legal adversarial proceedings, but that is not examined here.

Figure 7-1: Edgeworth-Box Diagram

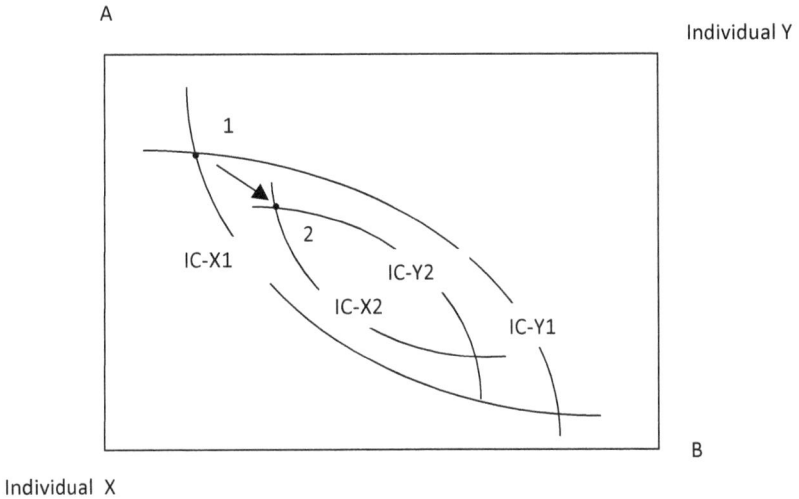

Figure 7-2: Edgeworth-Box Diagram

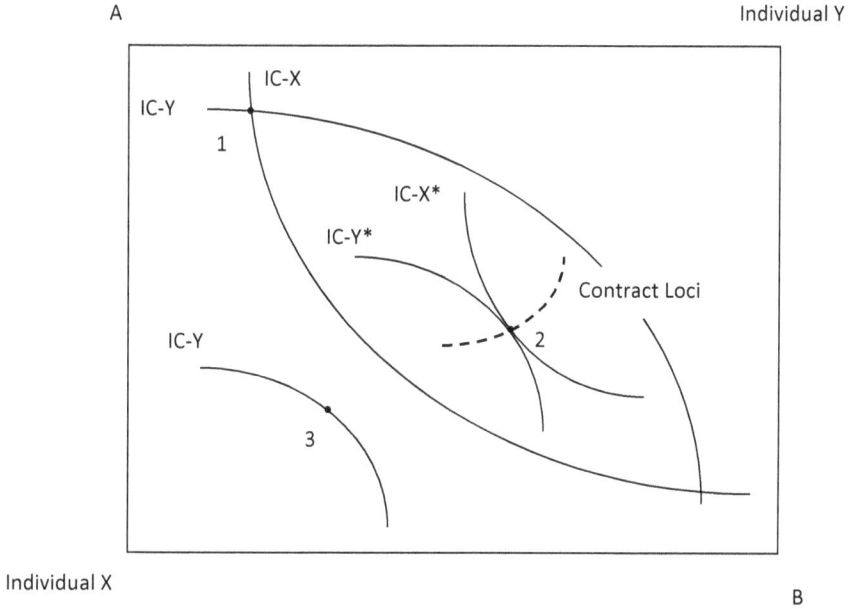

5. Definitions of *fair agreement* and *extent of negotiations*

We use the Edgeworth-Box analysis reviewed above to explore various questions:

1. Once negotiations have begun, if the *rules of fairness* are maintained, must any agreement lead to an interior position with both parties better off, i.e., a Pareto move?

2. If negotiations continue under the *rules of fairness*, will a position on the contract curve eventually be reached?

We argued so far that the answer to both these questions is "yes!" This is the very purpose of our exploration of the fairness issue: fairness facilitates both the continuance of negotiations and the ultimate achievement of a position on the *contract curve*. Such a position, where all parties are better off, promotes Kantian *harmony*, and perhaps of equal importance, it promotes a continuance of *harmony* as required of SWM. As a result, the Edgeworth-Box analysis facilitates a definition:

Definition of fair agreement:

A fair agreement is one agreed to by all counter parties, and that has been reached according to the rules of fair negotiations.

It might be argued that the negotiating parties could start at position "1" in Figure 7-2, meet all rules of *fair negotiations*, and move to some position that is not strictly interior, one that leaves only one person better off, but the other no worse off (on the same original IC). One must ask the question, however, why would the person who is not better off agree to the move? Was coercion involved, or some other violation of *fairness*? Perhaps some other side agreement was reached that left the apparent no-better-off negotiator actually better off? This is a particular problem that involves what we term *the extent of the negotiation*, and we explore this situation below.

The answer to our questions, however, must be "It is not possible!" If the *rules of fairness are followed*, then all parties will inevitably be better off, and therefore *harmony* is facilitated. We mean by this that if stakeholders, internal and external, have an *a priori* disposition to pursue Kantian *harmony*, then following the *rules of fairness*, they will inevitable be left better off as a result of the negotiations. They will therefore not be left *frustrated*. Their disposition to pursue *harmony* should continue.

6. The Extent of the Negotiation

As indicated above, negotiations are often multi-dimensional. Rather than simple negotiations over goods A and B, they may also be over C, D, and E, all simultaneously to be settled. It is useful for us to define the range of goods subject to the negotiations.

Definition of extent:

The extent of the negotiations consists of both the positive and negative goods to be distributed by the negotiated agreement.

A principle problem occurs if there is no clear understanding as to this *extent of the negotiations* prior to reaching the agreement. This is a problem that frequently occurs; one that can lead to considerable frustration and anger. The problem has considerable potential to disrupt the organization's *harmony*.

To clearly understand this problem, we use the employment negotiation example referred to above. In this example, a manager negotiates with an employee over the hours of employment. The manager understands the negotiation to be narrow in that it is only over the hours of employment. The employee mistakenly believes, however, that a willingness to accept difficult hours improves his possibilities for promotion. The manager does not make it clear that the hours negotiated will have no impact on the employee's potential for promotion. The negotiations continue for some years until the employee erupts in anger due to frustration over not being promoted, all because the manager did not make the *extent of the negotiations* clear. Any sort of harmonious cooperation from the employee is now difficult to achieve, or to even expect. The employee feels cheated, and is not likely to subsequently concern himself with the *moral maxims* management preaches. He sees management as hypocritical.

7. Negotiating the Special Case of Risk

One of the special and important situations we should consider for *fair negotiations* concerns the question of who bears certain types of risk. By this, we mean negotiation between owners, as represented by their agents, and other stakeholders. In fact, all stakeholders in one way or another negotiate with owners over risk. Some of these negotiations consist of the following:

1) *Consumers negotiate product safety and reliability issues.*

This is usually an implicit negotiation that takes place through the marketplace. For example, consider the purchase of an automobile, both new and used. The consumer often negotiates over price and add-on amenities such as rust-proof coating, electronic equipment, paint color, etc. Warranty and service reliability issues are also subject to the negotiated package. The consumer's objective is to negotiate a reduced risk of his or her expenditures on future service. The owner's agent negotiates over the same issue. The price (wealth transfer) and associated terms are the negotiated instruments.

2) *Debt holders negotiate indenture and default terms.*

Borrowing funds is usually associated with complex legal agreements (the bond's "indenture agreements") that specify the recourse provisions in case of default (the "priority of claims"), and also various provisions that the bond holders require in order to limit the probability of default. The more restrictive these terms, the higher the price the market will pay for the bonds, i.e. the lower the interest rate the borrower must pledge to pay. These "bond indentures," however, restrict the actions of management so that it is more difficult to pursue various opportunities. There is uncertainty associated with both the possible future opportunities that the firm may have to avoid in order to maintain the indenture provisions, and also with the possibilities of financial distress (default). The negotiation is therefore over the division of risk of default between the borrower and the lender.

3) *Community interests negotiate employment externality issues.*

Local governments often seek potential employers to move to their area. They negotiate by offering tax-break incentives for the promise of a certain level of employment. The amount of employment is often not entirely contractual in that there is some range of employment specified. Also, along with the tax breaks, the community often demands restrictions of externalities such as noise or water pollution allowed. There is, however, always uncertainty as to the final outcome for employment and pollution, and hence there is risk for both sides. A guaranteed minimum employment-level in case the product market declines results in a greater wealth loss for the owners. Granting tax breaks when employment is not as high as expected, or pollution is higher than expected, means a wealth and welfare loss for the community.

4) *Employees negotiate employment guarantees.*

As with the case above, union negotiations are often over guarantees for employment versus the wage rate. The commitments for employment are often conditional in that they specify who is to be laid-off first in case of distress. Both parties bear uncertainty. If the product market declines, the owners must uphold their commitments and therefore they suffer wealth losses that are greater than if no commitment is made. The employees try to lower the risk of layoffs, but in return, they must make wage concessions, i.e. they give up wealth for greater certainty of employment. The owners have similar tradeoffs.

It is natural for owners to want others to bear their business risk, while other stakeholders want the owners to bear the risk. Wealth transfers are generally the negotiating instrument in that the owners are often willing to give up some wealth in return for the other parties bearing more risk. The wealth transfers might be in the form of higher salaries for employees, higher tax payments for community interests, higher rates of return for debt holders, etc.

Consider the indifference curve analysis illustrated by Figure 7-3. The variable E(wealth) measures the expected wealth to the individual, either the owner or some counter-stakeholder party, that results from some negotiation over a business related issue. Risk is measured by the standard deviation of the relevant probability distribution for wealth, as symbolized by s. [Material in Chapter 4 reviews the concepts of expected value and standard deviation of a discrete probability distribution, E(wealth), s, and also the indifference curves in this space.]

The indifference curves in Figure 7-3 show the preferences for expected wealth versus the risk associated with obtaining that wealth. It is important that we allow the probability distribution for wealth to be entirely subjective for both counter parties. By this we mean that an objective third party might or might not discern any objective evidence for these distributions.

For example, the negotiation could be over an employment contract, and the indifference curves could be those of an employee. The contract negotiated could allow for increased probability of layoffs in return for higher expected compensation. This is a risky situation since the employee can only measure expected wealth given the uncertain compensation stream. The contract allows for layoffs but with some assurance of reasonable probabilities of employment. The owners are willing to allow for higher compensation provided they are granted greater ease of laying employees off. The higher the risk of layoffs, as measured by the standard deviation of the wealth probability distribution, the greater the expected wealth to the employee. The negotiation is therefore over the exact level of E(wealth) and σ.

We allow E(wealth) and s to be entirely subjective in that the counter parties might disagree as to the actual probability distribution for the potential wealth transfer. Nonetheless, we show below that the Edgeworth-Box Diagram can apply. If the employee measures E(wealth) at Ee and risk at se, and the owners measure these parameters at Eo and so, then the dimensions of the Edgeworth Box are Ee + E0 by se + so, and the initial point is determined. We argue below that as long as their indifference curves are not tangent at this point then a Pareto move can be negotiated. Under these circumstances, a Pareto optimal point should be achievable provided our *rules of fairness* apply.

The indifference curves in the space of E(wealth) and σ are positively sloped and concave from above. Also, as shown in Figure 7-3, IC-2 is at a higher utility level than IC-1. These constant utility curves are concave from above because at low initial levels of E(wealth), the employee is willing to accept substantial increases in risk in order to obtain an increase in E(wealth). At a higher level of risk, however, any further increase in σ must be compensated by a much larger increase in E(wealth) [65]. This is just another way of stating that the employees are risk averse. (See the Chapter IV for a review of this notion of risk aversion.)

We also allow the owners to have positive sloped indifference curves in the space of E(wealth) and σ, and also allow them to be concave from above, i.e., owners also are assumed to be risk averse. Given the initial endowments of E(wealth) and σ, we can form an Edgeworth-Box Diagram as in Figure 7-4. If the *rules of fair negotiation* are upheld, then the employee and owner will reach some point on the *contract curve*, and this point will be a Pareto optimal point. We can state that the division of risk and expected wealth is *fair*.

As stated above, points along the *contract curve* are defined by the tangency of the two sets of indifference curves for the two negotiators, or in the language of utility theory, equality of the marginal rates of substitution for each of the negotiators, i.e., for the employee and owner negotiation example above, $MRS_e = MRS_o$ where $MRS = -MU_\sigma / MU_E$. [66]

---

[65] This is well explored in Chapter IV. Allow E = E(wealth), and the employee's utility function be given by U = U(E,σ). Taking the total differential of U gives dU = (∂U/∂E)dE + (∂U/$\partial\sigma$)dσ. Along the constant utility curve, dU = 0, so that dE/dσ = -(∂U/$\partial\sigma$)/(∂U/∂E). The differential dE/dσ is the slope of the indifference curve at any point. Since ∂U/$\partial\sigma$ < 0, i.e. the marginal utility of risk is negative, then dE/dσ > 0.
[66] MRS = -(∂U/$\partial\sigma$)/(∂U/∂E) as presented in Chapter IV.

8. Negotiations with Multiple Counter Parties

The Edgeworth -Box analysis facilitates the understanding and logic of negotiations between two parties. As we reviewed, fairness requires an attempt to leave both parties better off as a result of the negotiations. Conducting fair negotiations with multiple counter parties, however, can be problematic when interests within one of the negotiating groups are divergent. How can one assure that a minority will not be hurt while the majority is better off?

Figure 7-3: Risk Return Preferences

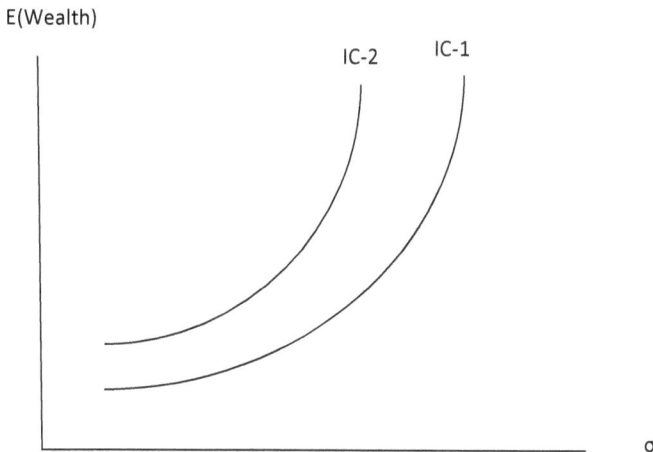

Figure 7-4: Edgeworth-Box Diagram for Risk Return Tradeoff

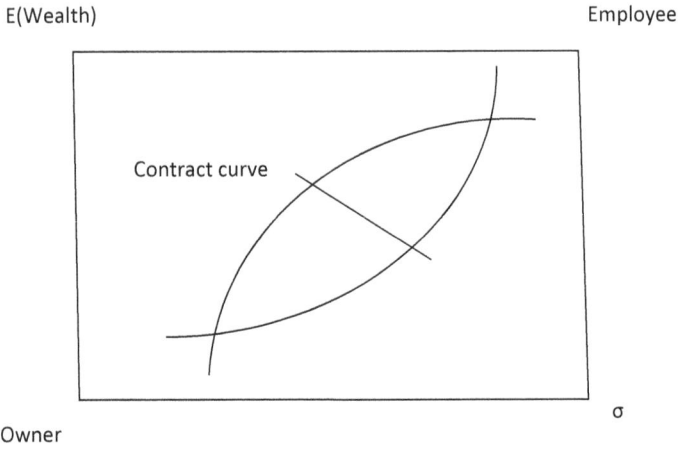

For example, consider the case of a manager negotiating with a union of employees. The negotiations might be over the wage versus benefits package. It is easy to claim that the problem is eliminated through an "a la carte" package-offer where employees select their optimal package, but benefit packages can seldom be that flexible. Often only two or perhaps three packages can be offered. The union employees may be segmented in interests due to age, gender, or other characteristics, while each segment has different preferences. It is certainly possible that one segment could actually be hurt by the new settlement agreed to by majority vote.

With group negotiations, we can revert to Rawlsian analysis to explore issues of representation within the group, i.e. are group members being coerced by other group members? Is information equally assessable to all? Are decision and voting rights equal within the group? To the extent that the management has any influence over these or other fairness issues involving the group dynamics of the counterparty, management should attempt to ameliorate these fairness issues. It is often the case however, that management has no such influence. (These Rawlsian issues are explored in Chapter VIII.)

It is important to remember that Kantian *harmony* within the counterparty group is likely to be in the interests of SWM. While pursuing SWM, it can be short-sighted indeed to try to exploit counter-party group dynamics in such a way as to prevent each group member from being better off. Why would this be the case? The answer is that conflict is likely to lead to disharmony and inefficiencies within the organization. These issues often involve the development of what we term *countervailing power*.

Power abhors a vacuum, and this is especially true with negotiating power positions. Counter parties who perceive themselves as weak will certainly be dissatisfied with the outcome of any negotiations. Disharmony results when stakeholders are unlikely to contribute to firm performance, but rather they might attempt to frustrate firm efficiency as a psychological reaction to believing they are weak. Even if the counter party does negotiate a position that leaves them better off, the belief that they are weak is likely to solicit a response that they could have done better. This frustration manifests a desire to seek some sort of power leverage, either by banding with other counter parties, or by seeking some position prior to negotiation that management must respect.

To obtain a team-like atmosphere where counter parties believe they have an interest in seeing the success of the negotiation and the firm, counter parties need a sense of power and ownership in the firm. To the extent that this power and ownership facilitates cooperation and therefore SWM, then it is obvious that management should not resist this development of *countervailing power*.

This problem is particularly amenable to the marginal analysis of neoclassical economics, i.e., SWM is achieved where the marginal tradeoffs of owner wealth for stakeholder wealth are equalized through the development of this countervailing power, but this is not explored in depth here.

As an example of this, consider negotiation with a community over possible tax breaks, transportation roads, or other amenities beneficial to the firm. Perhaps the firm has considerable leverage over this community in that if the firm withdraws its facilities, the community would be severely hurt. Management negotiators, however, must keep in mind the political power the community might have in the future if it economically develops. Using its current political power in current negotiations could lead to a disgruntled community that manifests disharmony, and attempts to hurt the firm in the future. A management team that attempts to intuit a solution of what they perceive as fairness need not overcome this disgruntlement. Allowing the community to at least act as though they have power in negotiation, or perhaps allowing the community to develop *counter-vailing power* so they can more properly represent their longer-term interests, is more likely to lead to an *harmonious* and therefore stable agreement. It is easy to perceive that this could be in the SWM interests of the firm.

Another example considers the pre-packaged bankruptcy problem. Modern bank-ruptcy is frequently pre-packaged in that lawyers negotiate with debt holders prior to legal filing in bankruptcy court. The negotiations are over debt reductions, changes in indentures, changes of debt to equity, and the like. The firm's legal representation generally argues that a pre-packaged agreement is in the wealth interests of all parties in that a lengthy court proceeding would erode the value of the firm's assets, and therefore the value debt holders would eventually receive. Given these negotiating tactics, an agreement is often reached, bankruptcy is then legally filed, the agreement is court approved, and the legal proceeding is quick. Frequently, all (or at least almost all) negotiating parties do benefit.

The prepackaged negotiating does allow certain power over otherwise holdouts who try to achieve a *free rider benefit*. A debt holder might decide that by being the last holdout to the agreement, or one of the last holdouts, he can achieve a better settlement than others who have already agreed. The *pre-packaged nego-tiations*, however, generally achieve agreement amongst almost all parties. The court, then seeing that few disagree, approves, and all must accept the agree-ment as negotiated.

The problem, of course, is that if the legal representation is overly vigorous in their power in negotiating the debt write-down, then the firm will suffer in the future when it reissues securities for sale. Investors will be wary about the firm's securities in that investors fear the firm might again vigorously negotiate for a prepackaged relief from the originally pre-bankruptcy stated terms. The firm should recognize the *countervailing power* of debt investors, that is that they may be coerced into a weak position now, but they may refuse to purchase the firm's future issued securities. This recognition should certainly be in the SWM interests of the firm.

One could easily develop other examples, perhaps union negotiation examples, or supplier negotiation examples, to further illustrate the dangers of exercising temporary coercive managerial power in these activities. Conducting all nego-tiations by following the *rules of fairness* can clearly assist management in multi-party negotiations. In this sense, Kant's notion of *harmony*, although we use this notion in the context of stakeholder relations rather than society overall, are in the SWM interests of the firm.

There are, however, certain criteria for multi-party negotiations which can be used as aids for assurance that *harmonious* results are achieved. These criteria are borrowed from the theory of *welfare economics*. [See Henderson and Quandt (1958, p. 219).] They are presented and explored next.

9. Criteria for Multi-Party Negotiations

Consider management negotiating with a multi-party group. The potential nego-tiated movement is from position B to position A, and this movement applies to all in the multi-member group. For this movement, the symbology of $A > B$ indicates here that we can state that moving from B to A leaves all better off. There are three criteria offered in the *welfare economics* literature that we can use to reach this conclusion:

(1) Kaldor criteria: $A > B$ if $A^* > B$ where A^* has winners compensating losers to move to A. If winners can compensate losers sufficiently to make them better off, then all are better off.

(2) Hicks criteria: $A > B$ if $A > B^*$ where B^* has losers compensating winners to prevent the move to A. For this case, the losers cannot pay the winners sufficiently to prevent the move and still be better off. If they could, and be better off as a result, then $B > A$, and therefore moving from B to A is not a Pareto move.

(3) Scitovsky criteria: $A > B$ if $A^* > B$, and $A > B^*$. Winners must com-pensate losers sufficiently to leave them better off, but losers cannot compensate winners sufficiently to prevent the move. For this crite-rion, after the compensation from winners to losers, both winners and losers are better off.

To illustrate these criteria, consider management negotiating with an employee union. An agreement is proposed, but some union members would be worse off as a result of this proposed agreement while the majority would be better off.

The union, however, is willing to shift a sufficient amount of dues to the losers so as to compensate them and leave them better off, and the amount of redistribution still leaves the majority better off with the proposed agreement. This illustrates Kaldor's criterion.

By Hick's criterion, we must allow consideration of the losers in the union compensating the winners to prevent them from accepting the agreement. If the losers can compensate sufficiently, then we cannot claim that the agreement does serve the general interest of the union. By Scitovsky's criterion, however, the winners can compensate the losers sufficiently, and the losers cannot compensate the winners sufficiently to prevent the move. The agreement is contracted, the winners compensate the losers (losers need not compensate the winners), and we are assured that all are better off.

Whether or not compensation must actually be paid is a controversial issue in welfare economics. It is generally claimed that compensation need not actually be paid, but that only that if it could be paid and be sufficient to leave all better off, then social welfare is enhanced. For our case of examination of *fair negotiation*, however, it should be that compensation be paid in order to leave all parties better off. This motivates an *eighth rule of fair negotiations*, one that applies only for multi-member group negotiations:

> 8) *Fair multi-member negotiations require that winners compensate all losers sufficiently to have all members better off.*

If *rule #8* is maintained, then the negotiated move must be a *Pareto move*. Continued negotiations should lead to a *Pareto optimal* position, i.e., a position on the *contract curve*.

10. Compensation Criteria When Violation of Rules is Unavoidable
Consider cases when some of the *rules of fair negotiations* are unavoidably violated. These situations could apply to rules #2 or #6, as repeated below:

> 2) *The counter parties are not disadvantaged due to any inequality of information access.*

> 6) *The counter parties communicate and explore various options for negotiations.*

Unlike the other *rules*, the two listed above might be unavoidably violated. For example, consider the example of a company that desires an expansion in productive plant, but this expansion requires purchase of real estate as required for the new plant. The firm's management is constrained from announcing this expansion because of competitive reasons, i.e., because it does not want its competitor firms to yet know of this planned expansion. An additional reason for temporary secrecy would be that if the firm is to purchase the necessary real estate parcels without a radical increase in price, it must do this quietly, one adjacent parcel at a time.

To make this problem more realistic and interesting, also allow the real estate where the planned expansion is located to be depressed so that prices are very low. The real estate market does not realize that a change in usage from residential to industrial is likely.

We note that this situation violates the equality of information rule, and also the rule concerning exploration and communication of various options. These rules are violated due to the need for secrecy.

Knowing that the negotiations cannot be entirely *fair*, what can the management negotiators do? We argue that the answer lies in the *Scitovsky criterion*. For any agreement where the two *rules of negotiations* indicated above must be violated, the management negotiators must have an *a priori* expectation that the following compensation rule will be met:

Compensation rule for violation of rules of fairness: When the two rules indicated above must be unavoidably violated, the fair agreement requires an expectation that ex post, compensation will be paid by those who benefit to those who lose. Only if both negotiating parties are expected to be better off after the compensation can the negotiation be deemed fair.

For the plant expansion example explored above, this *compensation rule* requires that management must form an expectation of the real estate prices if the expansion plan was known by all. Management must expect that it can and will be able to further compensate the real estate sellers once the expansion is completed. The expansion project must be judged as worthy even after the compensation is paid in order for the firm to proceed. This is the SWM solution. With the necessary compensation, the real estate sellers will not believe they are cheated. The community interests will not feel frustrated, and a Kantian *harmony* can continue.

11. Managerial Obligations

As effectively argued above, managerial pursuit of Kantian *harmony* through fair negotiations with stakeholders is clearly required for the wealth interests of owners. A lack of *harmony* leads to the sort of frustration that disrupts cooperation among stakeholders and this disruption cannot enhance any measure of firm performance. We must recognize, however, that there are instances when this pursuit is not possible.

For example, there may be proprietary information relevant to the negotiations that management cannot share with counter parties. Also, management may be in an authoritative position over the counter party, and this is unavoidable. When these aberrations of the rules occur, management cannot act strictly in the interests of shareholders even though they are the agents of the shareholders. The obligation of management under these circumstances is to attempt to assure a *Pareto movement*, and perhaps achieve what they envision as a *Pareto optimal* solution, as though the rules were able to be followed. This final solution may be judged as unfair by the counter parties, but there is no other possible action on the part of management but to try to reach this solution. Management can only hope that through time the solution will be eventually judged as fair after the information is discovered. The compensation rule reviewed above may be necessary to assure these *Pareto moves*.

12. Conclusion

In this Chapter we linked some of the principles of virtue ethics to Kantian ethics, and then linked these to some principles of utility theory to form notions of fairness, i.e., the *rules of fair negotiation*. We built this analysis around the concepts of *Pareto optimality*, the Edgeworth-Box Diagram analysis, and the *contract curve*. We justify *our rules of fairness*, on the basis of *Pareto movements*, but all of our rules are based upon, and in fact derived from, the Kantian *categorical imperative* and its three formulas: *universality, respect for the individual, motivation from the pursuit of harmony*. Our notions of *fairness in negotiation* are therefore part of the Kantian propositions for management.

We also briefly and partially explored the difficulties of applying these rules to negotiations under uncertainty, and also to multi-party negotiations. Management negotiators must be aware of these ethical difficulties in order to logically pursue solutions.

Review Questions:

(1) Consider some market transaction not reviewed above, but that involves implicit negotiation. Review in some detail (a paragraph or two should be sufficient) the implicit negotiation involved?

(2) Is it possible that some specific negotiation could be judged as *fair* even though the participants do not exhibit, or even have, the *noble nature* as reviewed above? Briefly review some negotiation when a lack of this *noble nature* would lead to unfairness?

(3) Is it possible that some specific negotiation could be judged as *fair* even though the participants do not exhibit, or even have, *sympathy for the pain of others*? Briefly review some negotiation when a lack of this *sympathy* would lead to unfairness?

(4) The Edgeworth-Box Diagram analysis is a utilitarian concept, but it need not serve the utilitarian philosophy's aim. Explain this? How can it be consistent with our Kantian exploration of ethics?

(5) Review the practicality of each of the 7 *rules of fairness?* Which of these rules is measurable ex post?

(6) How can we judge some negotiation as being *unfair?*

(7) How would the imposition of the 7 *rules* aid negotiators to reach an *harmonious* result?

(8) Present two other hypothetical examples of possible non-harmonious results of negotiation that could result from misunderstanding the *extent of the negotiations?*

Further Readings

For further readings in Pareto analysis and welfare economics, including compensation criteria, see Henderson and Quandt (1958).

Chapter VIII

SHAREHOLDER WEALTH MAXIMIZATION
AND THE SOCIAL CONTRACT

Chapter Abstract: *A Rawlsian political-philosophical analysis of the social contract is reviewed, especially in the context of distributional concerns. The capability of product and capital markets to work through SWM is also examined.*

1. Introduction

Can we claim that mere conformance with society's laws fulfills society's requirements for ethical behavior? Do our obligations extend beyond the law? These questions essentially concern the social contract and its expectations.

The Socratic dialogue initiates ideas of establishing the social contract as based upon reflective logical discussion. Although Plato's *Republic* envisions a philosopher-elite governing this hypothetical society, it still envisions a participatory democracy although with limitations on who could participate. (Females and slaves could not participate.) Kant envisions democratic social discourse as the filter for establishing the moral maxims we should live by provided the maxims are consistent with the categorical imperative.

One can still argue that "the social contract does not really exist" in that to claim that society agrees with some law or set of laws implies the need for periodic review and renewal of those laws. At a minimum, each new generation needs to renew the agreement since one generation cannot bind another. For example, our federal constitution was adopted by vote of the then existing states in 1789.

Other states joined the Union, and from this action, we can conclude they agreed with the existing constitutional law. Can we claim, however, that subsequent generations agree, particularly since amending the constitution requires more than a simple majority of states to adopt the amendment?

2. Two Principles of Justice

We should examine whether our corporate laws, which generally recognize shareholders as the owners although with some restrictions upon their control rights, express society's considered judgment as to an ethical social arrangement. For this reason we need to examine more closely the conditions under which we can claim some social agreement is itself ethical. To accomplish this, we examine the *Justice as Fairness* philosophy of John Rawls (1958, 2001).

Rawls' system is within the *social contractarian* school, which specifies that the demands of morality are fixed by agreement, that we should obey these demands because we have agreed to them. Its roots lie in Kant. These agreements must be freely reached by agents who are equal, and also via rational (or reasonable) means. The resulting *social contract* is only a device for establishing the moral statements; it does not constitute a moral statement in itself. [See Kymlika (2000) for a review of this school.]

In the Rawlsian system (1958), justice becomes an appropriate expression of the rules of fairness as established by the social contract.[67] Rawls presents two principles logically necessary for this justice system to be fair:

(1)   All have equal right to maximum liberty compatible with non-impingement of the liberty of others. This principle is termed *the universal principle of justice*, or UPJ, by Rawls.[68]

(2)   All positions and offices are open to all, and resulting inequalities are random. Violation of this can only occur if all benefit from the violation.

[67] MacIntyre (1981) argues that the enlightenment's attempt to establish a secularized morality free of metaphysical and religious assumptions has failed. He seeks a return to concepts of virtue similar to the Aristotelian system. This argument is consistent with Baier (1958), Gert (1976), Singer (1961), Tugendhat (1982), Apel (1980) and Habermas (1999), and are viewed by some as neo-Marxist reactions against democratic-capitalist assertions of being just and hence moral, which they also see in Rawls. (See Roberts, 2000.)

[68] Sullivan (1997, p. 11-13) also terms this the universal principle of justice, and is a restatement of Kant's *universal principle of right.*

Using these two "principles of justice," Rawls seeks to set the conditions necessary for a democratic approach to establish fairness as justice, a system that does not rely on intuitionist axioms. This system is the logical development of the categorical imperative of Kant, and requires that competent moral judges deliberate from an initial position of freedom, equality, rationality[69], reasonableness (defined as consistency with other logically founded judgments and decisions made under similar circumstances), and a willingness to engage in sufficiently sociable conduct to establish the social contract. Following the maximum freedom principle (UPJ as stated and restricted above), the processes or "practice" (the rules of the game) can be established which then develop the "well ordered society," which in turn manifests "justice as fairness." Figure 8-1 illustrates the Rawlsian system.

Given the appropriate initial position (examined in detail below), and provided deliberations maintain the two principles of justice, then competent judges (all participating parties to the democracy) logically establish a system of justice that becomes accepted by all as being fair. The Rawlsian system is therefore constructionist, i.e. society created and not naturally or theologically endowed. It follows that any real-world pronouncements that democratically established rules of justice are not fair, and by implication not ethical, must rely on pointing out the violations of the required initial position, or alternatively in some objection to Rawls' two principles of justice.

Figure 8-1: The Rawlsian System

Initial position: all parties are equal, free, rational and reasonable

ß

Rules of the game, or Practice, restrict freedom
consistent with the Principles of Justice

ß

The institutions of the "well ordered society" result
as an expression of justice as fairness

---

[69] Rationality is interpreted only in the sense of neoclassical economics or similar systems, i.e. a system of axioms such as if A is preferred to B, and B to C, then A is preferred to C. (For example, see Henderson and Quandt 1978.)

3. The Strength Of The Initial Position

To establish a social contract that allows fairness, participants of the Kantian social discourse must meet certain initial conditions for their debate, termed *the original position*. The conditions of the *original position*, as established by Rawls, include:

- all parties are free and equal (*freedom of equality*),

- all parties are rational (in the economic sense of knowing preferences and applying logic to ordering these preferences), and are reasonable in their discourse (*rational and reasonable*),

- a *veil of ignorance* exists for all parties in that they have no way of knowing the final outcomes for themselves personally,

- all necessary information is known by all (*publicity requirement*),

- the deliberators pursue the *two principles of justice* reviewed above.

If these initial conditions are met, then fairness follows by definition. It remains to be seen, however, how one would judge whether a society meets these initial conditions, or even how far a society is from meeting them. After all, the conditions represent ideal abstractions, not an actual list of laboratory observations.

The notion of *free individuals* is particularly abstract, and addressed by Kant as *a state of being unrestricted in following one's free will*. (Rawls, 1989, explores this definition in detail.) One can observe certain existence, or lack of existence, in society's institutions: freedom to petition courts and legislature, of association and expression, of movement, of occupation and education. All of these are important examples of the freedoms necessary for the democratic bargaining to result in fairness.

The notion of equality is more concrete than freedom, and institutions of equality are more readily observable. Equality means having equal positions in the bargaining sense. This does not require identical positions, indeed they may represent different groupings of people (such as managers, owners, workers), and these groupings may overlap. This may require the existence of countervailing powers in that labor unions could offset the power of owners in bargaining, or as is typically the case, lawyers represent debt holders in negotiations with owners. [70] Laws institutionalizing labor bargaining (institutionalized equality established by laws such as the Wagner Act), equal access to education, one person one vote, and laws against monopolies are examples of necessary institutions established for equality of bargaining in the initial position.

Equality, rationality, freedom (constrained by the UPJ), and reasonableness are all required in the initial position. In addition, Rawls specifies that initial endowments must not lead to bias in expectation; otherwise the deliberations will be skewed. This requires a certain *veil of ignorance* concerning the final result. Also, Rawls requires that all participants must be equally knowledgeable about relevant information. This requires, in turn, that the necessary information not be overly difficult to acquire or cumbersome to analyze. This information condition is termed the *publicity requirement*.

The *veil of ignorance* and *publicity requirements* are best viewed as joined. One cannot demand that all parties have homogeneous expectations as to the final outcome, but one can require that all have access to the same information (publicity requirement), and have the same ability to analyze this information. This requires adequate public disclosure laws, government institutions that disseminate sufficient information freely or near freely, and public access to education to establish equality in ability to analyze this information. All of these are observable institutions. Without them, some parties may have the advantage in knowing how some proposed rules might skew the results toward favoring themselves.

Since one can observe indirectly the evidence pertaining to the existence of the required initial conditions, and perhaps infer the establishment of these conditions, it is incumbent upon those who would argue that fairness does not exist in our democracy to indicate the conditional violations. Of course, observation of these institutions does not prove that any established justice system is moral in the purest sense. For this reason, Rawls (2001) restatement of *justice as fairness* focuses on the political aspects rather than the purely ethical.

---

[70] Galbraith (1985) uses the notion of countervailing power as necessary for the efficient functioning of an advanced capitalistic economy.

If the requirements of the initial position are met, then the result must be a system the public accepts as fair, and for this reason it will be stable (not because of any balance of opposing forces but because society accepts the system as fair). This establishes a Rawlsian method for analyzing any system of justice. Perceived degrees of unfairness must be linked to degrees of violation of the requirements of the initial position. These violations have strong implications for ethical decisions of business managers. For example, a system that requires managers to be legally responsible to shareholders (our current system of corporate law), and that also suffers from a high degree of income and wealth inequality (we only assume this as true for hypothetical argument), must expect the law concerning issues such as worker safety to be biased. Fairness, therefore, might require remedial establishment of what Galbraith (1960) calls countervailing institutions of power such as worker representation on the board of directors, or additional negotiation with a labor union, in keeping with Rawls' second principle of justice. In this sense, one deficiency in the initial position can be balanced with another to keep positions of power within the negotiations equal. Note that we did not offer as a solution that the manager must act as an ethical intuitionist and sacrifice the interests of shareholders, but rather that any flaws in the initial position be remedied by a patchwork of offsetting power arrangements. The Rawlsian argument still places trust in society to establish the ethical norms to be followed. Rawls was the strongest of modern Kantians in this respect.

Similarly, the information distribution may well be one sided (asymmetrical). This violation of the initial position requires remedial disclosure laws, or tort law, or SEC regulations such as those that prohibit insider trading under penalty of criminal and civil remedy. Again, it is not left to the manager-agent to remedy the situation, but rather society's imposition of rules imposed on the firm. To the extent that remedial rules should be imposed depends entirely upon the violation of the Rawlsian requirements for the initial position, not upon the ex post results of the economic system except insofar as these results might further violate the initial position.[71]

4. Shareholder Wealth as a Goal within the Rawlsian System

As reviewed above, the most commonly cited appropriate goal for the publicly traded corporation with diversified ownership is SWM, defined as maximizing the market value of equity.[72] The SWM goal, however, is often attacked as either *prima facie* unethical because it is motivated by greed, or as eliciting unethical conduct[73]. Balancing the interests of all stakeholders is often offered as the ethical alternative. Those who argue this appear unaware that the shareholder wealth goal is one of constrained maximization where the constraints consist of law, and negotiated settlements with other stakeholders such as workers, the community, and debt holders. In addition, those who argue the stakeholder approach appear unaware of three other important aspects, i.e. it requires either

- an arbitrary declaration of the weights assigned to each stakeholder group used in the balancing equation, or

- a pure utilitarian approach with all its inherent contradictions[74], or

- an intuitive approach that requires considerable intuitive managerial-insight in order to balance the stakeholder interests.

As explained above, however, the strongest implication of the Rawlsian system lies in its potential for the perfect expression of justice as fairness embodied in the

[71] Habermas (1999) argues that the Rawlsian initial position requirements are deficient in that an additional requirement restricting the form of the deliberations must exist, namely all parties must be capable of and exhibit empathy for each other's position. This position, however, appears to be so strong as to eliminate any notion that democracy would elicit fair rules. The author is clearly not this pessimistic in that he accepts that democracy, even if parties originate from unequal positions, can haggle towards sufficient fairness so that the elicited rules are more trustworthy in application than a system that relies on managers as intuitionists. Indeed, the author argues that society should be nervous, or at least questioning, whenever managers announce that their firm will do something particularly moral even though not required by law or negotiation. The action may, of course, just be motivated by public relations, but certainly managers are self interested and therefore biased parties. (See Chambers and Lacy, 1996, for elaboration on this problem.)

[72] As an example of a goal for a non-diversified ownership company, privately held small firms frequently sacrifice firm value for steadiness of income, employment for family members, or even the hobby interests of the owners.

[73] Michael Porter (2002) provides an example of this criticism. He links the shareholder wealth goal to recent accounting disclosure scandals, and corporate fraud. This claim is particularly ironic in that these scandals (Enron and other scandals) invariably involve theft from the shareholders, not for them. Managers who steal do so from the shareholders, and other stakeholders, not for them. In addition, all of the fraud scandals of the last few years involve massive erosion of owner wealth.

[74] By the pure utilitarian approach, it is conceivable that the interests of the worst off could be sacrificed for the interests of those most well off provided that total societal utility rises.

rule of law. Since SWM is constrained by society's law in all its form, or by negotiation with stakeholders, management need only follow the law and previously
reached agreements to exhibit ethical conduct. The existence of any problems
not covered by these arrangements implies that deliberations are incomplete.
The business manager would not impose her/his intuitions because of inherent
stakeholder suspicion of bias, i.e. the manager cannot fit the requirements of the
disinterested judge.

All of the business problems faced by corporations with diversified ownership
suffer the potential of agency conflicts in their resolution. The goal of constrained
shareholder-wealth maximization provides standard practical decision rules (NPV
for capital budgeting as an example) within which management-welfare pursuit
becomes difficult to hide. If boards of directors do their job, then these decisions
must be relatively transparent upon board review. Claims of satisfying multiple
stakeholder interests, or of satisfying intuited ethical considerations, can easily
lead to opaque specific-to-the-situation-at hand decision analyses that become
masks behind which the biased interests of management welfare can be hidden.

5. Distributional Fairness

Can we claim that society is better off if some policy or action leads to some
people having a higher level of utility while others are no worse off? This is
a fundamental question of welfare economics. It has no obvious answer. We
can, however, have serious reservations about society being better off if some
are wealthier while others remain at the same level of wealth. This is due to
the increase in wealth inequality. Many, such as Piff, et al (2012), argue that
increased wealth inequality strains the social institutions of society which leads
to political polarization and increased isolation of the wealthy class from lower
classes of socio-economic strata. Increased crime rates, lower civic involvement,
lower family stability, a wider dispersion of educational opportunities and other
cultural attainments have been cited as results. The very cohesiveness of society
might be strained. [75]

An exploration of these inequality issues is not intended here. We should, however,
explore the possibilities of the general perception of whether societal welfare

[75] Also see Gino and Pierce (2009), Adler, et al (2000), and Kraus, et al (2011) for reviews of empirical investigations
of wealth stratification and ethical behavior.

improves as a result of SWM? There are two general considerations which must be analyzed here:

- Does SWM necessarily lead to greater wealth inequality?

- If SWM does lead to greater income inequality, does this mean societal welfare is negatively impacted?

The past two decades witnessed an increase in US wealth inequality, although most corporate equity wealth is held through financial institutions such as mutual funds, pension funds, insurance-company managed funds, and the like. In part, this increased inequality may be due to the general aging of the population since people accumulate wealth as they age. Younger people are generally poorer as compared to older cohort groups that have similar initial backgrounds so that an aging population will naturally exhibit increasing wealth inequality. Note that progressive income tax, property tax and wealth inheritance tax policies should ameliorate this tendency so that SWM need not actually lead to greater wealth inequality at lease with respect to the aging phenomenon.

Smith (1776), Friedman (1969), and neo-classical micro-economics all point out the benefits to consumers of the functioning of the invisible hand of the market, and that free markets, with some restrictions on monopolistic behavior and nega-tive externalities, facilitate these benefits. More competitive markets have lower real prices, greater real wealth overall, and also develop improved products that benefit consumer welfare to a greater extent than less competitive markets. All of this requires that SWM motivates firms to respond to consumer preferences, hence SWM plays the crucial role in leading markets to benefit society.

Those who argue that free markets and SWM actually hurt societal welfare usu-ally argue from an empirical standpoint, i.e. that we can empirically observe the various defects of markets as they negatively impact some segments of society. For example, real wages have deteriorated over the last two decades, while global warming and other environmental degradations are often cited. From an empiri-cal standpoint, we should note that our 20th century experience with socialist countries exhibit far more severe environmental degradation, low real income, and political corruption than so called capitalist free-market societies. Friedman (1969) argues that the dispersal of power that results from capitalistic free-markets helps to keep these corruption effects in check. Socialism, he argues, means that the means of production are owned in common. This naturally requires and leads to government control which in turn means that power is concentrated at the top in government. Rather than having the marketplace determine what is produced, how much of it is produced, the price to be charged, and the allocation of resources for that production, under socialism, a government bureaucracy inevitably makes these decisions. This concentrates power in government.

It is also key to recognize that political power follows economic power. By concentrating power in government, how can we expect government to not abuse this power, especially with respect to allowing unfettered media access to political opposition? If someone is responsible to a government bureaucracy for their economic well being, can we expect her/him to engage in political opposition to it? Under free-market capitalism, however much it is regulated, there may in fact be a great deal of power held by corporate leaders, but there are so many corporations that power is inevitably dispersed. Still one can argue that since there is so much wealth generated through corporate institutions, then corporate expenditures on political campaigns warps the political process towards overly favorable regulatory environments. We therefore find it excessively difficult to regulate negative externalities, or to regulate various abusive employment practices such as the exploitation of undocumented illegal immigrants, or union busting and other business practices. This is the core of the rational "free-markets run-amuck" argument.

All of this political economic analysis can be placed under the umbrella of welfare economics, as well as in other academic areas of study. One of the essential questions here concerns the potential tradeoff of the wealth of one individual for another's. Consider the welfare (or social utility) functions exhibited by Figure 8-2. To explore this two-dimensional case, assume that some society consists of only two individuals with wealth endowments as shown. Iso-social-welfare functions are similar to the isoclines for utility that a single individual has for preferences among two goods. The social welfare function shown does allow for the possibility (the logic of which is challenged below) that a reduction in wealth for person 1 can be offset by a sufficient increase in the wealth of person 2 and leave societal welfare unchanged, i.e. a movement along the isocline. Note that the concavity of the isoclines (concave from above) exhibit diminishing marginal rate of substitution of wealth for each person. If person 1 has a great deal of wealth, and person 2 only a little, then we might consider changing the rules of the game by which wealth is accumulated. Allow this change in rules to necessarily result in a substantial decrease in wealth of person 1 as shown in Figure 8-2. Also allow this change in the rules of the game to necessarily result in an associated small increase in the wealth of person 2 which is also shown in Figure 8-2. With diminishing marginal utility, and assuming that social welfare is simply the sum of the utilities of each individual, then a large reduction in the wealth of one person need only be compensated by a small increase in the wealth of the second in order to leave societal welfare unchanged. This is essentially the utilitarian argument.

To consider this type of analysis further, allow the reduction in wealth of person 1 with associated increase in wealth of person 2 to occur via a simple income transfer (a wealth tax and transfer). As long as there is no bias towards one person and against the other, then given the initial unequal endowments and concave symmetric social-welfare function, then there must be a net increase in societal welfare as shown by a movement from SW1 to SW2 in Figure 8-3. This equality argument does not discriminate due to such factors as age, gender, or even the source of wealth (inherited wealth vs. entrepreneurial generated wealth as an example).

**Figure 8-2: Social Welfare
Function Exhibiting Tradeoffs**

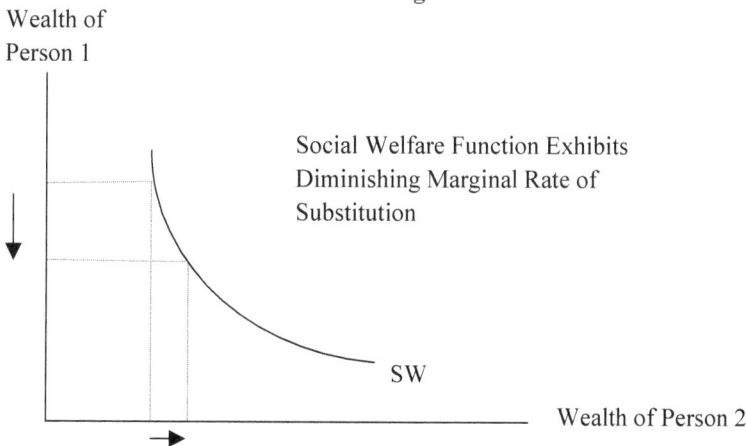

of the other, at least in terms of social welfare. This welfare function is for a two-person society that favors income equality in that only increases in the wealth of both result in society being better off. The 45° line (slope of one) indicates the wealth equality locus. To improve societal welfare, wealth must move along this locus.

**Figure 8-3: Social Welfare Function
With Equal Income Transfers**

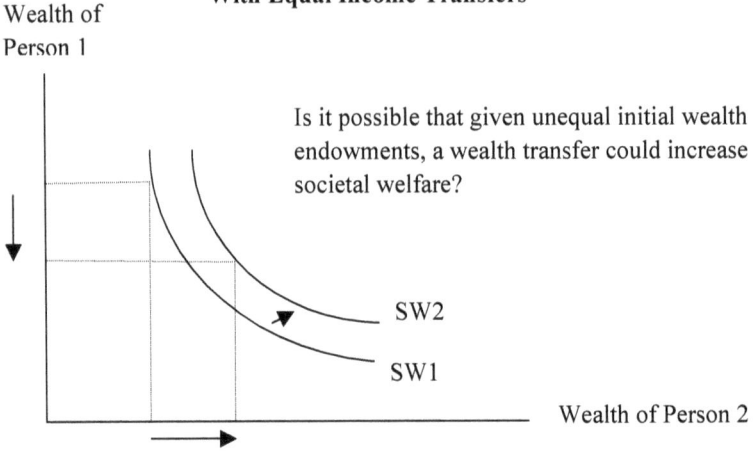

Wealth of
Person 1

Is it possible that given unequal initial wealth endowments, a wealth transfer could increase societal welfare?

SW2

SW1

Wealth of Person 2

**Figure 8-4: Social Welfare
Function No Substitution**

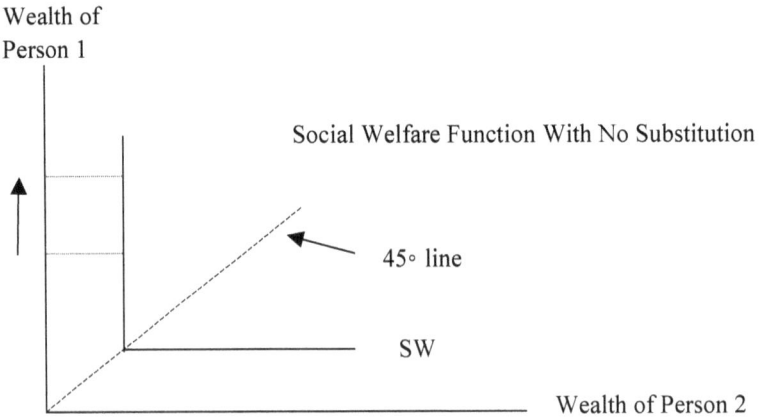

Wealth of
Person 1

Social Welfare Function With No Substitution

45° line

SW

Wealth of Person 2

Figure 8-5: Social Welfare Function No Substitution

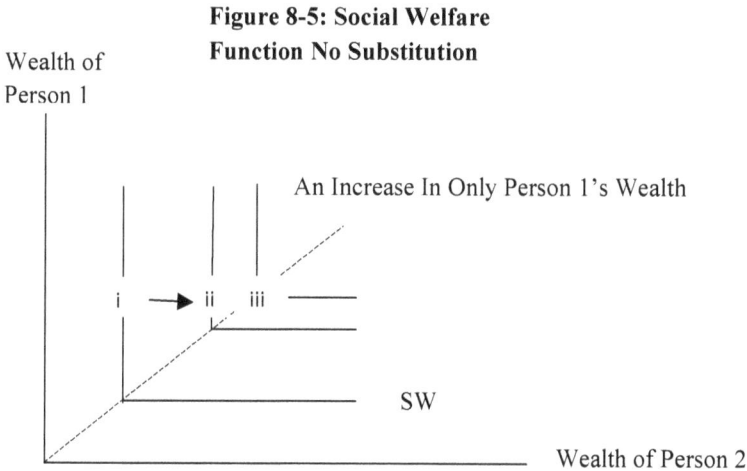

For example, consider the movements illustrated by Figure 8-5. The initial endowment of wealth is unequal as in position "i" where Person 1 has far greater wealth than Person 2. An increase in Person 2's wealth to position "ii" improves societal welfare (a higher isoclines is achieved) since it makes the income distribution closer to being even. Beyond position "iii," however, further increases do not improve societal welfare since at that position, wealth is evenly distributed. If Person 2 receives greater wealth, the movement is merely along constant isoclines since the distribution now becomes skewed towards Person 2.

A more extreme societal bias towards equality of wealth is exhibited by Figure 8-6. These isoclines exhibit bias against substitution in that while a change in the wealth distribution from position "i" to "ii" increases societal welfare because this makes the initial uneven distribution equal. A further change to position "iii" decreases welfare since the distribution becomes again unequal, although at position "iii" the wealth distribution is unequal in favor of Person 2 rather than 1. For this case, any movement away from perfect equality (the 45° line) decreases societal welfare. The smaller the internal angle of the isoclines, the greater the decrease in societal welfare associated with any movement away from perfect equality. Arguments in support of bias towards equality rely on citing the social strains that result from wealth inequality, i.e. that the political structure becomes skewed towards the wealth, that the lower socio-economic classes inevitably become exploited.

Figure 8-6: A Social Welfare
Function Biased Towards Equality

Wealth of
Person 1

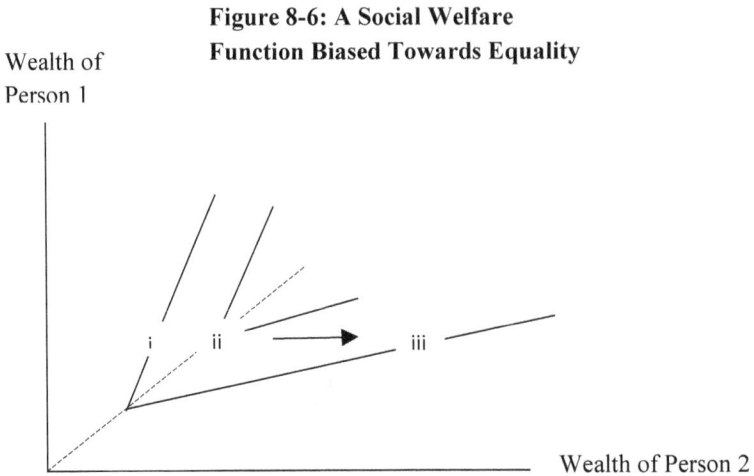

Wealth of Person 2

Yet another welfare argument concerns the source of the wealth possessed. For example, society might be biased away from inherited wealth (or other types of "unearned" wealth), and towards wealth generated from entrepreneurial activity or even common labor. The isoclines for this sort of social welfare function are exhibited by Figure 8-7. For this case, the isoclines are very steep in favor of Person 2, the entrepreneur. Even a large decrease in the wealth of Person 1, perhaps the inherited wealth, is compensated by a small increase in the wealth of the entrepreneur where this shift in wealth leaves society indifferent. This is further illustrated by Figure 8-8 where social welfare is increased from isoclines SW1 to SW2 by only a small increase in Person 2's wealth (position "i" to "ii"), whereas to move to SW2 through an increase in Person 1's wealth requires a very large increase in wealth (position "i" to "iii").

In addition to the source of the wealth, society may be biased towards to type of ownership. For example, consider wealth owned by the young versus older persons. The need for economic support after retirement might bias society towards more generous tax policies for the elderly versus the young. Health maintenance and the like might be offered as justifications for these policies.

Is it possible that SWM leads to greater wealth for any one group of society rather than others? Some argue that this does occur, that it leads to the wealthy becoming wealthier, and the poor becoming more impoverished, and that SWM leads to exploitation of the poor. To the extent that this sort of exploitation of the poor occurs, society can remedy this by other legal means. In fact, we observe these legal remedies in place in the form of numerous employment practice regulations. Unequal wealth, and in particular societal bias towards certain ownership groups such as entrepreneurs, can also be remedied through tax policies. Inheritance tax policies come to mind as ready examples as does short-term versus long-term capital gains tax policies which favor entrepreneurship-type wealth generations versus financial speculation and other forms of unearned wealth. Since SWM is one of the most critical tools that allow society to reap the benefits of free-market competition, and it otherwise can be entirely ethical if properly constrained by law and ethics, attacking it generally as a method of controlling the distributional aspects of capitalism is surely very much mistaken.

6. Societal Wealth and Distributional Fairness

In this section, we examine the various possibilities for the relation between the distribution of societal wealth and its generation. We do this within the context of the *second principle of the UPJ*.

Figure 8-7: Social Welfare Function Biased Towards Person 2

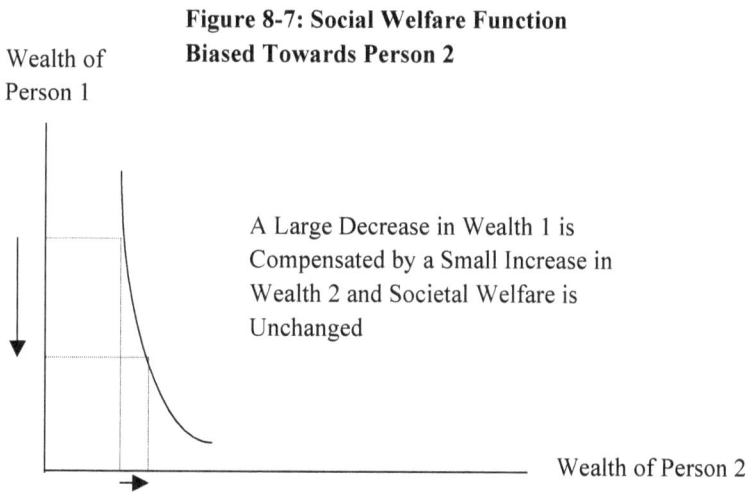

Wealth of Person 1

A Large Decrease in Wealth 1 is Compensated by a Small Increase in Wealth 2 and Societal Welfare is Unchanged

Wealth of Person 2

**Figure 8-8: Social Welfare Function
Biased Towards Person 2**

Wealth of
Person 1

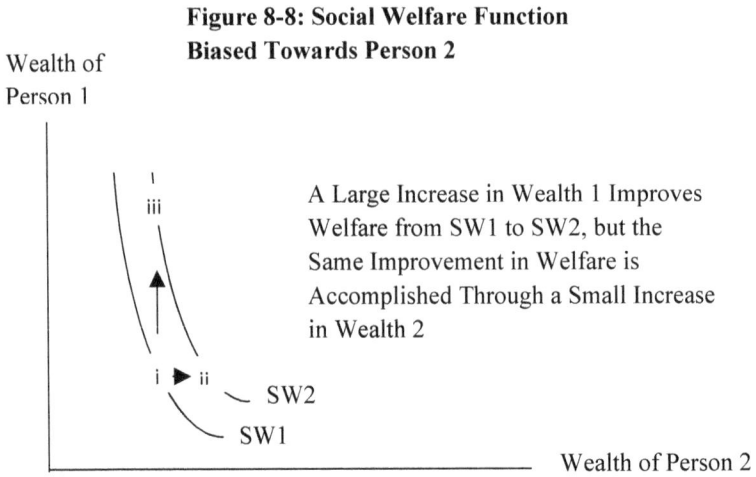

A Large Increase in Wealth 1 Improves
Welfare from SW1 to SW2, but the
Same Improvement in Welfare is
Accomplished Through a Small Increase
in Wealth 2

Wealth of Person 2

Consider the wealth production frontier exhibited by Figure 8-9 where the wealth distribution is strictly a zero-sum game, i.e. an equal increase in the wealth of person 1 requires an equal decrease in the wealth of person 2. As an example, this sort of distributional function would occur in a simple agricultural society of two people where the land cultivated is fixed in amount, and equal in productive possibility. The two farmers would also have to be equal in productive ability. A shift in an acre of land from one farmer to another implies a movement along the depicted production possibility frontier.

**Figure 8-9: A Societal Wealth
Production Possibility Frontier**

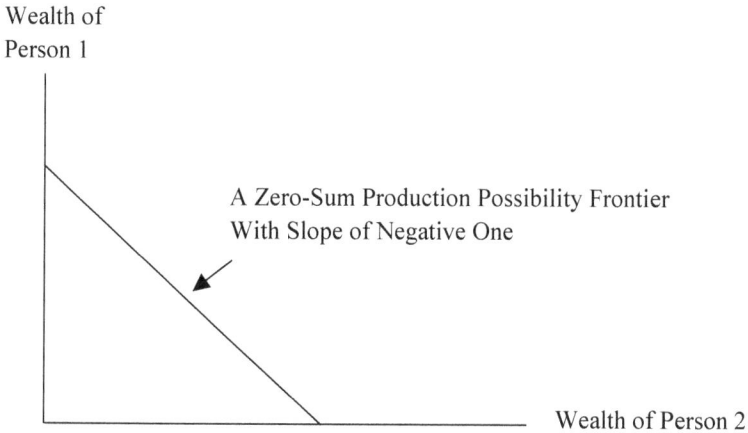

Wealth of
Person 1

A Zero-Sum Production Possibility Frontier
With Slope of Negative One

Wealth of Person 2

**Figure 8-10: An Optimal Societal
Wealth Distribution**

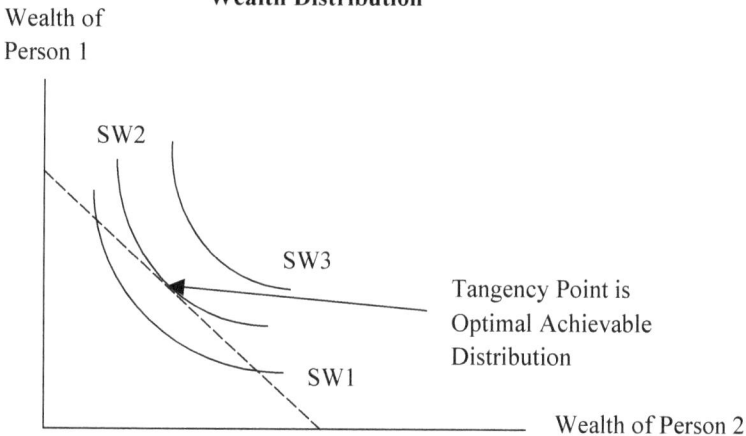

Wealth of
Person 1

SW2

SW3

Tangency Point is
Optimal Achievable
Distribution

SW1

Wealth of Person 2

In Figure 8-10, a social welfare function is superimposed on the wealth production frontier. The highest welfare function achievable occurs at the tangency
point where SW2 is the highest possible. The intersection points of the lower
welfare function SW1 with the production possibility frontier (there are two
intersection points) are both at a lower societal welfare than the tangency point of
SW2 with the frontier. In fact, the point of tangency of a social welfare function

with possibility frontier is the highest societal welfare achievable. This occurs at SW2. Points along SW3 are all superior to points on SW2, but these are not achievable. They are all outside the wealth possibility frontier. This tangency point of SW2 with the frontier indicates the optimal distribution, and whatever the institutions associated with this point, whether legal ownership restrictions, or tax, or other institutions, they should be enforced in order to achieve the optimal societal welfare.

The wealth production possibility frontier is very unlikely to exhibit a zero-sum property. Wealth generates income, which if saved and reinvested, becomes greater wealth which in turn generates income, and so on. If we assume that the wealth held by any single individual exhibits diminishing marginal productivity to generate income, but that the production capabilities of each individual are equal, then the wealth production frontier will be symmetric and concave from below, as shown in Figure 8-11. Here, the tangency point with SW2 still represents the optimal distribution.

Figure 8-11: An Optimal Societal Wealth Distribution

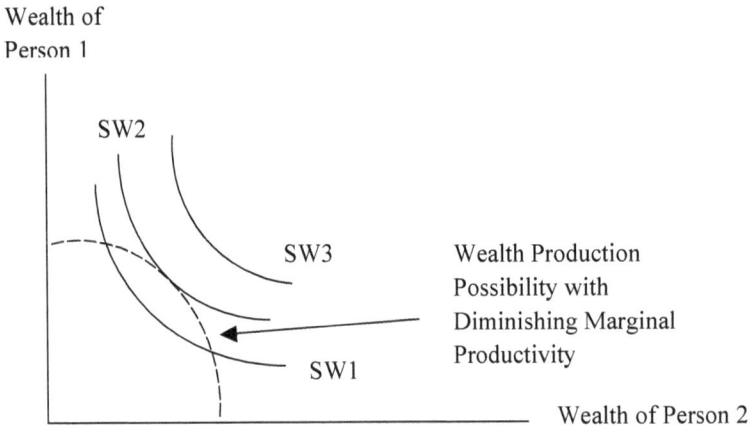

Rather than continuing to represent society as composed of only two individuals, the next step in our analysis is to consider two classifications of people. For example, we can consider non-entrepreneurs as Class 1, and entrepreneurs as Class 2. Allow the argument that wealth generates income at equal rates for each class, but entrepreneurs save and reinvest a larger portion of this income back into their capital (wealth). We could conversely argue that entrepreneurs manage their wealth better so that they are more productive. In either case, the wealth production possibility frontier becomes one that is more skewed towards Class 2, the entrepreneurs, as shown in Figure 8-12. The optimal distribution then favors the entrepreneurial class indicated by Class 2 as shown.

**Figure 8-12: A Skewed Wealth
Production Possibility Frontier**

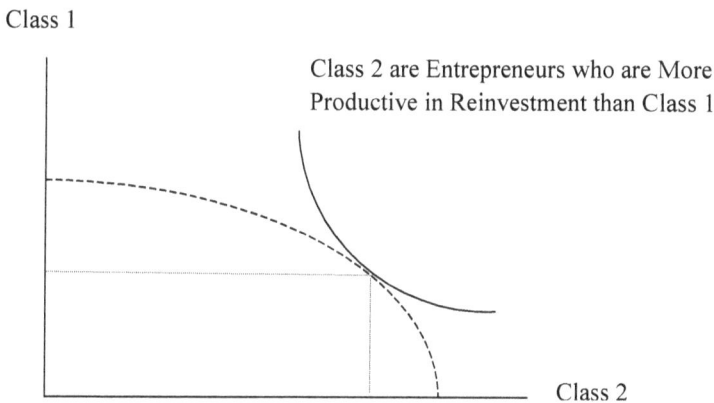

Class 1

Class 2 are Entrepreneurs who are More
Productive in Reinvestment than Class 1

Class 2

7. The Invisible Hand of the Market, Ethics and Justice as Fairness

What is not generally perceived is that the Rawlsian system of democratically established justice as fairness is entirely consistent with the goal of shareholder wealth maximization, and may require this as the ethical solution for business problems. The argument for this last proposition is made here.

Chambers and Lacey (1996) point out the democratic nature of managerial pursuit of the shareholder wealth goal. As envisioned by Smith (1776), the marketplace is essentially a voting place where the invisible hand moves participants to respond to meet society's needs. Under conditions of sufficient knowledge about the workings of the firm (especially about any externalities generated), the product market will democratically voice the concerns of the populace about perceived ethical lapses. Firms that pursue shareholder wealth as a goal must respond to society's sense of moral rightness. As evidence of this, note the numerous product market boycotts such as the California grape boycott in support of Migrant Farm Workers' Union during the 1960s, the tuna boycott of Bumblebee during the 1970s and 80s, the 1990s' Nestle Foods boycott due to their powdered baby-formula problems involving exports to Africa. Although not formerly an organized boycott, the rapid reduction in demand for Calvin Klein's products that occurred as a result of the public's negative view of that company's use of children in sexually provocative advertisements during the late 1990s can be categorized as an informal or implicit boycott. That company's policies changed too rapidly for any organized boycott to be formed. All of these boycotts, formally organized or unorganized, were effective in causing behavioral changes in firm policies. Perhaps the informal boycotts are the most effective in eliciting a quick response, and these are everyday occurrences in the marketplace.

Capital market boycotts also voice society's demand for moral reform of business behavior. Note the effective pressure exerted by the capital market boycott of firms doing business with South African companies during the apartheid era of the 1970s.

For boycotts of this type to take place, society must have knowledge of the perceived ethical lapses, but information concerning serious problems does have a way of surfacing in a free and open democracy. The pursuit of shareholder wealth as the overriding goal of the firm forces business behavior to conform to the democratic pressures of the marketplace and its declaration of moral reproach. If the Rawlsian requirements for the initial position are met, then the democratic marketplace is the complete expression of the person-centered notions of justice as fairness. The manager-as-intuitionist plays no role.

8. The Categorical Imperative and SWM

Business serves its own ends through serving customers, but by serving its own ends, it is meant that it serves its owners. Shareholders invest in corporations with other diversified owners in order to serve their own wealth interests[76]. As a result, it can be argued that the other business constituents are used as a means toward pursuing the business ends. Given the freedom of occupation and move-

---

[76] One should understand the principle of Fisher separation, i.e. by the firm maximizing the value of current equity, the individual investor can allocate her/his time preference for consumption (consumption now versus later), by either borrowing against this wealth, or further investing at the market rates of interest.

ments of employees, freedom of capital movement by debt holders (secondary capital-debt markets are very fluid, free and active), and given the freedom of communities to tax, legislate and regulate business, constituents use business toward meeting their own ends. If constituents possess the requisite freedom, then interfering with their pursuit of their own ends through business interaction should only occur in cases of fraud or deception about purpose or effect. It is for these reasons that laws regulating business behavior are democratically established, and negotiations with constituents are conducted, the purpose of which are to avoid exploitation, and assure that the intended ends of constituents are served. This follows from society's sense of fairness as an expression of the categorical imperative of Kant.

In addition, the *universal principal of justice* (UPJ) requires maximizing freedom, providing that laws constrain an individual's impingement of the freedom of others. The UPJ should be considered as a requirement for society, and is a necessary foundation for any democracy we would desire to live in. Freedom is as ethically important as sustenance or shelter. Its pursuit, subject to the UPJ, is clearly an ethical demand for both the individual and society.

9. Ethical Basis for the Stakeholder View

Solomon (2000) presents a complete statement of the stakeholder approach as an ethical system. He states that business is part of culture, part of society, and as such has ethical obligations to all stakeholders. He states, "The purpose of the corporation, after all, is to serve the public." (p. 361) In addition, he declares that the profit motive for business is a "myth," (p.356), that profits are just a way of keeping score, and that business serves higher purposes of society; that "The pursuit of profits is not the ultimate, much less the only goal of business. It is rather one of many goals and then by way of a means and not an end-in-itself." (p. 357)

Solomon does not recognize Smith's "invisible hand of the market" as leading business to serve the interests of the public (for which the profit motive is the motive force). As such, he also does not recognize the "invisible hand's" role in transferring society's sense of moral reproach to the firm, as in Chambers and Lacy (1996). Most importantly, as with all those who have the stakeholder view, he does not recognize the primary legal obligation of management to shareholders, as constrained by law and other agreements. Solomon's refusal to recognize this is willful, and certainly deceitful, since it is our current legal system. Shareholders are the legal owners of the firm; they are the residual claimants. They are not, as claimed by Solomon, entitled to just a "fair return" (except for those firms in regulated monopolistic-industries such as utilities), they are entitled to the residual claim, whether it be high or low or nonexistent.

Solomon's essay is an excellent example of stating the stakeholder view while not recognizing that SWM is constrained by law and stakeholder negotiations, that the social compact embodies society's sense of ethics and imposes this on the firm. That fact that those who hold the stakeholder view avoid recognition of the constructivist's complete argument is distressing in that it exhibits a lack of intellectual honesty. Denying legal realities of our system further compounds their ethical lapse.

By quoting the left's favorite whipping boy, Milton Friedman (1971), Solomon is consistent with those who hold his views. Friedman claims that viewing management as not having the fiduciary responsibility established in our legal system, i.e. denying management's primary responsibility to owners, and denying the profit motive, is socialistic. This was not used as a pejorative term, but rather as an attempt at a factual observation by Friedman. Solomon, however, resists this claim as embodying his own view. We should view Friedman's statement, however, as being based upon the common and objective definition of socialism: either society owns the means of production or individuals do, no matter the constraints on their actions established by the social contract. The former is by definition socialistic, but this does not fit the view of stakeholders. They allow ownership to be private, but the owners' interests are not fully served. Because of this, however, the benefits from the invisible hand as it influences consumer satisfaction and owner wealth, and allows society to voice its moral reproach against any particular lapse of ethics, would not fully occur. Balancing all the interests of stakeholders in the way viewed, especially by Solomon, impinges on the firm's response to market pressures.

Solomon lists several concerns of business behavior: charitable contributions, environmental problems, product safety, truth in advertising, labor problems. He then states the supposed benefits of the stakeholder theory for resolving those concerns. In a chapter below, we also review these problems, and some others, but we show the superiority of the constrained SWM method for resolution.

Review Questions:

(1) Can SWM be consistent with the Rawlsian notions of the social contract? Can the stakeholder balance approach be consistent?

(2) Could SWM lead to a lower level of social welfare than other managerial goals? Why?

(3) Can product and/or capital markets transfer society's sense of ethics?

(4) Is SWM consistent with the categorical imperative?

(5) Is there an ethical basis for the stakeholder balance view?

Chapter IX

—— ✦ ——

THE ETHIC OF THE MARKET

Chapter Abstract: *The conditions under which competitive free markets serve social-welfare are reviewed in the context of classical and neoclassical economics. Kantian ethics is shown to be not only consistent with this constrained free-market view, but also required by it. Note that sections 4. through 6. do require some knowledge of elementary calculus.*

1. Competition and the Kantian Kingdom of Ends

Is the competitive free market with its profit motive antithetical to ethical consideration, especially Kantian consideration? This is the essential question explored in this text. The argument presented throughout is that the profit motive and Kantian ethics are not antithetical. A sufficient exploration of this requires an exploration of the very foundation of economic analysis.

Adam Smith (1776) was an 18th century Scottish professor of moral philosophy at the University of Glasgow. His *Theory of Moral Sentiments* (1752) argued that ethical considerations stemmed from a natural sense of empathy in that we have a tendency to place ourselves in the position of others to envision their pain from our consequential actions. This motivates our moral sense and self imposed restraints. Smith accepted that ethical motivation must not be egotistical, but rather it must stem from our sense of responsibility to others and society as in Kant's notion of the *kingdom of ends* as explored in Chapter IV.

Adam Smith is generally recognized, however, for his five-book magnum opus, *An Inquiry into the Nature and Causes of the Wealth of Nations* (1776), where he argues that people's motives are generally very different than the pursuit of the *kingdom of ends*. In this revolutionary work, Smith argued that people do act from egotistical motivation, but nevertheless this motivation can lead to an efficient social result. Consider his argument for the economic motivation of producers:

"It is not from the benevolence of the butcher, the brewer, or the baker that we can expect our dinner, but from their regard to their own interest" (Smith, 1776, Book I, Chapter 2, paragraph 2.)

Also consider Smith's argument for the working of the *invisible hand of the market:*

"By directing that industry in such a manner as its produce may be of greatest value, he intends only his own gain, and he is in this, as in many cases, led by an invisible hand to promote an end which was no part of his intention." (Ibid, Book IV, Chapter 2, paragraph 9.)

Smith's argument is therefore that when producers act from the egotistical profit motive, they serve the public's interest. Knowledge of this allows producers and consumers to be both motivated by their egotistical pursuits while still believing they serve the broader social goals of society, at least under the constrained circumstances explored in this text. It is with this Smithian argument that we must remember that the *Kantian positive duties*, duties derived from real-world moral maxims which are themselves drawn from the categorical imperative, have practical limitations. These practicalities result because businesses must seek a competitive survival. After paying for their employee payroll and other input costs, business must provide for their owner-entrepreneurs; hence the existence of the profit motive, a motive that stems from serving the public through providing goods and services. This public service, however, requires that business must stay within ethical constraints.

These constraints involve ethical maxims that are consistent with Kant's *categorical imperative*, and socially imposed controls on broad classifications of externalities. This realization is the heart of the argument of this text, i.e. that self interest and free markets need not generate social conflict and disharmony, but rather they are uniquely capable of generating the *harmony* explored in Chapter IV. This is particularly true since free markets are necessary for generating freedom in general as in freedom to pursue both our individual and society's happiness. The necessary constraints placed on managerial action, however, are strong.

This chapter and this text in general, explore these constraints. For example, consider Smith's warning that business people seldom meet without forming some price-rigging conspiracy. We have antitrust laws against these price conspiracies. These conspiracies are unethical. In addition, there are a myriad of other ethical constraints on the actions of businesses in the market place. Still, the ethic of the market, that is the ethic of fairly competing to satisfy consumers, and also of fairly compete for factor inputs to generate the goods the consuming public wants, a competition that must be constrained by ethical considerations to be deemed as fair, serves the *kingdom of ends.* It is argued in this chapter, that means of economic organization other than the free market are unlikely to serve this broad social end.

2. The Classical and Neoclassical Models of Competition

Free markets ration goods by the price mechanism. The classical and neoclassical economic views are that free markets essentially provide a democratic voting mechanism that indicates society's sense of what is valuable but costly to produce. Under certain controllable circumstances, explored in this chapter, free markets allocate resources so as to yield the maximum social welfare.

The classical economics model of Adam Smith (1776) established the motive force of competition as acting through the "invisible hand" of the market in deciding what is produced, what and how resources are allocated to that production, how production is distributed through society, the prices charged, and the returns to that production. Smith showed the superiority of the marketplace for making these decisions as compared to the "mercantile system" of his age, i.e. a system of government charters granting the right to produce (frequently monopoly rights) and to sell to the public. Smith posed the theory that the marketplace responds to consumer demands by producing what is wanted and at a price equal to the minimum average cost of production. In addition, Smith also envisioned that through a free market, producers and consumers have the freedom to move to the area of production they wish. There are no legal impediments to their movement[77]. Freedom is a paramount aspect of this market driven economy.

The neoclassical economic model developed during the first half of the 20th century is the completion of Smith's classical model. It envisions atomistic producers who earn only a competitive profit. Juxtaposed against this competitive model is the opposite extreme of monopoly, where the monopolist charges higher prices than competitive firms, and produces less. Hence consumers are less well off (enjoy a lower state of welfare) under monopoly.

In particular, the neoclassical model of competition points out three strong ethical implications for society:

- A high level of competition has strong implications for notions of fairness in income distribution to entrepreneurs and other factor inputs.

- By responding to consumer preferences, the competitive free marketplace of atomistic producers innovates to provide the goods society wants, and at the minimum possible prices and costs of production.

- In the competitive market, the impersonal forces of supply and demand allocate resources and establish prices that in the absence of externalities, and with the appropriate subsidies to the disadvantaged, maximize societal welfare.

- The examination of this neoclassical economic model is also beneficial for reviewing the real-world deviations from the model's underlying assumptions. These include

- The ethical and economic-efficiency implications of firm's establishing monopoly power.

- The ethical and economic-efficiency implications of firm's generating negative externalities such as pollution.

---

[77] Recall that in 1776, merchantilistic and imperialistic governments generally required government grants or charters to produce in various locals, and large segments of the population were restricted by either serfdom, slavery or indentured servitude.

- The ethical and economic-efficiency implications of societal response to those so disadvantaged that they cannot compete.

The ethical implications for management that result from this vision of highly competitive atomistic producers is somewhat declared by society through trade regulatory laws such as the Sherman Antitrust Act and the Clayton Act. The resulting ethical implications for managerial behavior, particularly with respect to what is termed "business strategy," are strong. In addition to the laws that seek to enforce competition, we also have societal laws and controls applicable to negative externalities, and we also have social programs to assist the disadvantaged.

In order to proceed in this exploration of the ethics of the marketplace, we must assume that the reader is sufficiently familiar with elementary economics as it would be covered in an introductory university-level course. We must assume, as an example, that the reader has some knowledge of the role of supply and demand in establishing market clearing prices, of the effects of government imposed price controls in creating either shortages or surpluses, and of the role of markets in satisfying consumer demands and innovation in productive technology. Although some degree of reinforcement of these concepts is warranted and presented, our real task here is to further penetrate the study of markets so as to explore the implicit underlying ethical assumptions and implications.

3. A Brief Review of the Forces of Supply and Demand

Prior to proceeding in this exploration, it is necessary to have a clear understanding of the elements of market supply and demand. Although we assume the reader is familiar with these elements, perhaps it is beneficial to review this subject here, at least for the purpose of reinforcement. We establish the motive forces of the supply function, and also of the demand function in sections below. Here we merely assert that as shown in Figure 9-1, the market supply function is positively sloped, and the demand function is negatively sloped.

The positive slope of the supply function indicates that as prices rise, the quantity supplied to the market increases. For example, we could consider the market for wheat in that as prices rise, more land is converted to wheat production so that the quantity of wheat on the market increases. In a similar, but opposite way, as the price of wheat increases, the quantity of wheat demanded decreases as consumers seek substitute goods (perhaps barely or rice) and economize on their consumption of bread, pasta or other wheat products. We should recall that when we say "the quantity of wheat demanded or supplied varies" we are moving along a static supply or demand function. When we say "the demand or supply has changed" we are stating the either the entire demand or the entire supply function has shifted. Although we explain the forces that generate the demand or supply function below, for now we should merely recall that the demand function depends upon the consumers' preferences for wheat versus other products, and also the incomes and wealth of the consumers. The supply function, as shown below, depends upon the underlying costs of production.

As shown in Figure 9-1, as the price of wheat changes, the quantity of wheat demanded changes as we move along the static demand function. Similarly, as the price of wheat changes, the quantity supplied changes as we move along the static supply function. If the underlying costs of production change, the supply function shifts its position. If preferences for wheat consumption change, the demand function shifts its position. In either case, a new equilibrium price emerges.

As shown in Figure 9-1, if the price of wheat is above the equilibrium of Pe, say at P1, then there is a surplus of wheat on markets, i.e. the quantity supplied is greater than the quantity demanded. Prices fall towards Pe in order to clear the market. In a similar way, if the price of wheat is below the equilibrium, say at P2, then there is a shortage where the quantity demanded exceeds the quantity supplied, and the price rises towards Pe. At the equilibrium price Pe, the quantity supplied equals the quantity demanded so that there is no pressure to push the price either up or down, hence the use of the term "equilibrium price."

Suppose governments impose a price below equilibrium, i.e. a price control. The quantity demanded exceeds the quantity supplied. There is excess demand, or in other terms a shortage. In this case, the quantity supplied must be rationed by some means other than the price mechanism, perhaps by queues or government imposed rationing by demographic characteristics, or the like. In these cases of government regulatory imposition, often black markets emerge to circumvent the government price ceiling.

Suppose government imposes a price floor above equilibrium. In these cases, there is an excess supply, and government must purchase this surplus to remove it from the market. Otherwise a black market emerges where sellers charge prices below this government imposed price ceiling.

Government imposed prices always have consequences such as surpluses or shortages, consequences that must be managed by government, such as the control of emerging black markets. One of the beauties of allowing the free market to set the prices and quantities traded is that the forces of supply and demand appear impersonal like the forces of chemistry or gravity. Assuming there is no price conspiracy by producers or consumers, the equilibrium price appears fair, i.e. not manipulated by those interested in the result. In this sense, the price is generally more socially acceptable.

For examples of the opposite of free market prices, consider the situations of rent controls in New York City, or of agricultural price supports for a multitude of crops such as wheat or corn to be converted to ethanol. In the former case, landlords leave their properties less than developed and maintained, and there are tenant queues waiting for these rent controlled properties. There is also less rentable real estate developed in the City because the incentive for that development is not present.

In the latter case of agricultural price supports, we have surpluses that are purchased by government (out of general tax revenues that could be spent on other government services) that are usually sold overseas at lower prices, but with government subsidies. As a result, there is more land and resources devoted to the production of the price controlled good than if the market was without government interference. There are also US taxpayer subsidies of foreign consumers. These cases illustrate what we call "distortions" that result from government interference in free markets.

**Figure 9-1: Market Supply and Demand
With Equilibrium Price P$_e$ and Quantity Q$_e$**

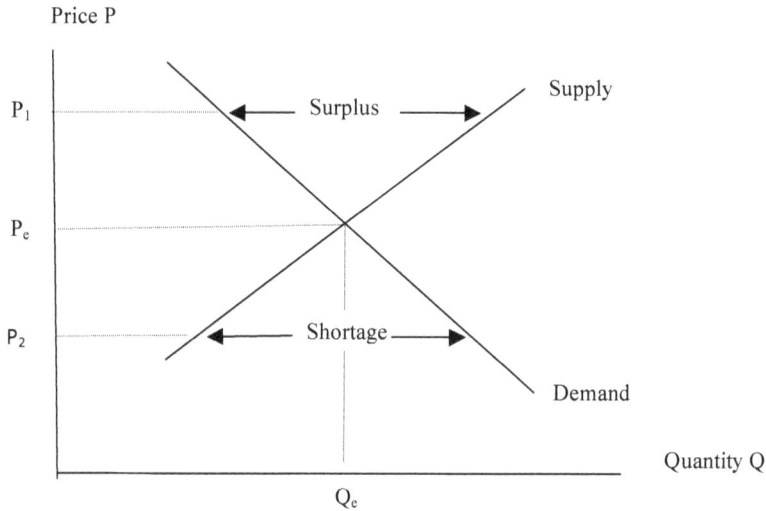

The perception of fairness is certainly a characteristic of free markets. People can move into or out of that particular production as they see fit. They take their chances, and without attempting to manipulate government to favor them over others by either subsidies or price restrictions. This perception, however, is partially flawed in that there are government institutions, such as legal

courts, law enforcement, and many other arrangements that are required for markets to function efficiently. In addition, the disadvantaged (the elderly, the handicapped, etc.) may need subsidies in order to fulfill society's sense of what is fair.

4. A Brief Review of Production and Cost Analysis

Production analysis is simplified by envisioning a production function of only two broad categories of inputs. The generalities of this theoretical exploration are not compromised by this broad categorization. Although in classical and neoclassical economics the two broad categories examined are capital and labor, we could just as well sub-classify labor into line employees and management, or capital into long-term versus working capital, or any other useful classifications. Our purpose here, however, is to simplify so that we might reveal some basic principles involving costs and productivity. These principles can be generalized later when we seek to examine some specific problems involving efficiency associated with production. For this general purpose we will stay with the classical categories of homogeneous labor and homogeneous capital.

Allow a production function to be specified by equation (9-1) where Q is the amount produced, K is the amount of input capital, and L is the amount of input labor. Conditions (9-2a) and (9-2b) specify that the marginal product of both capital and labor are positive but decreasing. This means that as either factor increases, the consequent increment in production is positive, but this increment decreases as each separate factor increases.

$$Q = q(K,L) \qquad\qquad\qquad\qquad\qquad\qquad (9\text{-}1)$$

$$\partial Q/\partial K = MP_K > 0, \ \partial Q/\partial L = MP_L > 0 \qquad\qquad\qquad (9\text{-}2a)$$

$$\partial^2 Q/\partial K^2 < 0, \ \partial^2 Q/\partial L^2 < 0 \qquad\qquad\qquad\qquad (9\text{-}2b)$$

Equation (9-3) gives the total cost of production (TC) where c is the per unit cost of capital, and w is the wage rate per unit of labor employed. Equation (9-4) gives the average cost per unit of production (AC).

$$TC = cK + wL \qquad\qquad\qquad\qquad\qquad\qquad (9\text{-}3)$$

$$AC = TC/Q \qquad\qquad\qquad\qquad\qquad\qquad (9\text{-}4)$$

We assume positive economies of scale that are exploited over the lower stages of production, i.e. starting from a zero level of production, as we expand our level of input usage, these factors learn to combine, specialize, and thereby learn to produce proportionately greater output increments so that average costs drop. Over higher levels of output, however, diseconomies eventually occur so that average costs rise. This occurs because further employment of combinations of inputs cannot yield the same increments in output enjoyed at lower levels of production. Factors are not as productive as over lower levels of inputs. Figure 9-2 illustrates this by showing average costs AC as a "U" shaped function when graphed against output Q.

**Figure 9-2: Average Cost and Marginal Cost Functions
Where AC is the Average Cost and MC is the Marginal Cost.**

AC, MC

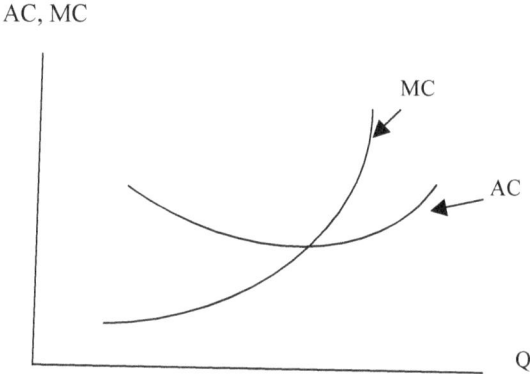

Q

At the minimum average cost point, marginal costs (MC) intersect the average cost curve (AC) at its minimum. This is demonstrated mathematically by (9-5) which expresses the first order condition for the minimization of costs. (This extreme point must be a minimization since we assume the "U" shape for AC.) This is apparent since if the increment (marginal addition) exceeds the average, then the average must increase. If the increment is below the average, then the average must increase. Only at the minimum average point can the increment and average equal.

$$\partial AC/\partial Q = \frac{\partial TC/\partial Q}{Q} - \frac{TC}{Q^2} = [MC - AC]/Q \quad \text{where } MC = \partial TC/\partial Q \tag{9-5}$$

Equation (9-2a) presents the marginal product of labor, i.e. the increment in output from employing an additional unit of labor. Together with (9-2b), we know this function is concave from below. We also define an important concept termed *the marginal revenue product of labor* as defined by (9-6). This represents the increment in total revenue earned by the firm from employing one more unit of labor. This marginal revenue product is an important concept for ethical explorations of the returns to labor as presented below and is illustrated by Figure 9-3. As we shall review, it forms the demand function for labor provided labor markets are competitive.

$$P(\partial Q/\partial L) = P \bullet MP_L = MRP_L \tag{9-6}$$

where MPL is the marginal product of labor, and P is the output price level. MRPL is the marginal revenue product.

Figure 9-3: The Marginal Revenue Product of Labor

MRP$_L$

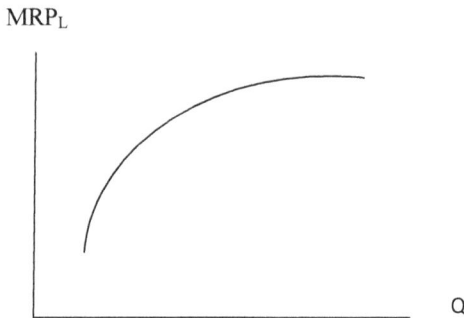

Q

5. The Neoclassical Theory of the Consumer

Chapter IV, *Utilitarian Philosophy and Utility Theory*, presented the elements of consumer demand. Equation (4-5) is a mathematical expression of that elementary theory. It is repeated below as equation (9-7). Its derivation and explanation are contained in that chapter. In applying equation (9-7), we develop a very simplified and stylized model in which there are only two goods for the consumer to purchase, X and Y. For example, they could be envisioned as consumption of material goods versus leisure, or two classifications of other consumer goods such as consumption versus investments. In either case, we equate at the margin so that (9-7) holds where MUX and MUY are the respective marginal utilities, and PX and PY are the respective prices. The neoclassical economic theory states that the consumer's budget is allocated so that the increment to utility per dollar of consumption is equal across all consumer goods considered broadly. If MUX/PX > MUY/PY, then the consumer's budget is reallocated towards good X and away from good Y until (9-7) holds.

$$MU_X/P_X = MU_Y/P_Y \tag{9-7}$$

We can use (9-7) to develop the consumer's demand curve for the product X. First we rearrange (9-7) to obtain (9-8). We use the relative price of X in terms of Y (PX/PY) as our price index which we vary on the vertical axis in Figure 9-4. As this relative price decreases, then MUX must drop as a ratio of MUY. Given that we have diminishing marginal utility to consumption of X, this is achieved by expanding our consumption of X. As a result, we establish a negatively sloped demand function for consumption of X.

$$MU_X/MU_Y = P_X/P_Y \tag{9-8}$$

Figure 9-4: The Demand Function for Good X
With Relative Prices $P_X/P_Y = P$

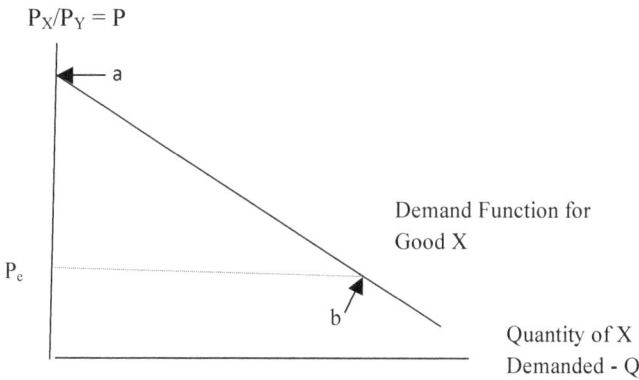

Suppose Pe is the equilibrium market-clearing price for this good. This being the case, there is an important interpretation of the area under the demand curve above this equilibrium price, i.e. the triangle Pe, a, b. This interpretation stems from the fact that Pe is the price paid for all units consumed of good X, even though the consumer was willing to pay a higher price for the initial units consumed that is the value of the initial units exceeds the price paid. Consider the area of the triangle mentioned, and as mathematically measured by the integral of equation (9-8) presented by (9-9).

$$\int \left(\frac{P_X}{P_Y}\right) dQ = \int \left(\frac{MU_X}{MU_Y}\right) dQ \tag{9-9}$$

= Total Utility of Consumption of X in Terms of Y

We call the area of this triangle the *consumer surplus*. It measures value received by the consumer that is not paid for. This can be an important concept for two reasons, as we shall see below:

- Since monopolies produce less than competitive markets, and charge more (as we shall demonstrate below) they deprive consumers of some of this surplus that they would have had if markets were competitive.

- Any producer conspiracy to raise prices above what would exist under competition deprives consumers of some of this surplus.

These problems of monopoly and pricing conspiracies are examined in more detail below.

6. The Profit Maximization Motive for Competitors

Neoclassical economics assumes that the profit motive moves competitive businesses to produce and distribute goods. To be more precise, it assumes they are driven to attempt to maximize profit[78]. This neoclassical model, however, is an abstract model in that it is a stylized view of the economic world, a view that is based upon certain abstract assumptions designed to give us a foundation for analyzing certain notions of efficiency (notions explored in detail in this and other chapters). This view (termed a model) also gives us a foundation for building more complex or complete views. It is useful to compare this neoclassical economic model of *perfect competition*, or of *monopoly* or *monopolistic competition* (all explored below), to the classical physics model of gravitational attraction.

Consider, for example, the problem of shooting a cannon ball and calculating the point at which it lands. How would we calculate this point? We would first proceed to make certain assumptions such as

- We know exactly the angle to the horizontal of the cannon barrel.

- We know exactly the velocity at which the ball leaves the barrel.

- The ball is perfectly and round and symmetric with respect to density.

---

[78] The appendix to this chapter shows that in the real world of uncertainty, this profit maximization motive becomes the maximization of the expected future profit stream. This is the same as wealth maximization.

- There are no atmospheric conditions that would affect the flight of the ball.

With these abstract assumptions, together with the knowledge of the constant of gravitational attraction, we can calculate where the ball will land. We should not criticize our model by stating that since the assumptions are unrealistic, our calculations must be wrong. We fully acknowledge that our abstractions produce some error, but our calculations would probably be reasonably accurate. Furthermore, if we enrich our model by gathering additional information, we know we can build upon our abstract positioning to make a more accurate calculation. For example, we might first calculate that the cannon ball will land in a direct line from the barrel 650 feet in distance. After considering a possible strong left to right wind, however, we might modify our estimate by several inches to the right.

Our neoclassical model of *perfect competition* should similarly be considered as a foundational initial estimate of the behavior of competitive firms. It forms the basis for more accurate models of firm behavior as explored below. The assumptions of *perfect competition* are

- The industry at question consists of a large number of small equally-sized firms called *price takers* who produce an homogenous good. This means that there is no difference between the product of one producer and another. This also means that producers are incapable of affecting the market clearing price of the good, i.e. these small firms could double or triple their production without sufficiently affecting the total market supply so that prices would drop as a result. For example, we might consider wheat or corn farmers as perfect competitors in that even if any single farmer radically expanded production, they could not so affect the total supply of wheat or corn that the world market-clearing price would change. Note that we assume there is no difference between the "hard red winter wheat" produced by one farmer as compared to another.

- We assume that the increment in costs per unit of expansion of output increases with this expansion. (More about this is explored below.)

- All producers know with certainty the affects of their decisions on production.

- There is no time dimension to examine for implications, i.e. the production decision is made now, and its effects occur immediately after.

- Producers are profit maximizers. If they do not seek to maximize profit they will be driven from the industry by those who do. This process of competition is explained in more detail below.

Profit Maximization for Perfect Competition

We specify that profit is given by equation (9-10) where P is the price of the product sold, and Q is the output produced and sold.

Profit = Total Revenue – Total Cost   (9-10)

$= P{\cdot}Q - TC$ where TC = Total Cost

An application of some very elementary calculus allows us to discern the profit maximizing level of output. Equation (9-11) specifies the first order condition for profit maximization.[79] Note that given the assumption that the firm's output is too small to affect price, then $dP/dQ = 0$.

$d(\text{Profit})/dQ = (dP/dQ)Q + P - d(TC)/dQ = P - dTC/dQ$ (9-11)

= Marginal Revenue – Marginal Cost

= 0 if Marginal Revenue = Marginal Cost

The condition "Marginal Revenue = Marginal Cost" is the profit maximizing condition for output Q. This means that profit is maximized at this particular level of output. Marginal revenue for the perfectly competitive firm is simply the increase in revenue per unit of increase in output. For the price taker, this is simply the price (P) of the output, i.e. it is constant at price. The marginal cost is the increment in costs per unit expansion of output.

Equation (9-12) specifies the second-order condition for the maximization with respect to output Q. This condition specifies that marginal cost increases as output expands, which we assume is true for competitive firms.

---

[79] As specified by (9-10), profit is a continuous function of Q. For an extreme point, either maximum or minimum, we need only set the derivative of profit with respect to output (dProfit/dQ) equal to zero. If the second derivative is negative $(d^2\text{Profit}/dQ^2 < 0)$, then this extreme point is a maximum. This is termed the second-order condition for a maximum.

$$d^2\text{Profit}/dQ^2 = -d^2TC/dQ^2 \qquad\qquad (9\text{-}12)$$

$$< 0 \text{ if } d^2\,TC/dQ^2 > 0$$

Figure 9-5 depicts the conditions necessary for profit maximization for the perfectly competitive firm. As shown, price is horizontal for the price taker, and
marginal costs are increasing. Also, as exhibited, as long as price is above marginal cost, that is as long as the increment to revenue is greater than the increment
to cost, profit is earned. Starting at an output level below Q*, output should be
expanded up to the point that P = Marginal Cost. Beyond Q*, the marginal cost
exceeds marginal revenue so that expansion of output beyond this point decreases
profit below its maximum point as shown in Figure 9-5.

We perceive from Figure 9-5 and from the profit maximizing condition that
marginal cost = P, that as price changes, the quantity supplied changes for this
competitive firm, i.e. the marginal cost function is the supply function for this
competitive firm. To obtain the market supply function, we need only sum the
marginal cost functions for every firm in the industry.

Figure 9-5: The Output Decision for the Price Taker
With Increasing Marginal Costs

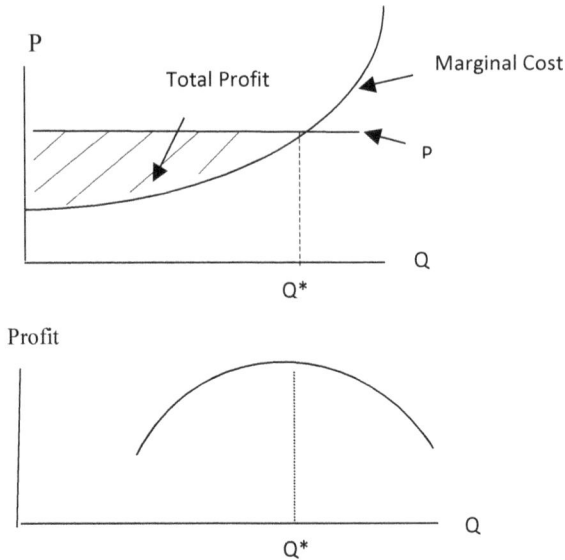

The analysis examined so far also explains entry and exit from the competitive industry. Consider the situation illustrated by Figure 9-6 for a single competitive firm where the marginal costs (MC) and average costs (AC) are shown. Note that as explained above, the MC curve intersects the AC curve at the minimum average cost for the firm, and assuming that all firms in this industry are homogeneous in their cost structure, the industry. It must be kept in mind that the cost curves reflect more than just the direct costs of production. They also include the required profit necessary to keep each firm operating in this industry. If P1 is the market clearing price, and as shown, it is above the average cost, then the difference P − AC is the *excess profit* per unit of production, i.e. the profit above that necessary to keep firms in this industry. This excess profit will induce new entrant firms into the industry, industry supply will expand, and prices decrease towards PM. If, however, the market clearing price is P2, where P2 < PM, the firm is not earning the required competitive profit necessary to keep it in the industry. This firm, along with others, will exit the industry, supply will decrease, and prices rise towards PM. Hence the equilibrium price will be at PM where only the required necessary competitive profit level is earned. This occurs at the minimum average costs. Society, therefore, obtains this good at the minimum average cost of production, and the producers earn only the minimum competitive profit level necessary to keep them producing.

Figure 9-6: Competition, Minimum Average Costs
Excess and Competitive Profits

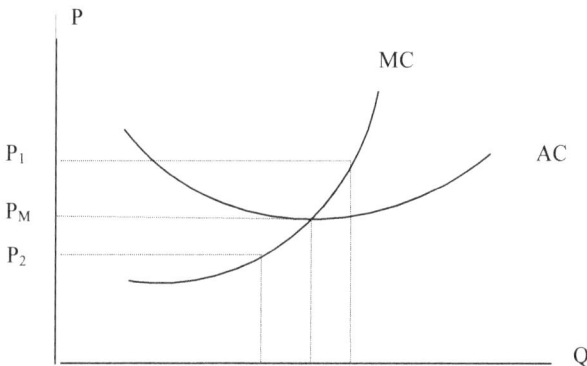

Excess and Competitive Profits

This analysis of competitive industries has strong implications for income distribution. If all industries were competitive, where only the minimum competitive profits necessary to keep entrepreneurs operating in their industries are earned, then the returns to capital investment would be relatively flat and low. If producers can establish artificial barriers to entry, say by legal-legislative means, where when market clearing prices are at P1, other firms are restricted from entering this industry and thereby pushing supply higher, and prices and profits lower, then artificially high profit levels will be maintained. The resulting distribution of income will be more skewed.

This analysis of competitive industries is also applicable for examination of problems associated with negative externalities. If there are no externalities to be concerned with then the cost functions depicted in Figure 9-6, reflects society's true costs of production. The competitive market therefore allocates resources in- and out-of this market so that prices reflect and cover the true social costs. The price, it has been argued above, reflects society's marginal value so that a production level that equates social marginal value with social marginal cost is one that maximizes the total net value to society. As is argued below, this is a substantial contribution to notions of societal efficiency. If, however, there are externalities such as pollution, externalities not reflected in the costs paid by the firm but are nonetheless paid by society, then market prices will be below the marginal social value. In this case, the competitive equilibrium does not maximize net social value, i.e. it is not socially efficient. This externality cost problem is considered in more detail below.

The Monopoly Pricing

Note that from equation (9-11), the profit maximizing condition for any firm is given by (9-13).

$$\text{Marginal Cost} = \text{Marginal Revenue} \tag{9-13}$$
$$\text{where Marginal Revenue} = (dP/dQ)Q + P$$

For a monopoly, we consider the derivative dP/dQ as the slope of the market demand function. For monopolized industry, a single firm faces the entire market demand function which has a negative slope (see Figure 9-1), that is $dP/dQ < 0$.

Whereas for the competitive price-taking firm, $dP/dQ = 0$, so that profit maximization requires that marginal revenue equals price, the profit maximizing condition for the monopolist requires that production occur at a marginal cost that is below price. This is the consequence of $dP/dQ < 0$ together with condition (9-13).

If we differentiate the marginal revenue function for the monopoly, as given by (9-14a), we find something interesting. (This derivative is the slope of the marginal revenue function.)

$$\text{d Marginal revenue}/dQ = (d^2P/dQ^2)\, Q + 2(dP/dQ) \tag{9-14a}$$

For a linear demand function, we have $d2P/dQ2 = 0$, and therefore we have (9-14b).

$$\text{d Marginal revenue}/dQ = 2(dP/dQ) \tag{9-14b}$$

This indicates that the marginal revenue function has a slope that is twice the magnitude of the linear demand function with slope dP/dQ, i.e., it bisects the angle made between the linear demand function and the vertical axis as shown in Figure 9-7.

The profit maximizing output level for the monopoly is given by "marginal revenue = marginal cost," but unlike the case of the perfect competitor, and as shown above, marginal revenue is not constant, but rather it has a negative slope. This occurs because as the monopolist increases output, the price not only decreases for the last unit sold, but also for every other unit produced and sold. The profit maximizing level of output is again given by Q*, but it is less than the quantity that occurs at the intersection of the industry marginal cost (the competitive supply function) and the demand function as shown by Figure 9-8. We perceive that one of the social problems with monopoly is therefore that a lower amount of production occurs, and the price charged is therefore higher than under competition.

Figure 9-7: Monopolist Marginal Revenue for a Linear Demand Function

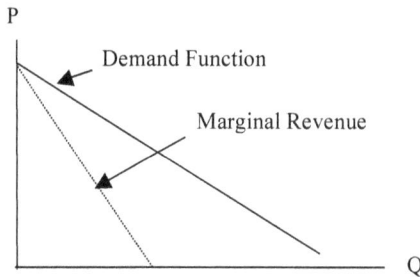

The reduction in the quantity produced under a monopoly as compared to what would occur if the industry were highly competitive is of considerable interest because of the consumer surplus lost. Figure 9-8 illustrates this loss where Pc is the price under competition (where the industry MC curve intersects the market demand curve) and PM is the price charged by the monopolist. As shown, the consumer surplus is much lower under monopoly. The consumer surplus under monopoly is the area of the triangle PM – a – b. The consumer surplus under competition is Pc – a – c.

**Figure 9-8: The Profit Maximizing Level of Output
For a Monopolist**

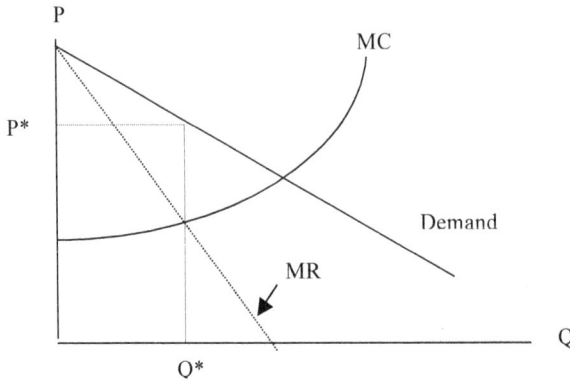

Our society generally attempts to eliminate monopolies, but is also recognizes that some industries are characterized by considerable economies of scale for which average costs fall even up to the point that there is only one very large producer, a monopoly. Electric utilities are good examples of this where each locality of the country has a single electric utility provider. Under this circumstance, prices and supplies are regulated by various public service commissions, and this regulation is designed to assure that prices and supplies approximate what would be produced under competition.

**Figure 9-9: Comparison of Consumer Surplus for Competition
and Monopoly**

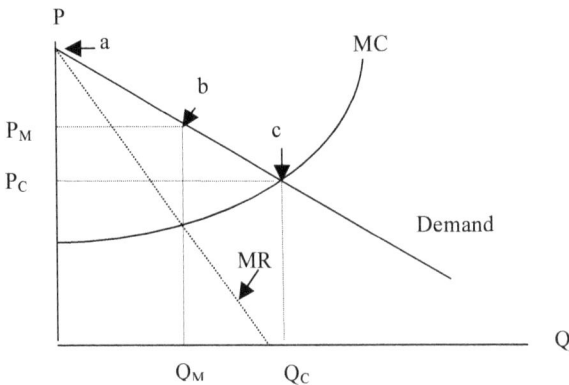

Monopolistic Competition

Between the abstract extremes of perfect competition and monopoly lies the very realistic industrial case of monopolistic competition. These industries consist of a few firms who differentiate their product so as to establish some monopoly (or market) power as indicated by the definition below. (Recall that with perfect competition, the produced good is homogeneous.)

Definition: *Monopoly power,* frequently termed *market power*, is the ability of a firm to raise price without losing all of its demand.

Perfectly competitive firms must be price takers since any attempt to raise their price above the market level results in an inability to sell any product. In perfectly competitive industries the product is homogeneous. Firms try to develop monopoly power so that they can raise price above marginal cost and as a result, increase total profit. This increase in total profit does not always happen, especially if there are substitutes for the firm's product. *Market power* is not an easy thing to develop. To do so, producers must differentiate their product. Often this is attempted through advertising. For example, the cigarette industry has long advertised that one cigarette fits or establishes one image for the smoker, and another creates a different image. A price increase by one of these brands will not eliminate all sales for that product, as occurs with a perfectly competitive industry. As a result, for the monopolistic competitor, there is some slope to the firm's demand function. Price will be above marginal cost, at least by some small amount. This is illustrated by Figure 9-10 where the attempts to rotate its perfect-competitor horizontal demand function to one with negative slope. In effect, this firm obtains its own market by differentiating its product. It produces where marginal cost equals marginal revenue, and prices are above marginal cost.

Establishing monopoly power is generally the objective of the business subject of *strategy*. As we shall examine below, there are ethical implications to establishing market power in any industry.

**Figure 9-10: Establishing Market Power by
Rotating Demand Function to have Negative Slope**

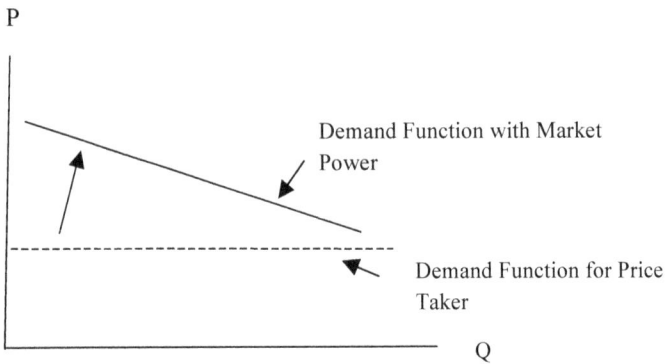

P

Demand Function with Market
Power

Demand Function for Price
Taker

Q

Price Discrimination

Price discrimination occurs when companies with monopoly power charge different prices to different buyers even though the costs of producing or delivering these goods do not differ.

Firms cannot do this in perfectly competitive markets because customers would merely turn to an alternative producer, one who does not discriminate. Price discrimination requires that the discriminator has some monopoly power. For example, a discriminator might establish different prices for delivering to government in volume as compared to private buyers who purchase smaller quantities.

Monopoly power often comes with regional suppliers where transportation costs limit customers ability to travel to obtain the same good at lower prices. An inner city supermarket, therefore, might charge higher prices for the same good because buyers do not have the flexibility to travel to suburban markets.

Figure 9-11 illustrates the problem with price discrimination. For the case illustrated, the producer charges P1 for quantities produced up to Q1, P2 for quantities between Q1 and Q2, and P3 for quantities between Q2 and Q3. By doing so, the producer expropriates some of the consumer surplus in the form of profit which consists of the differences between the prices and the marginal costs. For the case of perfect price discrimination, every buyer is charged a different price equal to the maximum they are willing to pay. The entire consumer surplus is expropriated by the producer as an increase in profit.

Figure 9-11: Price Discrimination Occurs if Different Customers are Charged Different Prices

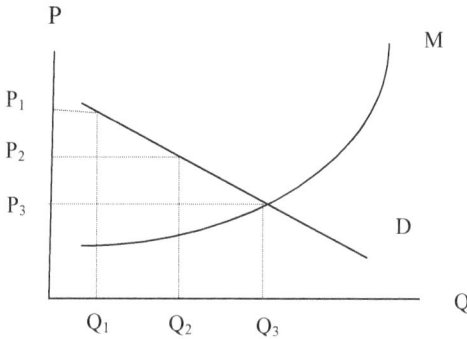

As we shall see below, some forms of price discrimination is prohibited by US law.

Returns to the Factors of Production

Allow two factor inputs to production: inputs A and B with unit costs WA and WS. Equation (9-15) gives profit with costs specified as consisting of WAA + WBB. In (9-15), P indicates the price of the output, and A and B indicate the quantities of the respective input. Equation (9-16) presents the first-order condition for profit maximization involving the usage of input A. MPA is the marginal product of A.

Profit = Total Revenue – Total Cost   (9-15)

$$= P{\cdot}Q - (W_A A + W_B B)$$

$$d(Profit)/dA = (dP/dQ)(dQ/dA)Q + P(dQ/dA) - W_A \quad (9\text{-}16)$$

$$= [(dP/dQ)Q + P]dQ/dA - W_A$$

$$= [Marginal\ Revenue]MP_A - W_A$$

$$= Marginal\ Revenue\ Product - W_A$$

$$= 0\ if\ Marginal\ Revenue\ Product = W_A$$

As above in our section concerning production, we assume that dQ/dA > 0, but that d2Q/dA2 < 0, i.e. the marginal product of A is positive but decreasing. This results in the factor's marginal revenue product decreasing as input A expands. Figure 9-12 illustrates this maximization condition. As shown, the marginal revenue product for A decreases as A expands. If in the market for this factor input, the firm is a price taker (the firm is too small to affect the market price of this input), the factor price (W_A) is constant. The quantity A* is the optimum quantity demanded for this factor in that this quantity satisfies the profit maximizing condition of (9-16). In this sense, the marginal revenue product is the demand function for this factor on the part of this firm. A summation of all these functions across all firms composes the market demand function for this factor.

To better understand Figure 9-12, consider that for every quantity of factor input below A*, the factor's contribution to gross revenue exceeds the cost of the input. This generates profit for this employment. Beyond A*, the factor input's contribution to revenue is less than its contribution to cost, and a loss for this extension of employment would be earned. A* is therefore the efficient usage of this input.

Figure 9-12: Marginal Revenue Product and the Demand for a Factor Input A

Marginal Revenue Product

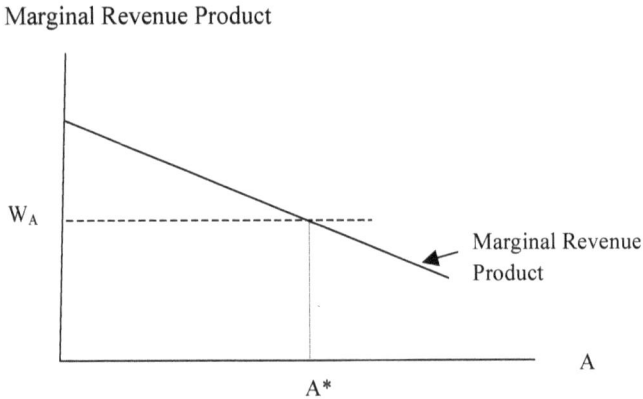

Monopsony

A *monopsony* is similar to a *monopoly* except that it is on the buying side rather than the selling side. A firm is a *monopoly* if it is the only seller. It has *monopoly market power* to the extent that its quantity of output affects the price of the product. A *monopsony* is a single buyer of a product. A firm has *monopsony market power* if the quantity that it purchases affects the price of the good. Typically, if *monopsony market power* occurs, it does so for inputs to the production function rather than for a final consumer product. Consumers tend to not be so unique as to be the only buyer of some consumer good.

Monopsony market power and *monopoly market power* tend to go together. For example, a large local supermarket, the only one in some geographic area although there might be a few small competitors, will normally have some *monopoly market power* over the demand for its produce. Because it will likely be the largest buyer of local produce, it will also have some *monopsony market power* over the supply of local produce. Firms that dominate their output markets tend to also dominate its input market.

7. Legal Prohibitions Against Anti-Competitive Practices

During the late 19th century, the political power of *trusts* spawned a populist movement to limit the political influence of big business. A *trust* was an arrangement whereby the shareholders of several separate companies rendered their shares to a group of trustees who ran the combination as a monopoly. The original shareholders were granted shares in the resulting combination. In response to this practice, in 1890 Congress passed the Sherman Anti-Trust Act, named after senator John Sherman of Ohio (the Civil War General William Tecumseh Sherman's brother). This Act takes its constitutional authority from *Section 8's* (of the Constitution) granting to Congress the power to "regulate commerce among the several States." There are two important sections to this Act:

Section 1: "Every Contract, combination in the form of trust or otherwise, or conspiracy, in restraint of trade or commerce among the several states, or with foreign nations is declared to be illegal."

Section 2: "Every person who shall monopolize, or attempt to monopolize, or combine or conspire with any other person or persons, to monopolize any part of the trade or commerce among the several states ...."

Violation of either section is declared by this law to be a felony punishable by imprisonment and fine. The law is the US society's first declaration that anti-competitive practices are both unethical and illegal. It essentially declares that a competitive market economy is desired.

Initially enforcement of the Sherman Act was a failure in that the courts refused to apply the common understanding of the Act's language to limit monopoly. Initially the Act was only applied against labor unions as restraints of competition in the labor market. This was clearly not the intention of Congress, and in fact the courts had a history of hostility to labor unions prior to 1890. The right to strike was viewed as an attack on private property rights, and interpretations of the Sherman Act as being anti union was merely a continuation of this hostility. In 1895, however, in an infamous case involving American Sugar Refining Co., who monopolized 98% of sugar refining in the US, the monopoly was found to not be in violation of Sherman because the court differentiated between manufacturing and trade, a very warped interpretation of the intention of Congress.

With the election of the William McKinley – Theodore Roosevelt Administration in 1898, anti-monopoly enforcement became much stronger. In 1904, the Northern Securities Corporation, a railroad trust, was dissolved. In 1911, the Standard Oil Co. of New Jersey was also dissolved where the Court articulated a new "rule of reason" under which the conduct that led to the monopolization became the key as to whether the Act was violated. [80]

Partly in response to the courts application of the Sherman Act to labor unions, and partly for other reasons, Congress passed the Clayton Act in 1914. This Act expressly stated that the anti-trust laws should not be applied to labor unions. This did not stop the courts, however, from this application. This Act did outlaw price discrimination (charging different customers different prices for the same

---

[80] In a famous dissent in the Standard Oil case, the great jurist Judge Learned Hand stated that "Congress did not forbid bad trusts and forgive good trusts, it forbid all trusts." His dissent emphasized that motive was not important, but only the result, i.e an unregulated monopoly hurts the public good whether formed through good intentions or bad. This has been a controversial issue since the Standard Oil decision.

product), outlawed interlocking directorates (where seeming competitors have common directors so that conspiracies in restraint of trade are enabled), prohibited the buying out of competitors, and established the Federal Trade Commission to enforce many of these prohibitions. Laws against price discrimination were strengthened by the Robinson-Patman Act of 1936. Laws against mergers among competitors were strengthened by the Cellar – Kefauver Act of 1950. With respect to labor union exercise of the power of strikes, the Wagner Act of 1936 established the right of unions to both organize and strike. Subsequent to this law court decisions upheld this law.

Society has therefore indicated its distain for pricing conspiracies, consolidations that tend to establish monopoly power in manufacturing or distribution of goods, and against price discrimination. Society has also recognized the rights of unions to organize and strike even those these actions could be, and have previously been recognized as restraints in trade.

8. Problems with Externalities

Externalities consist of third-party type effects associated with market transactions. For example,

Suppose you and I agree to an exchange, one that generates some garbage. If we dump our garbage on another's property, this would be a negative externality to our transaction. Positive externalities are positive third party effects. To be efficient, that is to maximize social welfare, we want to discourage negative but encourage positive externalities.

To illustrate one of the economic problems associated with negative externalities, consider two sets of costs, one with pollution-abatement costs internalized, and one with these pollution costs externalized. If these costs are not internalized, then as a result, the firm without the internalized costs produces a greater amount and charges a lower price. This is illustrated by Figure 9-13 where the higher marginalized costs curve occurs with the pollution costs internalized. As shown, moving to internalize these costs reduces the amount of the good produced, and raises the price. Without this internalization, the social cost of the negative externalities is passed onto society through the form of costs associated with pollution. If these costs were internalized in the form of pollution abatement, a smaller output would be produced, and the firm that generates the pollution would bear the cost of abatement. This latter case appears to be fair, and is more efficient in enhancing social welfare.

Figure 9-13: Marginal Cost Curve MC₁ Externalizes Pollutions Costs While MC₂ Internalizes these Costs to the Industry

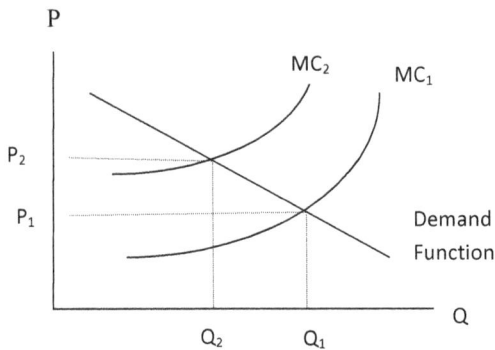

Ronald Coase won the Nobel Prize in Economics in 1991 for his contribution to understanding the efficiency of free markets with respect to resource allocation even when externalities are present. (See Coase, 1960.) His contribution consists of his *Coase Theorem*, a version of which is presented here.

Coase Theorem: In the absence of transaction costs, free markets allocate resources efficiently (maximizes social welfare) even in the presence of externalities provided private property rights are well defined.

The idea of the *Coase Theorem* is that if property rights can be sold, then in the presence of negative externalities, the losers will either compensate the winners so as to prevent the negative externality, or the winners will compensate the losers so as to compensate for their absorption of the externality. Transaction costs are those associated with bargaining, i.e. the time and expense of finding the appropriate parties and conducting the actual bargaining associated with property right exchanges. The *Coase Theorem* emphasizes the combination of well-defined saleable property rights and low transaction costs as the keys to economic efficiency with respect to externalities. Of course, transaction costs might make this compensation either very expensive to arrange, or even impossible to arrange. Finding losers and winners, and forcing them into negotiating compensation schemes is problematic at best. Transaction costs are seldom negligible, and the initial allocation of property rights has the potential to affect the final outcome. Even if transaction costs were non-existent, we still have a problem with the fairness of having compensation for negative externalities.

Consider the problem of noise pollution generated from a manufacturing plant. Does the manufacturing firm own the right to pollute the nearby neighborhood with noise, or do the nearby residents own the right to a quiet area? If the former is true then perhaps the nearby residents could join to pay the manufacturing plant to either move or adopt a quiet technology. If the latter is true then the manufacturing plant would pay the residents compensation to move? If property rights to having or not having quiet in the area are not defined, then bargaining will not occur, and perhaps endless and expensive litigation over the issue results. Even if the property rights are well defined, inhibitions to bargaining could occur associated with reaching a legal contract of resolution. Lawyer and court costs can be expensive and these could inhibit an agreeable resolution.

Positive externalities also pose difficulties with respect to the *Coase Theorem*. These third party effects are benefits such as those we observe frequently in the marketplace. For example, we note that the costs associated with the retail development of some areas are frequently born by only a few large retailers, although many smaller businesses tag along to that area so as to have a viable business. The large retailers draw shoppers, and the smaller retailers are "free riders" in attracting these customers. The same is often true of major manufacturing areas where transportation, zoning arrangements with government, and energy costs are initially born by large businesses. Smaller businesses do not bear a significant portion of this infrastructure development. Anticipating these positive externalities, and having all fairly bear the costs that reflect the benefits, are difficult. The market is not entirely efficient without considerable government regulation and encouragement.

One of the benefits of the *Coase Theorem* is that it emphasizes a particular role for government, namely that it should create institutions that minimize transactions costs. Note that establishing well defined property rights is one of these institutions along with establishing an efficient low-cost court system for dispute resolution. The issue of fairness with respect to externalities is essentially handled by society's definition and allocation of property rights. For example, do I have the right to prevent my neighbors from affecting my property in ways I do not approve? If so, and if my neighbors find this action to be extremely beneficial, then they can compensate me for their actions. This negotiation, however, must be low cost to all in order for this system to be efficient.

9. Ethical Implications with Competition

Ethical Issues with Industry Structure

Using the analysis of negative externalities, perfect competition, monopoly, monopolistic competition, and monopsony we can examine a variety of associated ethical issues. These include the following:

- Do the costs underlying the supply function for some industry reflect all the social costs associated with production? For example, are there external pollutions costs not incorporated in the production price of the product? If not, then costs will be lower, the market price charged will be lower, and more than an efficient level of production will occur, i.e. a level where the true social marginal cost of production is above the market price.

- Are industries sufficiently competitive so that profits are low, i.e.do profits equal just what is necessary to keep firms in this industry? Are artificial barriers to entry established (legal restrictions on entry) so that excess profits are earned? If the answer to the latter is "yes!", then in the lack of other governmental regulation, there are implications for consumers, income distribution, and overall economic efficiency. An associated question concerns whether producers respond to consumer demands. This may not occur to an optimal degree if artificial barriers to competition exist.

- Do returns to factor inputs reflect their productivity, i.e. their marginal revenue product? Factor inputs might create artificial barriers to competition so that their compensation exceeds their marginal contribution.

There are then at least three broad categorical questions to the organization of production that pose strong ethical questions:

(i)   Do product prices reflect true social costs?

(ii) Are there artificial barriers to producer competition?

(iii) Are their artificial barriers to factor input competition?

Society addresses issues ii. and iii. through several laws designed to maintain competition.

Ethical Issues with Business Strategy

Michael Porter, often called the original guru of *Business Strategy*, gathered this subject's material from a graduate course in Industrial Organization (IO) at Harvard University. His original works became the substance of capstone courses in *Business Strategy* or *Policy* at business schools across the Country. This same IO material has often been used as the basis for courses in *Managerial Economics* also often offered at business schools across the Country, although the faculty who have offered these courses often have not recognized the material as being in common. Those who instruct the *Strategy* course usually have their PhDs in Management. Those who instruct the *Managerial Economics* course have their PhDs in Economics.

Michael Porter reduces his *Strategy* material as dependent upon five basic forces that determine the financial success of the firm. From these five basic forces, Porter derives three generic strategies. The first three of these five forces that Porter lists are:

(1)   The current degree of competition in the market for the firm's product.

(2)   The threat of entry into this product market.

(3)   The threat of substitutes for the firm's product.

These three forces determine what we have called the firm's *monopoly market power* for the sale of its product.

Note that the first of these listed forces, the degree of competition for the firm's product, depends upon the ability of the firm to differentiate its product, and/ or build brand loyalty. This can be quantified as the elasticity, or slope, of the demand for the firm's product, which in turn is a measure of the firm's *monopoly market power* on the selling side. In the longer run, however, the threat of substitutes, the third of Porter's forces, can erode this market power. We have seen this erosion in the past, for example when the energy crisis of the 1970s elicited conservation and more energy-efficient technology.

The energy example presented above is also a good example of Porter's second force, the threat of substitutes. We explored this subject through a standard and often used strategy o "pricing to avoid entry," i.e. establishing prices below the minimum average cost of an entry-level start-up firm, a lower price than strict current profit maximization warrants, but a price that maximizes the firm's profit stream while avoiding the potential competition.

Porter's other two forces are:

(4) The degree of *monopsony market power* the firm's customers have in the product market.

(5) The degree of *monopsony market power* the firm has over its input market.

Monopsony market power over the firm's input market is often linked to the degree of *monopoly market power* the firms has in its product market, that the latter is often a necessary precondition to the former. If the latter does not exist, it is very unlikely that *monopsony market power* can be developed in the input market.

Porter suggests three generic strategies to develop financial success for the firm:

(1) Become the cost leader for this product market.

(2) Differentiate the product so as to develop *market power*.

(3) Develop *focus* by narrowing the product line so as to exploit either or both of the above.

We have already noted the social implications of establishing market power in that society is deprived from some of the benefits of greater competition, benefits such as consumer surplus. Nevertheless we note that there is nothing unethical inherent in Porter's three generic strategies, at least in the sense of our Kantian moral maxims, although there might be utilitarian implications. There are, however, some actions aimed at establishing market power that could be considered as unethical such as consolidations (mergers and acquisitions) to substantially reduce competition, or certainly conspiracies among sellers to not compete by price. The former action would be considered illegal under the Clayton and Cellar-Kefauver Acts. The latter is illegal under the Sherman Act.

Buyer-Beware and the Free Market

We have already indicated the Kantian moral prohibitions against purposeful deception. This certainly applies to trades in free markets. The *buyer beware* model of free markets can never be wither social welfare maximizing, nor ethical. The purposeful hiding of important information related to goods to be sold not only is inefficient in that it imposes unnecessary information- gathering costs onto the purchaser, but also it violates the *categorical imperative*.

The notion of the free market applies to entry and exit from industries, it does not imply "freedom for those who wish to commit fraud to participate." Deception is neither Kantian nor utilitarian.

10. Kantian Considerations Concerning Freely Competitive Markets

As briefly reviewed in a previous chapter, one of the important Kantian principles is the *universal principle of justice,* or UPJ, which requires that our system of moral maxims and legalities maximizes the freedom of individuals provided that we establish laws that prevent individuals from impinging the freedom of others. Allowing markets to act freely without societal interference, and provided externalities are internalized or controlled, and provided our other moral maxims apply, appears a requirement of the UPJ. In addition, as pointed out by Chambers and Lacey (1996), free markets allow society's sense of ethics to impact the competing firms through the price mechanism, i.e. consumer and capital market boycotts.

The problem with the opposite extreme from free market capitalism, that is socialism, is that it concentrates power in the government to direct the allocation of resource. This is essentially a coercive system with respect to individuals where the rights of private property are not existent. Society claims the property rights and resources are allocated to production by government bureaucrats. The freedom of individuals to try-their-hand at meeting some market demand is not present. If society objects to some ethical lapse, they must complain directly to the bureaucracy in the hope of change. Individuals do not get to vote in the marketplace through their purchases.

In free markets, however, we cannot expect individuals to exercise this marketplace voting if violations of the *imperative of the respect for the dignity of individuals* are hidden. For the marketplace system to work, information must be available and unbiased, hence some of our rules with respect to public audits. Whether our rules for this information divulgence are sufficient is certainly not certain given that our society continues to be plagued by a variety of business scandals.

Another ethical problem that plagues free markets is best described as a modern version of merchantilism, i.e. the government granting of monopoly-type market-power. Artificial barriers to entry are often established through government influence. For example consider the recent establishment of restrictions on street vendors in Atlanta. (See the Wall Street Journal story, August 15, 2011, page A12.) previous to 2009, vendors paid $250 per year for the street cite for selling their wares. Under the leadership of Mayor Shirley Franklin, and motivated by "enhancing the downtown aesthetic," the city granted monopoly rights to the Chicago-based management company General Growth Properties, who charged vendors between $500 and $1,600 per month for one of their pre fabricated uniformly-constructed and designed kiosks. Many of these kiosks currently stand empty.

During early August, 2010, an organization called the *Institute for Justice*, representing the street vendors, sued in Fulton County Georgia *Superior Court* on grounds that the new monopoly interferes with the vendors' right to "earn an honest living free from unreasonable and anticompetitive government restrictions." The suit challenges the city's contract with the management company, which requires it to prevent lessees from directly competing with nearby businesses. The WSJ editorial states that "The Atlanta case is one more example of the way that governments tend to collude with private interests to benefit the powerful."

We find many examples of local government restrictions on competition, generally offered under the guise of benefiting the public. For example, most municipalities restrict taxi cab competition by only offering a limited number of licenses. The rational for these restrictions is usually that the public is thereby protected from fly-by-night competitors. One can argue, however, that these fly-by-night competitors are really start-ups who would survive by offering a better service at a better price, and that the government granting of monopoly market power to a limited number of taxis results in poorly conditioned vehicles, slower service and higher prices.

The problem with these government established restrictions on competition is that business is always willing to pay through political contributions, *pay-to-play* as it is termed, for this market power. It is this *pay-to-play* action that is unethical. This is the curse of what we term free-market capitalism that is that the free-market is restricted because of these unethical contributions. They do not serve a greater public good, a *kingdom of ends*. In addition, they are essentially deceptive in that they are generally hidden from public view.

11. Competitive Markets for Explicit and Implicit Contracts

When goods and services are sold on open markets, they are generally associated with some sort of either explicit or implicit contract. Explicit contracts are those that are legally enforceable. Implicit contracts are those with an ethical, but not legal, obligation. We understand that various goods and services are sold with certain legal obligations such as warranties or contractual service obligations, but most markets involve implicit obligations pertaining to the quality of good or service.

For example, consider supermarket transactions. We trust that the markets' claims to selling fresh and nonpoisonous food pose their obligations which they will honor. We do not expect that we would sue in the courts because we purchase an item that does not turn out to meet our expectation for freshness. Nevertheless, we certainly might complain and demand some compensation, and good markets will honor that obligation upon presentation of some basic evidence. One must suspect that in fact most transactions bear some ethical-contractual obligation. Hence there is a role for examination of these ethical obligations in the marketplace.

A previous chapter examined certain notions of fairness as they would apply to these contractual obligations, both implicit and explicit. Certainly deception violates all our notions of fairness. Coercion also violates notions of fairness, and by coercion we mean some sort of forced transaction. This could occur because of some sort of tie-in agreement, such as if you wish to purchase this, you must purchase that. Also, a monopoly or monopsony forces us to deal with only one seller or buyer. Companies that attempt to establish this degree of market power patently commit unfair acts, and this is the reason why these acts are unlawful. In fact, the political movement behind these antitrust laws was essentially motivated by the public's perception of this unfairness.

Review Questions

(1) Briefly review Adam Smith's argument concerning the role of competitive markets in serving public welfare? How can this be consistent with Kant's *kingdom of ends* and notions of positive duties?

(2) What benefits do we obtain from examination of the neoclassical economic model?

(3) Briefly review how the twin forces of supply and demand explain price movements?

(4) Explain the notion of consumer surplus and how monopolies deprive society of this surplus?

(5) What are the conditions necessary for perfect competition? Define competitive profit level? Explain how perfect competition assures that prices equal minimum average cost to the producers and only competitive profits are earned? Explain why monopoly assures that prices are greater than average cost and that excess profits are earned? Explain the role of negative externalities to the production levels of competitive firms?

(6) How does monopolistic competition differ from perfect competition and monopoly?

(7) Explain the demand function for factor inputs in competitive markets?

(8) Explain the benefits to fairness of competitive markets?

(9) Explain the role of externalities to fairness and social welfare? Explain the *Coase theorem* and its importance in welfare arguments?

(10) Briefly summarize the Kantian considerations associated with competitive markets in particular the *UPJ*?

Appendix: Wealth and Profit Maximization

The goal of maximizing profit is generally cited in introductory economics texts. It is used to develop various notions of social-economic efficiency. The models used for this development, however, assume certainty, and a world of only one period. We must extend this model to multi periods, and uncertainty. This is what we do later in this course, and this extension leads to shareholder wealth maximization rather than profit maximization.

What is the relation between profits (which we recognize as the net earnings of the corporation) and the wealth of the shareholders? This wealth is in the equity value of the firm, i.e. the total market value of the outstanding common stock. Consider the Figure A-1 below where the risky but expected profit stream of the firm. This expectation is formed by the owners and by the financial markets in general.

A publicly owned corporation is legally owned by its common stockholders. They have the legal power to hire or fire management, they also must select and approve the company's board of directors, and they own the company's residual cash earnings (profits). These profits must either be paid back to the shareholders in the form of dividends, or retained back in the firm for the purpose of generating future growth in earnings.

Figure A-1: The Expected Future Profit Stream

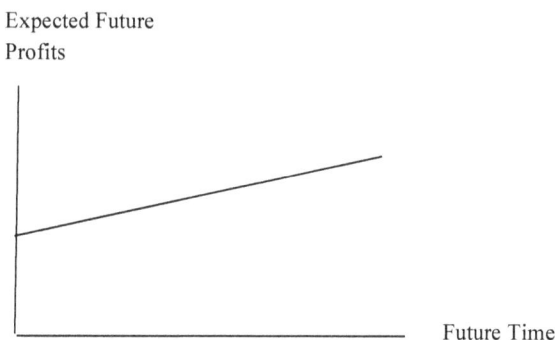

In competitive financial markets (such as the US stock market), a publicly traded corporation's market value of equity (the market value of the company's common stock) reflects the present value of the expected future earnings (or profit) stream. Because of compound interest, money has time value. You would rather have $100 now than $100 one year from now if for no other reason than investing the $100 now would give you more than $100 one year from now. So it is with common stock investors, except that they only have an expectation of future earnings. They know that obtaining their expected earnings is risky. Based upon this consideration of future expected earnings, and the risk involved, they will offer a price for the company's shares. In competitive financial markets such as the NYSE or the NASDAQ, prices of shares will be bid to reflect the market consensus of expected earnings and risk.

In making key financial and other business decisions, the goal of the management of a publicly traded company with diversified ownership (many owners) should be to maximize the current market value of equity. We often call this *shareholder wealth maximization*. This amounts to maximizing the present value of the expected future earnings (or profit) stream. All other firm goals and strategies are subsidiary to this, and are only valid in so far as they pursue this goal.

There are four reasons why management typically pursues this overriding goal:

- Management has an ethical and legal obligation to pursue the interest of the owners.

- If financial markets believe that a company's equity value is depressed, a hostile takeover is likely to occur. [81]

- If management does not pursue this goal, they may be fired by the owners.

- Management often owns a portion of the company's shares (or at least they own stock options issued by the company), and will therefore act in the interests of the owners since it is also in management's interests.

In the business school's curriculum, other goals are often mentioned as possible goals for the firm. They include:

- Maximizing market share.

[81] A "hostile takeover attempt" is one resisted by management because they know they will likely be fired if it succeeds.

- Maximizing the satisfaction of customers.

- Maximizing social welfare.

- Maximizing profit.

The first two of these alternative goals are on their face ridiculous. You maximize market share by giving the product away for free, and you maximize customer satisfaction by giving them the best product possible for free. Companies that pursue these first two goals quickly find themselves in bankruptcy.

In the neoclassical economic analysis of introductory economics, one discovers a great deal about economic systems and social welfare maximization. Competitive economies will, to some extent, lead naturally to social welfare maximization with the exception of various difficulties involving externalities such as pollution and some other problems. These are problems we seek to manage by various regulations. It is important to note that the goal of shareholder wealth maximization is a constrained maximization. The constraints are legal and ethical; they are expressed by society through law and contracts. Because of these constraints, we hope the invisible hand of the marketplace, operating in part through shareholder wealth maximization, will also lead to social welfare maximization.

It is natural for management to want to treat the firm they manage as their own private property. To some extent, they may be able to get away with this because shareholders are generally so diversified, they often pay little attention to what is going on in the particular firms they own. This poses the problem we term *the agency problem*: *How do owners get management to behave in the owners' interests?* Today this is generally accomplished by giving owners sufficient shares in the company to motivate them to not exploit the company via perquisites and such, but rather to be interested in shareholder wealth.

What about the small firm that is not publicly owned and traded? For these firms, the goal may be different from owner wealth maximization if for no other reason than an active market for the firm's equity may not exist. The owner may never know what his company would sell for. The owner may never be interested in the sale value of his company, but rather may only be interested in reliable, steady income. It is sufficient to recognize that when we seek the solutions to various business problems, these solutions depend upon the pursuit of an overriding goal and not a multiple of conflicting goals. In fact, when you read business propaganda about some firm pursuing a multiple of goals (which are usually conflicting), this most often is just a mask to hide management's pursuit of their own welfare. For example, what does management mean when they state that *they are trying to satisfy or balance the interest of all constituents*? That is such a vague statement that any action by management could be justified by it. What is the formula for this *balance*? Statements such as these are generally smoke-screens that have little substantive content.

It states above that there are legal and ethical constraints on a firm's pursuit of shareholder wealth maximization. Violation of law can certainly hurt the firm's bottom line because it often involves expensive litigation. But it should also be kept in mind that legal violations and unethical behavior are often considered by customers as reasons to not purchase the company's product. Examples of this involve various product boycotts such as the grape boycott of the 1960s, and the tuna boycott of the 1970s and 1980s. [82] In addition, when society judges a firm as being involved in unethical behavior, the capital markets (stock markets) often depress the price of the company's shares. The successful South African invest-ment-boycott by large foundations in the 1960s and 1970s is an example of this. [83]

---

[82] The grape boycott involved migrant farm workers who sought to form a union. Grape growers resisted, but the boycott eventually lead to the union being recognized by the farmers. The tuna boycott involved customers wanting to protect dolphins (the mammal) from being depleted by tuna nets. The boycott resulted in the major tuna canners verify-ing that they only canned tuna (previously there was a significant portion of dolphin being labeled as tuna), and fishing techniques being changed.

[83] During the 1960s and 70s, South Africa was a segregated society. College students protested university founda-tions holding shares of South African firms. This boycott spread to mutual funds and other institutions during the 1970s. The boycott worked in that shares were divested, and South Africa did eliminate all legal segregation.

Chapter X

ETHICAL IMPLICATIONS FOR
SOME GENERAL BUSINESS PRACTICES

Chapter Abstract: Ethical issues of management compensation, perquisite consumption (as broadly defined), negative externality generation, employee management, community relations, and board of directors composition are explored in this Chapter.

1. Management Compensation

How much compensation is necessary to elicit management's best performance, and what do we mean by "best performance?" Also, in what form should this compensation be? The general topic of management compensation is full of ethical issues. Many of these issues involve shareholder wealth maximization (SWM) versus management welfare maximization (MWM)? The latter management goal involves the general topic of management perquisites, i.e. the nonmonetary compensation received as part of the overall compensation package.

These perquisites take numerous forms from golden parachute contracts in case of a hostile takeover or other forms of termination, to having living and/or recreational expenses paid by the company. Management acts as the legal agents of the owners, and therefore has a moral obligation to pursue the owners' interests. Management could be saintly and pursue the owners' interest, within ethical and legal constraints of course, without deriving any compensation above the absolute minimum necessary to induce them to pursue SWM. The moral quandary occurs because for a publicly traded corporation with diversified ownership, management has considerable discretionary latitude in deciding its own perquisite consumption. The larger the corporation, the easier it perhaps is to hide perquisites from the shareholders, and therefore the greater the perquisite consumption. As we explore below, this is a very different situation from the narrowly owned business or the single owner-manager company. For this latter business, perquisite consumption directly leads to lower value of equity. The owner-manager therefore expends his own resources so as to maximize his own welfare. This is not the case with separation of ownership from management where MWM for the less-than-saintly manager comes at the expense of the owners.

Consider Firm A as depicted in Figure 10-1 where we measure this firm's equity value on the horizontal axis, and the value of some perquisite stream on the horizontal axis. Management always has the opportunity to expend some of its resources so that if the value of the company's equity is reduced by $1 the value of some perquisite stream that management enjoys increases by $1. This is merely a shift of resources from productive assets to unproductive perquisites enjoyed only by management. The problem is that management will own some of the company's equity, so that this shifting in expenditures need not leave management with a higher level of welfare.

Allow Firm A to be entirely owner managed with one-hundred percent of its equity owned by the manager. For the management of Firm A, an expenditure of $1 of equity on perquisites generates a one-for-one tradeoff of perquisite consumption versus equity value. The tradeoff function therefore has a slope of -1 along the constraint $V0 - P0$ as shown. Given this tradeoff, and given that management's utility function will include both equity wealth and the perquisite consumption, the tangency point of indifference curve ICA with the tradeoff constraint indicates that the optimal combination of $V1$ equity value and $P1$ perquisite consumption maximizes the owner-manager's welfare. For Firm A, the owner-manager can either consume no perquisites and enjoy a company's equity value of $V0$, or maximize its own welfare by consuming perquisite level of $P1$ where the tangency point with the owner's indifference curve (ICA) occurs. The later will be selected. This perquisite consumption could take many forms including an extra luxurious office, or a managerial jet, or some other forms explored below.

We compare Firm A's solution to the situation for Firm B. Allow this firm to be in the same industry as Firm A, and have the same equity value at the point where there are no management perquisites and equity value is maximized. For Firm B, however, the manager owns only α portion of the firm's equity, where $0 < \alpha < 1$. For this manager, the tradeoff of perquisites for firm value is only α, i.e. the manager loses only $\$\alpha < 1$ for every $\$1$ of equity value sacrificed.

Figure 10-1: Perquisite Consumption for the Owner-Managed Firm A and Firm B with Managerial Ownership of α.

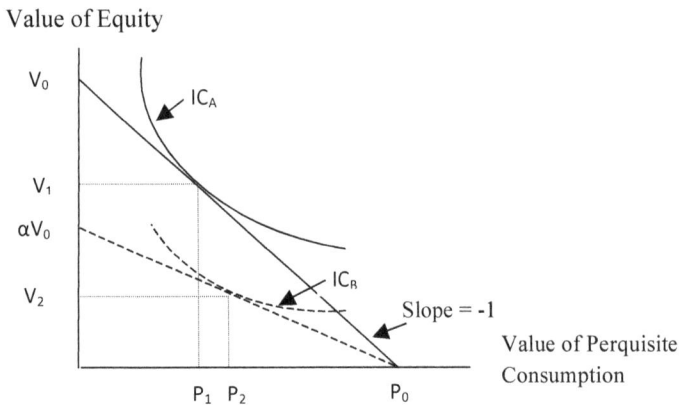

This occurs even though $\$1$ spent on perquisites decreases the total value of Firm B's equity by the same $\$1$. This being the case, and with the manager having the discretionary authority to select the level of perquisite level, the tradeoff constraint function has slope of only $-\alpha$, and the MWM level of perquisites is given by P2 with equity value of V2. This latter point represents the tangency (utility maximizing point) of the manager's indifference curve ICB with the lower tradeoff constraint of αV0–P0. Note that P0 is the horizontal intercept for both firms A and B since if all of V0 is expended on perquisites, then P0 becomes the value of the perquisite steamed consumed by management.

This analysis indicates the problem with managerial welfare pursuit. Even with managers owning some of the equity of the firm, it is in their welfare interests to sacrifice some firm value in order to consume perquisites of all sorts. Non-saintly behavior leads to MWM and the stronger the managerial preferences for this sort of consumption, the greater the equity value sacrificed. This non-saintly behavior could be considered as unethical, but we do note that even for the case of the manager with one-hundred percent ownership, we still have perquisite consumption. We could conclude that consumption beyond this point, P2 – P1, is unethical, but we must explore the ethical-logical grounds for this claim.

When management is hired, the compensation package usually includes both some equity ownership and a perquisite package. This is a contractual package. If we assume there is no deception involved in the negotiations involving this package, and if P1 is the perquisite package agreed upon fairly, then the amount actually enjoyed above this (P2 – P1 in our example) is unethical.

One way to reduce the amount of unethical perquisite consumption, P2 – P1, is to increase the portion of the firm's equity value owned by management, i.e. α. If we assume that the management utility functions for firm's A and B are identical, then increasing α towards 1 decreases P2 towards P1. This, however, would be a drastic strategy since giving nearly all of the company's equity away defeats the purpose of equity investment.

The question becomes why would the owners give management some of the firm they manage? The answer is that the owners hope that doing so increases the value of the firm from V0 to V0* as shown in Figure 10-2. By making management owners of some of the company's equity, the management team has an incentive to expand the value of the company since this would be in their own interest. The relevant question then becomes if after consumption of perquisites, if the outside ownership (the non-manager equity value) is greater after a portion of the equity is given.

**Figure 10-2: Perquisite Consumption for the Owner-Managed
Firm After the Portion α of the Company's Equity is Given to Management.**

Value of Equity

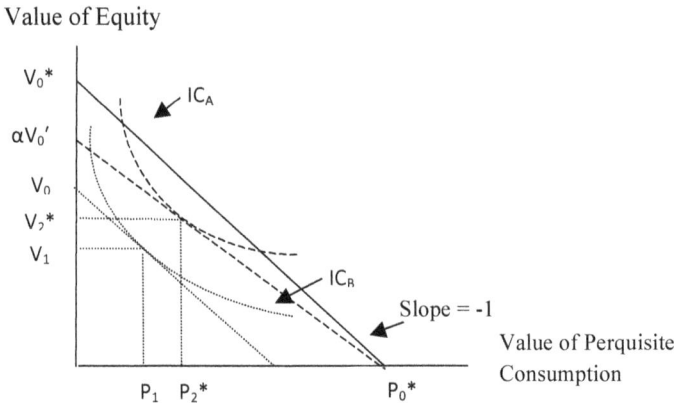

As shown in Figure 10-2, if inequality (10-1a) holds, then giving the equity shares to management is wealth beneficial to the outside ownership. This occurs since $(1-\alpha)$ portion of the shares is owned by the outsiders. Note that (10-1a) reduces to inequality (10-1b). This inequality is merely stating that if the value of the outside equity (after shares are given to management) exceeds the value of equity with no shares given to management, then giving these shares to management is wealth enhancing for the outsiders.

$$(1-\alpha)(V_0^*-P_2^*) = (1-\alpha)V_2^* > V_0 - P_1 = (1-\alpha)V_1 \qquad (10\text{-}1a)$$

$$V_2^* > V_1 \qquad (10\text{-}1b)$$

In giving shares to management, the contracting problem for the outside owners is to anticipate the value of perquisites management will consume and decide if this is an acceptable amount. Once this amount is contracted, it would be unethical for management to consume more than this agreed upon amount.

One method of reducing the unethical consumption of perquisites is to monitor management. Monitoring can occur through both internal and external auditors who report to owners, or by establishing budgeting procedures that require review by the board of directors. If monitoring indicates excessive consumption, then a turnover of management is warranted. Excessive consumption indicates unethical actions by the management team in that their contract is violated. Monitoring, however, can be expensive, and therefore also erode equity value.

2. Types of Perquisites

We often consider management perquisites as merely direct consumption of a lavish lifestyle at the expense of the shareholders. The business press is filled with stories of lavish birthday parties for management, or yachts, luxury planes, and lavish corporate headquarters at the expense of the firm. Perquisite consumption, however, extends far beyond these more obvious abuses of corporate expenditures. They include behaviors such as excessive risk aversion by management that limits equity value to being below what owners want, expenditures on the pet projects of management (those projects with negative value), and even corporate charity contributions to the pet charities of management. These perquisite abuses are examined here.

Excessive Managerial Risk Aversion

Shareholders typically have a diversified portfolio of investments. Their investment in any one company is usually a small fraction of their overall portfolio value. By diversifying their portfolio, they reduce the type of risk termed *firm specific risk*. The idea is elementary. *Firm specific events* are those that happen unrelated to the overall economy, while *market related events* are those that happen to all companies because the overall economy fluctuates. In any diversified portfolio, some firms will have *good firm specific events* happen, while others have bad firm specific events happen. In a diversified portfolio with a sufficient number of companies included, the good and bad firm specific events should washout. This leaves only the *market related events* for the investor to worry about. This diversification strategy leaves risk reduced to below the sum of the risks of each firm in the portfolio, i.e. the portfolio's firm specific risk is the thing for investors to eliminate so that only the *market related risk* of the firms in the portfolio remains to be managed.

Management, however, is very likely to earn most of its wealth directly in the form of compensation from the managed firm. Even if management has a portfolio of outside investments, the value of this outside portfolio is likely dominated by the value of the compensation stream from the firm. For this reason, management is likely to be more risk averse when it comes to decisions regarding the managed firm than the outside owners would prefer. Outsiders express their preferences through the prices they offer for the firm's securities, both equity and debt. They typically want a bit more risky behavior by the firm than what fits the preferences of management, and as a result, the firm's securities are at a lower market value than what would occur if the risk preferences of management matched those of the outside shareholders.

This excessive management risk-aversion is manifested in several key firm-related decisions. For example, consider the *capital structure decision*. This decision is illustrated by the simplified analysis represented on Figure 10-3 where the firm's debt-ratio decision is presented. Consider a company with a homogeneous debt represented by D. By homogeneous, we mean that all debt has the same maturity and associated legalities (indenture agreements). If Q stands for the total market value of the company's equity, then we seek to explore the factors that lead to the debt ratio decision, where this ratio is given by $d = D/(D+Q)$.

As shown on Figure 10-3, if the firm starts with no debt but then increases the debt ratio by issuing debt, i.e. by selling bonds, and then using the proceeds to repurchase equity thereby only changing the debt ratio and no other aspect of the firm, then the total equity value at first rises. This rise occurs because of two reasons:

(1) Financing with debt rather than equity allows for the chance for a big rate of return to equity. With fewer shares outstanding, the earnings per share increases if the firm's investment turns out to be profitable. The payments on debt are fixed. If sales are particularly large, all of the earnings in excess of these payments can be distributed as dividends among a fewer number of shares. This is called the advantage of *leverage* associated with debt. It gives shareholders a chance for the larger rate of return to equity, and this increases the total market value of the remaining outstanding shares.

(2) The interest paid on debt is tax deductible, while dividends paid on equity are not. When a company finances with new equity, the dividends are not tax deductible, but financing with debt has the interest paid as deductible.

Figure 10-3: The Optimal Capital Structure Decision Where D is the Company's Homogeneous Debt, and Q is the Company's Market-value of Equity, and d is the Debt Ratio

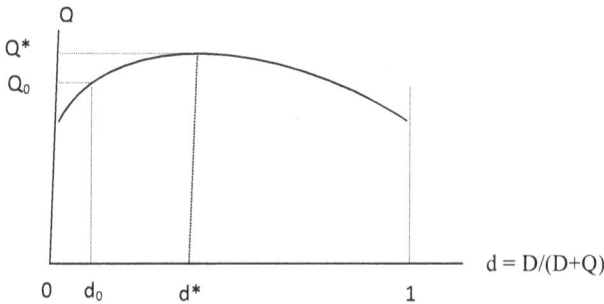

For the two reasons cited above, the total value of equity profile rises with the initial increases in the debt ratio d from zero towards one, but beyond some point, the profile falls. This occurs because the probabilities of insolvency and bankruptcy become overly large. As soon as any debt is issued, the probabilities of insolvency and bankruptcy increase. It is important to differentiate between these two onerous events.

(1) Companies often survive through trade credit from suppliers where inventory goods are shipped to the company, but payment is made later. This given the company an opportunity to produce and sell the finished product, sells it, and then repays the trade credit. Insolvency means the company is unable to pay its due liabilities, including trade credit. If suppliers believe that the company has a high probability of not being able to pay on time, then credit will not be extended.

In addition, many products, such as consumer durables, are sold with warranties. If a company is insolvent, it cannot honor its warranties. If customers believe that the probabilities are high that the company will be insolvent and not honor its warranties, they will not purchase the product.

(2) Bankruptcy is a legal term involving going into bankruptcy court and requesting relief from creditors. Once bankruptcy is filed, under

Chapter 11 of the bankruptcy law, management typically submits a "reorganization plan" that indicates how much of its liabilities will be paid and when. The court can accept or reject this plan. The bankruptcy court, however, is in charge of the management of this company, and the interests of the creditors are paramount in the court's decisions. The company is no longer managed primarily for the interests of the owners. The market value of equity is particularly affected.

For these two reasons reviewed above, if the probabilities of insolvency and/or bankruptcy become too large, the market value of equity falls. Note that the company need not actually be insolvent or bankrupt for this decrease in equity value to occur.

If as the debt ratio increases from zero towards 1, the profile first rises and then falls, there must be a peak at some point. Since the goal is to maximize the market value of equity, the debt ratio of d* should be selected. Note that since this is the market value of equity, it is the shareholders in financial markets who decide what this optimal debt ratio is. This is essentially a democratic process where management is trying to satisfy the preferences of the shareholders, and not their own preferences.

As reviewed above, management does not have the ability to diversify its wealth in the way the typical investor has. Most of management's wealth is generated by its compensation stream from its firm. Financial stress (insolvency and/or bankruptcy) is particularly onerous to management in that their whole career is disrupted, and consequently they suffer much greater wealth loss than the typical shareholder of the firm. For this reason, management is usually much more risk averse than shareholders. Management prefers a debt ratio that is below d*, say at d0 in Figure 10-3. This is a management perquisite in that the firm is kept at a lower risk level than shareholders want. This is a loss of wealth for share shareholders. Capital structure decisions are monitored by the board of directors, and if these decisions are deemed to be overly conservative, a change is often forced on management.

A decision that is associated with capital structure is the liquidity level decision, and this is often particularly contentious between owners and management. The probability distribution of financial distress is determined by the probability distributions for revenues and costs, and the amounts and liquidity of the firm's assets. The greater the expected value of sales revenue and the lower the variance, the lower the probability of financial distress. The lower the expected cost of producing the firm's goods and the lower the variance, the lower is the probability of financial distress. These appear obvious, but what about the "liquidity of the firm's assets?"

This property of liquidity has a rather nebulous definition. *The liquidity of an asset is its ability to be sold quickly at a known price.* It's a property of the asset's probability distribution for its sale price. This distribution has a time dimension to it in that if the owner of the asset can wait for a better price, then the expected price might be higher than if the asset needs to be sold immediately. Every asset has some degree of liquidity, but some are more liquid than others. For example, US Treasury securities can be sold quickly, and short-term Treasury securities have very stable prices so that they can be sold quickly and at a very foreseeable price, i.e. they are very liquid. Corporations usually keep a certain amount of cash on hand to cover unforeseen expenditures, especially if the firm's revenues and costs are unstable. Since short-term Treasury securities are so liquid, and they also pay some interest, these are also kept for contingency against financial distress. The question is how much should be kept? Cash and liquid securities are not the earning assets for a company. If excessive amounts are kept, then the real earning assets are lower than they should be. As a result, the expected level of net earnings is lower, and therefore the total market value of equity is lower.

Figure 10-4 illustrates two different scenarios for the same firm. For this company, profile A has less is cash and liquid securities, but more in longer-term real earnings assets, than profile B. As a result the equity value profile is everywhere lower for profile B. In addition, because the cash and liquid securities are higher for profile B, the probabilities of financial distress is lower, so financial markets indicate that the optimal debt ratios have dB > dA.

Which profile should the management select, A or B? If A is selected with debt ratio dA then equity value is maximized. This selection is preferable for the shareholders than profile B, but profile B may have much lower probability of financial distress than A, and therefore be in the welfare interests of management. Selection of B, even if the optimal debt ratios are selected, would deprive the shareholders of equity value of QA − QB. This would be perquisite consumption on the part of management. If management compounds their welfare pursuit by selecting B with a debt ratio that is less than dB, then the probability of financial distress is even lower, but management welfare higher.

Figure 10-4: Profiles for the Same Firm With Different Liquidity levels

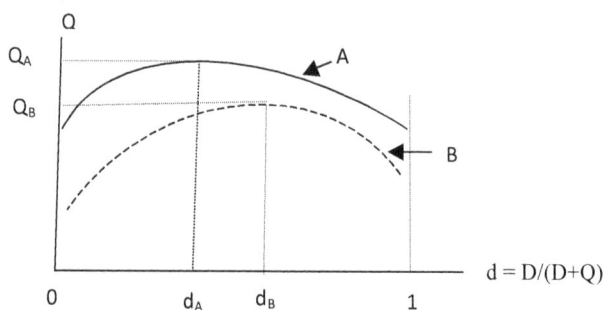

For risk aversion reasons, management might also select long-term projects that do not enhance the total value of equity. This is often associated with the pursuit of corporate diversification. By goring the company into different industrial product lines, those that have different correlations with the business cycle, a firm can "smooth out" their earnings stream. This means reducing the variability of the firm's earnings stream by combining products such as financial services, consumer durable production, food consumption, and the like. This diversification produces what we often term a *conglomerate*, a firm with unrelated product lines. The idea is that if one product line goes bad the other will keep the company afloat.

The problem with conglomerates is that they are usually managed poorly since no single top-level management team can be experts in widely divergent product lines. Most conglomerates are worth more broken up into separate companies than they are together. Breaking off a product line is called *spinning off*. When we observe new companies spun off, the combined value of the spun off company and the remaining company is generally greater than the original conglomerate. The motive for conglomeration is that it enhances management welfare because it lowers the probabilities of financial distress. Shareholders, however, can easily achieve all of the benefits of conglomeration by diversifying their portfolio, a task that today is inexpensive. For example, one can purchase shares in a diversified mutual fund and achieve all the benefits possible from diversification. Still, large corporations often pursue conglomeration only because it enhances management welfare. In this conglomeration process, one frequently sees the purchasing company's equity value drop. Conglomeration is a perquisite consumed by management. It generally should be the responsibility of the board of directors to only approve purchases that are shareholder wealth enhancing.

Corporate Charity Contributions
Corporations do give to charities for the purpose of community relations, and this sort of giving may obviously be in the interests of shareholder wealth maximization (SWM). One could consider charitable contributions as projects with expenses and possibly a positive rate of return. It could be merely a method of advertisement for the company's products, or it could be an attempt to influence the community in its regulations or employee relations. For example, corporations often promote civic efforts with contributions to children's programs or local sport programs. These generally are accompanied by advertising the company's name in public banners at the sport venues, or in event programs or public announcements. "This civic event is brought to you by …..," is typical of civic events.

These community advertisements can be a relatively inexpensive method of generating sales, or helping to hire employees. In addition, communities regulate businesses in many ways such as zoning laws, taxes, and community-subsidized programs for employee training, and the like. As a result of the votes of elected officials, these regulations could either be favorable or not to the bottom line of the income statement. As a result, these community relation investments may be beneficial to the company. In this respect, and provided that these business efforts are otherwise ethical, we could have no argument with them. Such efforts could be considered as a multi-way negotiation. They would need to meet our standards for fair negotiation as reviewed in Chapter 7.

There are, however, certain moral objections to corporate charitable contributions when there is separation between ownership and management. For the case of the owner-manager, charity contributions are essentially contributions of the owners that come at the owners' discretion. It is their funds to be given to any legitimate charity they wish. The contributions might lower the net earnings of the company, but these belong to the owner to begin with so it makes no differ-ence whether these contributions occur prior to the earnings being distributed to the owner, or after the distribution and as a personal contribution. This is a very different case, however, for publicly traded corporations with separation between ownership and management.

For the publicly traded corporation, earnings belong to the shareholders. Earnings can either be distributed back to shareholders in the form of dividends, or rein-vested in order to generate greater future earnings. In the latter case, at least for the situation of charitable contributions that are community related, the share-holders would have no objection provided the rate of return for these community investments warrants the contribution. We must realize, however, that in the case of charitable contributions that are not warranted by the rate of return, these funds should be redistributed back to the legal owners, i.e. the shareholders, as divi-dends. Whether they should then be contributed to management is a matter for the owners' personal discretion. Since these funds belong to the shareholders, it is not under the discretion of management to select these charitable contributions.

Management acts as the legal agents of the owners. They have a moral obliga-tion to manage the owners' funds in their interests, not merely in the interests of management welfare maximization (MWM). This would be a violation of man-agement's ethical obligation to the owners. Management also has charities they favor for their own personal reasons, perhaps because their families are involved in the civic organization, or because they favor some cultural charity for personal taste. Giving to these pet charities of management is not in the interests of SWM although perhaps in the interests of MWM.

It is also clearly more democratic to pay these contributions back to the sharehold-ers in the form of dividends, and allow them to decide the appropriate charities and contributions. We claim this because there are more shareholders in any pub-licly traded corporation than there are in top management, i.e. the management level that would make decisions about these charitable contributions. Perhaps those who manage their own funds take greater care than those who manage the funds of others. For these reasons, the market for raising charitable contributions might well be better served in the sense of serving general social preferences if the discretion were strictly left to the shareholders and the funds were distributed back to them. The funds belong to the shareholders to begin with, and using these funds for charity can only be justified if in the interests of SWM. The manager is the owner's agent, and giving funds that belong to the owners to their own pet charities constitutes fraud.

Stock Options as Management Compensation

Rohatyn (2002) argues that compensation in the form of stock options has encouraged management to stray from SWM. Giving management options was previously thought to be an incentive consistent with motivating management to pursue SWM. The options, however, are now generally recognized as stimulating management to ignore the downside risks of their actions as long as upside possibilities are exaggerated. To explain this, a two-state model with Scenarios A and B are presented by Table 10-1 and 10-2 are useful.

Table 10-1: Value of Shares

State	Scenario A	Scenario B	Probability
1	$50	$60	½
2	$50	$30	½

Table 10-2: Option Payoff for Management With Exercise Price of $55

State	Scenario A	Scenario B	Probability
1	$0	$5	½
2	$0	$0	½

As illustrated, Scenario A actually gives perfect certainty of share price at $50. Scenario B, however, is risky with expected price of $45, that is ½ ($60) + ½ ($30) = $45. If we allow management the choice of having the firm follow either A or B, then shareholders clearly prefer A. If management compensation is in the form of an option with an exercise price of $55, then management only receives a payoff under Scenario B (State 1). It will have the firm follow B. This has an excess of risk, and is not in the interests of SWM. It is important to note that management may prefer bonding-compensation in the form of options rather than shares, and management may arrange this if the board is not properly monitoring.

This violates the categorical imperative in that SWM is violated (the ends of the shareholders are not pursued) for the purpose of pursuing the ends of management.

This illustration shows that giving management shares, rather than stock options, is in the interests of SWM. Previously, stock options were thought to align the interest of management with owner, but it does not do this, and it certainly is opposed to other stakeholder interests.

3. Aspects of Social Responsibility

The broad subject of business ethics is often linked to social responsibility. In fact, the two terms *ethics and social responsibility* are often present in the titles of college level courses as though one implies the other. The latter term should be a subject contained within the former. In this section, we review the subjects of positive and negative externalities generated by business, corporate charity contributions, and community relations as subjects within this domain.

Negative Externalities

As reviewed in Chapter 9, negative externalities, such as with pollution, is generally inefficient as far as social welfare is concerned. Societal costs are not internalized to the production decision, i.e. how much of the good is to be produced, and at what market price. Since, as shown in Chapter 9, the market supply function is the market's marginal cost function, and if these costs do not reflect all of the costs that society bears, then the amount of the good produced is greater than if all of these costs are internalized. This is illustrated by Figure 10-5. In addition, because of the artificial increase in supply, the amount of the good produced is greater than what social welfare would warrant.

**Figure 10-5: Marginal Cost Curve MC$_1$ Externalizes
Pollutions Costs While MC$_2$ Internalizes these
Costs to the Industry**

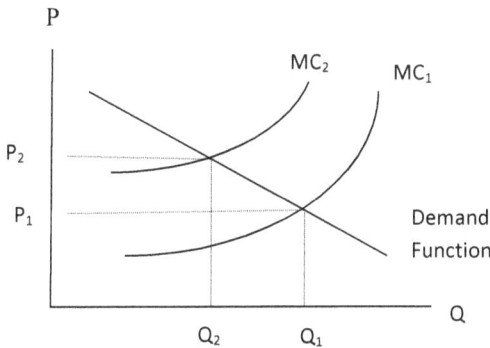

Generally negative externalities are regulated by society's laws, or by heavy taxation. Pollution amounts, such as air and water pollution, are limited by law, and/or the firm is taxed heavily for the amount of pollution as in the proposed *cap and trade* laws for global warming air emissions. Clearly it is unethical for business to avoid these laws.

The argument against pollution controls usually relies of the preservation of jobs, although pollution abatement and cleanup also generates jobs. (Note President Obama's withdrawal of ozone regulations as of September, 2011, as an example of an attempt to argue that jobs are preserved by not limiting certain pollution controls.) Also as pointed out in Chapter 9, considerations around the *Coase theorem* are also relevant, i.e. in the absence of transactions costs, producers of pollution might be able to compensate those who suffer the effects of pollution, and compensate sufficiently so that all are better off.

Almost all human activity results in some sort of environmental effects, i.e. some sort of pollution. Social welfare considerations concerning pollution abatement are subject to marginal analysis, society should reduce pollution as long as the marginal social benefit of the abatement exceeds the marginal social cost. The benefits include health and other environmental positive effects such as enhanced sight value, noise reductions, and/or nature restoration. The costs include reduction of consumer product consumption and employment opportunities. Effective analysis that might lead towards an optimal solution requires uniform measures of these effects, usually in monetary terms such as measured by enhanced property values, reductions in health costs, salary reductions, consumer product prices, and the like. Figure 10-6 illustrates the applicable marginal analysis, where MSB stands for the "marginal social benefit," and MSC stands for "marginal social cost." The pollution abatement is measured in terms of percentages of the existing level, with one-hundred percent being the maximum possible cleanup. The level A* gives the socially optimal abatement percentage, and 100%–A* gives the optimal remaining level.

Figure 10-6: Marginal Social Benefits (MSB) and Marginal Social Costs (MSC) of Pollution Abatement

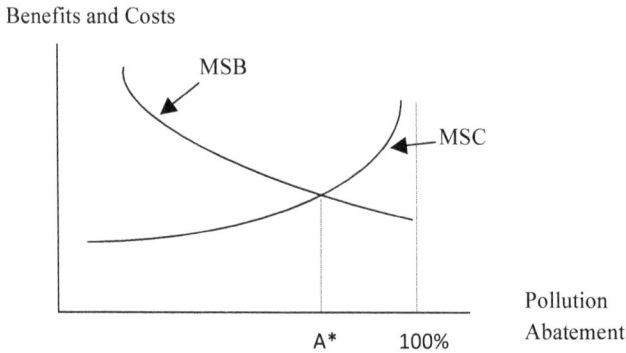

It is evident, therefore, that there is theoretically an optimal level of abatement and pollution.

The relevant argument concerning negative externalities therefore becomes, "If as long as business conforms to the pollution regulatory laws, is pollution otherwise ethical?" Consider that the generation of pollution has been long associated with industrial development, which has in turn generated considerable societal wealth. For this reason, certain levels of pollution are tolerated by society. The arguments that legal pollution is ethical have three limitations:

(1) intergenerational equity, (2) uneven impacts across society, and (3) in pollution externalities that occur between transitional laws.

The first of these arguments, the intergenerational equity argument, concerns our basic philosophy of fairness. Degrading the environment for future generations is essentially unethical, it can be argued, even if it is currently legal. Future generations do not have a voice in this legal arrangement, so it cannot be argued that they have given consent. This is the intergenerational social contract argument. It is particularly troubling if current business has achieved the pollution regulatory laws through their own political efforts since future generations do not have this current opportunity. The analysis of Figure 10-5, however, could possibly still apply provided future benefits and costs are included and given equal weight to current benefits and costs. For example, discounting future health costs to being below a one-for-one current value would pose problems of fairness for intergenerational equity.

The second argument, the uneven impacts across society argument, has often been posed as a strong criticism of current pollution regulatory law. The vast majority of society might approve some level of pollution, but most of society may be able to avoid the effects by living in locales that do not suffer from its harmful effects. For example, the poorer classes of society are usually (not always) the only people living in highly polluted areas. Approval by the majority does not make this fair or ethical. A utilitarian argument, that the total sum of individual's utility might warrant some particular level of pollution, becomes especially invalid if there are uneven impacts across segments of society. Such impacts would be anti-egalitarian, and in our egalitarian society, this would not be considered welfare enhancing. Businesses that generate this pollution clearly have a positive duty to remedy and compensate for these problems.

The third argument, that pollution may be only temporarily unregulated since laws are on their way, may have merit particularly with new types of pollution. The regulatory process has not yet had a chance to catch up. For this situation, since society has not declared its intention yet, business has an obligation to act fairly towards all those affected, and thereby delay until the problem is resolved.

Community Relations

Firms issue public relations announcements, and this publicity poses serious ethical questions. In resolving these issues, the notion of statistical bias is applicable, particularly in the context of SWM. Publicity should be honest in expectation, not biased to paint a more favorable picture of future prospects than the evidence warrants. Biased publicity is akin to lying, and therefore violates Kant's categorical imperative. Biased publicity will also disappoint on average when reality becomes clear through repetitive trials. Management with a reputation for biased publicity loses an important tool usable in the interests of SWM. Stock analysts, as an example, will discount management pronouncements so that possible truthful publicity is not recognized. The interests of SWM require unbiased publicity.

4. Human Resource Management Issues

There are a myriad of issues surrounding the fair treatment of employees. Legal practices need not be fair practices when it comes to problems of deception, and implicit contracts. Some of these issues are reviewed in this section.

Assignment of Decision Responsibilities,
Evaluation, Reward Systems, and Fairness

One of the fundamental problems of business is the assignment of decision responsibilities. This incorporates day-to-day decisions such as hiring and firing, worker and other resource allocation, and setting daily production targets. Decision responsibilities also include the higher-level decisions of business expansion, publicity disclosure, dividend policy, board composition, promotion, and pay raises. Firms have evaluation and rewards systems geared to the level of employee responsibility and effort. Fairness, as embodied in the implicit and explicit contract rules, requires transparency of the linkage between the responsibility, effort, and compensation received. The a priori rewards, however, are also linked to the uncertain success of the firm, and they must therefore be stochastic. Nonetheless, fairness requires the reasonable expectation of reward for effort. Misleading employees about this expectation constitutes lying and violates the categorical imperative. To some extent, laws limit this sort of fraud, but a great deal of leeway is allowed. SWM, however, motivates management to give systematic, explicitly-offered transparent and proper incentives for employees to absorb more responsibility, and expend more effort towards the success of the firm. Misplaced reward and incentive systems lead to stagnant companies.[84] It is the explicit system that is fair and effective, not some personal and hidden arrangements between managers and employees.

Discrimination, Affirmative Action, and Fairness

Neoclassical economics has long argued that discrimination is inconsistent with SWM that the firm that discriminates in employee hiring will be at a competitive disadvantage, and therefore will probably not survive. Affirmative action, however, may not be consistent with SWM, but if it is judged as being in the long-term fairness or other interests of society, it may need to be imposed on the firm by law. Assuring that some class of citizens who are discriminated against receive temporary favorable treatment is a societal decision, not appropriate for the firm as a separate entity (not appropriate for the manager-intuitionist to make) since a single firm cannot have the societal impact required.

Growth Issues

In the interests of SWM, in recent years firms have often sacrificed one plant in order to open another in an area of lower employee costs. This may be viewed as a tradeoff of some jobs for others. At first glance this tradeoff appears to be ethically neutral. Disrupting ongoing lives and careers, however, in order to relocate production with new jobs are not equivalent. Careers are disrupted at mid-stream, possibly at ages that do not allow new careers to begin. The younger new workers at the new location have more opportunities to explore options. It is for this reason that communities make these sort of relocation decisions costly for firms, and rightly so. Nonetheless, this argument only goes so far in that a sacrifice of X number of jobs in order to compete and grow to a greater number of Y jobs, usually in a poorer undeveloped area, is more than just a utilitarian tradeoff. It is surely the ethical action when society assures sufficient compensation for their job loss. With a clear understanding of the dictates of SWM, society is obliged to establish the rules of the game for business mobility, including the compensation schemes necessary.

The categorical imperative demands that management must be open in communicating career opportunities with employees. If implicit or explicit agreements

---

[84] See Brickley, Smith and Zimmerman (1999).

concerning career sustenance are reached, these commitments should not be breached for SWM reasons, at least not without fairly negotiated compensation for the employees affected.

Rules of the Internal Labor Market

Employees, pursing their own welfare, will typically seek to establish artificial rules for competing in the internal market for promotion, compensation and demands for worker effort. Economists call these arrangements "insider-outsider" arrangements. They are arbitrary in that they are unrelated to productivity, but are related to exerting the market power of those who are insiders. They are not in the interests of SWM, and are exploitive in that they primarily meet only the interests of the insiders.

Chapter 9 presented the marginal revenue product as the demand of employment services. This analysis is repeated below in Figure 10-7. In this analysis, L* is the optimal employment of this human resource factor, but insider-outsider rules can restrict this employment to a lower level L0. The reason for these rules is strictly to raise the employee compensation to a higher level W0. The rules to establish this restriction are generally unrelated to productivity or fairness. For example, they include training programs that are artificially expensive, artificially restrictive as to who qualifies to enter these training programs and artificial overall in that the skills developed are unrelated, or only weakly related, to productivity. They include seniority rules that are unrelated to productivity, and are unfair to junior employees.

These artificial rules of restriction of employment do not meet the categorical imperative. They use both the outsiders, and the resources of the firm, as means towards only the insiders' ends. Insiders obtain this power only because management selects not to struggle with workers over these rules, the effort and strife required being avoidable without proper board monitoring. Essentially, the rules of fairness are violated. For example, employment is not open to all, but only to relatives of employees (or management). Bonuses and other compensation are geared only to seniority and not effort or responsibility or any other performance measure. These arrangements represent cozy relations between management and other employees in that managerial effort towards evaluation are not required. The firm's culture becomes unconnected to pursuit of performance. [85]

Figure 10 – 7: Marginal Revenue Product (MRP) as the Employee Demand, and Effects of Insider-Outsider Rules

Marginal Revenue Product

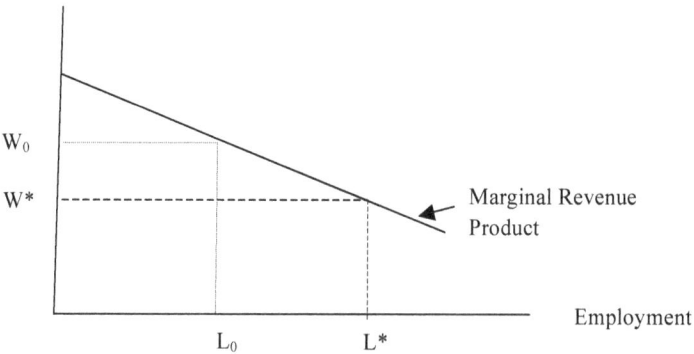

5. Board Composition

The board of directors plays the crucial role of monitoring management. They act as agents of the shareholders, who typically have highly diversified portfolios so that their personal interest in monitoring the firm is small. Because of the diversified nature of shareholders, and the consequent low motivation of owners to monitor the firm, management has often been able to nominate the majority of directors from insiders to the firm, or from otherwise friendly monitors. Monitoring is decreased in this way, and because of this, management is better able to pursue their welfare interests. Note that even if management owns shares in the firm, their portfolio can never be well diversified since their human capital composes a large portion of their wealth, and this human capital is invested in the single firm they manage. Agency exploitation of shareholders is always in management's interests if allowed. A board dominated by insiders is never in the interests of SWM.

[85] See Brickly, Smith and Zimmerman (1999)

It can also be the case, however, that outside but ineffectual board members allow insiders to dominate. In this scenario, a twenty-member board may have six insiders, but a dozen ineffectual members. Their ineffectiveness stems from the lack of knowledge about the industry, the firm itself, or even business in general. Fraud and management welfare pursuit requires that management be able to hide their activities from the board. [86]

Ineffective board members are often nominated by management, and often are posed as representing community interests. To the unknowledgeable, these ineffective board members may appear as paragons of virtue (religious representatives, charity representatives, or even academic philosophers posing as experts of ethical conduct), but not knowing the right questions to ask, or the right sources of information, they can be easily deceived. Knowledgeable outsiders are necessary for SWM, and necessary for oversight of the ethical conduct of management.

Review Questions

(1) Should owners expect management consumption of perquisites be zero? Will giving ownership in the company to management eliminate excessive consumption of perquisites? How much of the firm's equity should be given to management?

(2) When are corporate charitable contributions ethical, and when are they unethical?

(3) Review some consequences of excessive risk aversion by management? Why should this be considered as part of perquisite consumption?

(4) What is wrong with compensation via stock options?

(5) When might legal pollution be unethical?

(6) Review some ethical problems associated with employee management, community relations, and board compensation?

---

[86] This is a violation of what Sullivan (1994) calls "the principle of publicity," i.e., open publicity acts as a strong constraint on unethical actions.

Chapter XI

—— ❦ ——

THE PHILOSOPHY OF EVIL AND THE ABANDONMENT OF BUSINESS CODES OF ETHICS

Chapter Abstract: Avoidance of well established ethical business-codes currently continues as a prime societal problem. Examples of proper business codes of ethics, as based upon Kant's (1996) categorical imperative, are reviewed, but these codes have a tendency to be ignored for reasons inherent to competitive firms. These inherent reasons are examined in the context of Arendt's (1971, 2003) theory of why ethical codes are abandoned. Svendsen's Philosophy of Evil (2001) is shown to provide insights relevant for preserving these codes. In addition, the evidence from recent experimental psychology is shown to reinforce these devolution theories of Arendt and Svendsen.

1. The Process of Evil

Ethical norms and codes are essential to what we consider to be civilization. Historically, however, they have been periodically abandoned both within cultures and sub-culture organizations. In studying and explaining why these abandonments occur, philosophers offer the theory of *destruction by evil*. Rather than viewing this "evil" as a separate entity, such as some demon, we more properly can view it as a characteristic of a process, and/or an adjective that describes the result of this process. This is the approach taken here where the abandonment of business codes of behavior (ethical business codes) are examined.

Business codes consist of the behavioral norms manifested in law, custom and various explicit and implicit contracts. A variety of documents internal to the firm express portions of these codes: manuals that concern employee management, external firm communications, capital budgeting procedure-manuals, and internal control and auditing procedure manuals. All of these documents manifest ethical maxims, although some are more explicit in this manifestation than others. For example, employee management manuals generally specify grievance procedures for those who perceive they were treated unfairly. External communications are often restricted to particular executives, and even then only after approval by other managers. Capital budgeting procedures are generally designed to prevent firm resources being spent on the "pet projects" of management that add no value to the company. It is obvious that internal control procedures are designed to prevent fraud. Hence all of these embody ethical codes.

Perhaps most of the social interactions in Western civilization occur through business. As a result, the study of how we establish ethical business codes and why we ignore them forms a considerable subject for practical philosophy and management. The study presented here, however, primarily relies on the philosophical works of Arendt (1979), Svendsen (2001) and Kant (1996) who study the broader aspects of cultural degeneration and cataclysmic resulting evil. It is shown, however, that the principles established apply well to recent business scandals where ethical business codes of conduct were ignored. As such, perhaps the effort presented here is of considerable value.

Notions of evil have been well explored in Western philosophy. In Socratic-Platonic philosophy evil is anything that hinders our pursuit of the good (*eudaimonia*). It has often been interpreted in a narrow sense as purposeful harm to others. Both of these definitions are suboptimal when we seek to explain group processes resulting in severe damage to others, whether this damage results from purposeful avoidance or cavalier ignorance of ethical codes. It is the process of devolution from the ethical code that we seek to focus on, not merely an individual's actions.

Kant (1902) argues that evil is caused by an absence of *reflective thought*; that this absence results from "stupidity caused by a wicked heart." This is the form of evil that Hannah Arendt describes as "banal." In particular, we argue that although this "stupidity" may be an initial step that leads to resulting evil actions, we find that there is much more to the process. The initial stages, we argue, can be interrupted so that the devolution is halted.

Of course, we seek insights into the processes that led to massive evil such as the holocaust of World War II, Stalin's and Mao's purges and similar events, and from these insights we seek to draw parallels to the ethical-process deterioration of widespread business scandals such as Enron and Madoff. We find that it is more than only an absence of reflective thought that generates this dynamic ethical-process devolution. This devolution, whether in broader society or in business, contains common elements such as authoritarianism (or its more severe form of totalitarianism), group think, teambuilding, and humiliation of dissenters. These elements can easily be developed within the competitive business firm. All forms of evil exhibit a lack of respect for the dignity of others, but we must ask ourselves, "How can this lack of respect be developed within ourselves? What process could bring this about? More particularly, what principles of managerial leadership are necessary to prevent this process in business?"

Svendsen (2001, p. 85-87) indicates four anthropological types of evil:

(1) Demonic evil: Evil committed for the sake of evil. This is a classical concept generally based upon religious notions of demonic subversion of individuals.

(2) Instrumental evil: This evil is a side result from pursuing some goal that is itself not inherently evil. The evil itself in not intended but is nonetheless a consequence. An example could be the pursuit of wealth where that pursuit causes harm to others.

(3) Idealistic evil: This evil is intended, but the pursuit of some other goal that is considered good necessitates it. Social reforms might provide examples where these reforms require the coercion of some subgroups.

(4) Stupid evil: This is evil that result from a lack of reflective thought. As shown in this paper, it is particularly present in business, and remedying this is the primary purpose of our proposed preventative action.

Forms (2), (3), and (4) can result in abandoning the well established ethical norms of either society in general or some organization. They are the forms we focus on here.

There are four overlapping inherencies to the competitive firm that make these organizations particularly subject to systematic violations of society's ethical norms:

(1) The competitive firm encourages management and employees to abstractly identify with the organization to develop an attitude of *us-versus-them* towards their competitors.

(2) Individuals within these firms usually must participate in team building exercises and efforts so as to develop business efficiency. These team building efforts help exacerbate these *us-versus-them* tendencies.

(3) These firms generally exhibit considerable division of labor in accomplishing important tasks. This division also often allows a division of responsibility when it comes to enforcement of ethical codes.

(4) Competitive firms tend to be authoritarian where each individual's career depends upon the authority above them.

These inherencies make group-think prevalent and dissent difficult even when the question concerns some moral standard. We shall see below that these inherencies allow the elements that make it easier for individuals to accept evil results. The prevention of these results, however, always begins with and relies upon *reflective thought* as pointed out by Arendt, but more is required for this prevention.

This required *reflective thought* follows Kant in that certain characteristics are necessary. In particular, these necessary characteristics include the following:

(1) Participants must have *sympathy* in the Smithian sense, i.e. they must be capable of envisioning a substitution of themselves into someone potentially hurt by the violation of the ethical norm. This generates

a potential for remorse in the actor who might violate the norm. But this is not sufficient.

(2) The actor must also be able to apply logic to envision the potential consequences of their actions, and be willing to apply this logic consistently. This may eliminate a mere application of a-priori ideology to the potential problem at hand, an ideology that poses a bias in analysis of possible results.

(3) Finally, the actor must be willing to spend the time and effort necessary for this reflection. This last requirement might pose the most significant problem necessary to overcome the tendency to abandon normal codes of ethical behavior.

This *reflective thought*, even if fully characterized as above, need not be sufficient to overcome abandonment of ethics if there are no actors who are willing to exhibit what Arendt terms the *noble nature*, i.e. the willingness to speak out in a social setting that some action is wrong, that it violates the ethical code, and that this code is necessary for harmony in society or within the firm. Without this willingness to publicly defend the code, all the reflective thought, however proper, will be ineffective. Much more about this *noble nature* is presented below.

2. Thoughtful Reflection and Codes of Conduct
A basic premise of Greek philosophy is that people do not commit evil voluntarily, but only out of ignorance about the consequences of their actions. This is basic Socratic (the *Gorgias* dialogue) and Platonic philosophy. Yet history, and particularly the history of the 20th century, illustrates how very common evil is. Late 20th century philosopher Hanna Arendt presents us with a particularly cogent argument as to why this evil occurs, and this argument is reviewed here. It concerns people who follow what we might consider a proper code of conduct but who do so with an absence of reflective thought.

The list of *maxims* presented above could be considered, or reduced to, a *code of conduct*. If we follow Kant, however, it is *reasoned thought* that is at the core of his *categorical imperative* and the associated *maxims*. Any attempt to simply apply these *maxims,* as in the case of following an established *code of conduct,* can lead to substantial difficulties. We are not saying that carefully established codes are not a positive way to provide a framework for workplace behavior, but rather if the *code* is not associated with reflective reason, it can still allow what we would judge as misconduct and possibly even evil.

For example, consider the first three moral maxims posed in Chapter V.:

(1) *We ought not to make lying promises.*

(2) *Within practical limitations, we ought to help others pursue their own ends where and when we can.*

(3) *We ought to behave as though all our actions were publicly known, even when some actions must be kept private.*

Consider the following question concerning *maxim1*, the prohibition against lying promises. When corporate management signs its annual reports, it is assuring the company's owners and the rest of the financial markets as well, that all the data is accurate. No manager, however, could possible know that every transaction and account is recorded accurately. Management has a positive duty to verify, but this practical limitation on authentication of accuracy could be easily considered by some managers as less than fully serious so that unintentional inaccuracies are allowed. The self justification would be that the requirements of accuracy and authentication are overly severe; that no one manager can know all. The more serious inaccuracies could be prevented, however, by reasoned reflection about their impacts. Without this reflection, a cavalier attitude could develop, one that is likely to lead to serious problems.

The second and third *moral maxims*, the demands for benevolence and behavior as though all were publicly known, also have practical limitations. Without reasoned reflection, these positive duties and there practical demands can also be treated cavalierly. This attitude towards any ethical code might easily lead to what we term an *evil result*.

Hanna Arendt (1906-1975) won Denmark's "Sonning Prize" in 1975 for her "considerable contributions to European Civilization" which resulted from her contributions to Western philosophy. Her main philosophical subject was the explanation of the existence of evil in Western Civilization, i.e., the breakdown of that civilization as built upon both Greek philosophy and the philosophy of the enlightenment (including Kant). Her major works include *Eichmann in Jersusalem: a Report on the Banality of Evil* (1963), *The Origins of Totalitarianism* (1951), *Thinking and Moral Considerations* (1971), and *Responsibility and Judgment* (2003), the latter being a compendium of her other published works.

Arendt witnessed the rise of Hitler's Germany and left that country for the United States in 1933. She witnessed Adolf Eichmann's trial in 1959, and wrote about her observations. World War II and its aftermath formed the basis for her contributions. We argue here, however, that she has a great deal to say about ethics especially as it applies to business decisions.

Arendt perceived that the evil which occurred on such a gigantic scale during the 20th century, such as the holocaust of WWII, did not result from the wickedness of the people involved, but rather from their extraordinary shallowness and refusal to think. She argued that a lack of reflective thought that stems from the bureaucratic behavior associated with following simple codes of conduct was the ultimate cause. Indeed, she saw that standardized codes of conduct protected people against this reflective thought, that "conscience" essentially consisted of this reflective thought, and that since the evil she witnessed occurred without this thought process, it was essentially without motive. Note that Arendt's view is consistent with the Socratic view that people select evil only out of ignorance.

Kant argued that reasoned thought provided the foundation of ethics, and that the reasoning ability of the ordinary average person was sufficient to establish an ethical society. This idea was challenged by Arendt. [See Arendt (2003), p. 164.] Her argument begins with this statement:

If the ability to tell right from wrong should have anything to do with the ability to think, then we must be able to "demand" its exercise in every sane person no matter how erudite or ignorant, how intelligent or stupid he may appear to be. Kant, in this respect almost alone among the philosophers, was much bothered by the common opinion that philosophy is only for the few precisely because of this opinion's moral implications. In this vein, he once remarked, "Stupidity is caused by a wicked heart," a statement which in this form is not true. Inability to think is not stupidity; it can be found in highly intelligent people, and wickedness is hardly its cause, if only because thoughtlessness as well as stupidity are much more frequent phenomena than wickedness. The trouble is precisely that no wicked heart, a relatively rare phenomenon, is necessary to cause great evil. Hence, in Kantian terms, one would need philosophy, the exercise of reason as a faculty of thought, to prevent evil. [Arendt (2003), p. 164.]

The substance of Arendt's argument proceeds as follows:

(i)   It is true, as Kant argued that thinking is a trait of all people.

(ii) When we reach conclusions as a result of our thought processes, we typically have considerable uncertainty as to their validity, especially with respect to our moral thought. As a result, we seek dialogue with others, and perhaps democratic debate that acts as a filter for our ideas before we accept the conclusions of our reflective thought.

(iii) By its very nature, reflective thought leads to a period of abstraction from the real world, a "paralysis" from other actions.

(iv) Because of ii. and iii. above, there is a cultural bias against reflective thought.

(v)   Because of iv. above, there is a cultural bias towards following simple rules, or codes of conduct. Because these rules have no basis in our own reflective thought, they are therefore supported by only shallow belief.

(vi) Because of v. above, people are willing to disregard codes of conduct. People are quick to follow others who appear to have a passion for alternative actions that violate the code. These others argue that they have given the new action careful thought.

Arendt argues that "thinking is a marginal affair" in society, "except in emergencies." (2003, p. 188) Evil is a violation of rules based on rational thought. As a result, the counter to evil lies in what Plato terms the "noble nature," that is the desire to participate in rational thought in a social context. It is not, Arendt argues, the common reasoning person who is responsible for maintaining societal ethical conduct and thereby avoiding evil, but rather it is the person who exhibits the "noble nature" of reflective thought as voiced in the social setting who is necessary to avoid this evil.

With respect to the above mentioned "emergencies," Arendt writes:

At these moments, thinking ceases to be a marginal affair in political matters. When everybody is swept away unthinkingly by what everybody else does and believes in, those who think are drawn out of hiding because their refusal to join in is conspicuous and thereby becomes a kind of action. The purging element in thinking, Socrates' midwifery, that brings out the implications of unexamined opinions and thereby destroys them – values, doctrines, theories, and even convictions – is political by implication. For this destruction has a liberating effect on another human faculty, the faculty of judgment, which one may call, with some justification, the most political of man's mental abilities. (2003, p. 188-189)

One should not perceive Arendt's argument as applying only to the large mass political movements such as the National Socialism of Germany, or the communism of the Soviet Union. This argument applies to our business scandals as well. The bureaucracy we typically find in business, which is certainly essential for efficiency, often regulates behavior by a code of conduct that subsumes rational or reflective thought. Mob psychology sweeps through organizations just as in political societies. If people do not have clarity as to the thoughtful reasons behind the code, then these rules can be easily discarded and unethical pursuits result. Managerial leadership must provide this *clarity*. In addition, we know that the clever person can always find ways around the rules through actions that violate the spirit, but not the letter of the code. Keep in mind that the Kantian ethic is based on the motive for the action. Violation of the spirit of some code is a violation of the code itself. Managerial leadership that violates this spirit will likely lead to evil results within the organization.

3. The Competitive Firm and Tendencies Towards Code Abandonment

As briefly reviewed above, there are inherencies that naturally lead the competitive firm towards abandoning any rationally adopted ethical code that is consistent with a Western tradition. Paramount among these inherencies is *group think*. Groups cannot have a conscience, only individuals do. As such, groups can feel no remorse; only individuals manifest this character. Groups can, however, spread a generally accepted ideology among their members. Problems with ethical content that are viewed through the lens of ideology probably remain unanalyzed. Where beating the competitors, or contributing to the team effort, or other ideological versions of slogans become the firm's mantra, then no matter how devoid of unethical content the slogan might appear, when applied to ethical problems the group emotions can move the individual actors away from their better logical sense and towards unethical actions they would not adopt as individuals. For example, top managerial leaders might allow the individual to be humiliated, coerced or even deceived since they might believe that competitors do the same, and that this is therefore necessary for motivating employees.

Gourevitch (1998) claims that genocide is essentially an exercise in team building, an extreme version of *us-versus-them* activity. Ethnic identities are a more typical method of identification, but no matter how abstract the in-common traits that link some team together, all versions of team building separate the human bonds between the groups at least to some small degree if not to a considerable degree. Competitive firms seek to also establish these common traits among employees, and to separate from those of competitors. In the more extreme cases, the other firms become evil in the view of each competitive firm. These sorts of group identities may motivate ethical code abandonment for the sake of defeating the perceived greater evil posed by the competition.

Bonheoeffer (1997) identifies the thoughtlessness of Arendt's *lack of reflective thought* as *foolishness*, where the fools become manipulated tools of the leader. This is essentially Arendt's perception that someone offers an alternative to the code for which the followers have little commitment. Bonhoeffer points out that under these circumstances, new shallow slogans replace the code as guides to behavior. The *noble nature* is then seen as betrayal of *us* in favor of *them*. Individual thought that questions the *group think* is then seen as betrayal. It follows then that "our most basic moral understanding crumbles in the face of (this) ideological conviction." (Svendsen 2001, p. 127) In addition, perceptions of outside forces and communications become warped in which (1) the group perceives all external forces and communications as aimed at it personally, (2) the group focuses on those interpretations of circumstances that reinforce it's a-priori notions of being threatened, and ignores aspects that contradict, and (3) the group interprets even positive external statements as malicious. Facts that contradict the new warped vision are merely disbelieved. **The authoritarian firm is therefore changed into a totalitarian firm, the latter exhibiting the elimination of individual thought where even the individual doubts their own conscience so that ultimately we see that individuality is eradicated.**

There are certain conformity characteristics manifested by this totalitarian firm, i.e. the firm that abandons a logical ethical code:

(1) Dissenters, whether internal or external, are humiliated, or at least attempts at humiliation are made.

(2) The group manifests contempt for weakness among its members in that any sign indicating anything less than enthusiastic support for its new adopted slogan-oriented code is strongly discouraged.

(3) To reinforce the new code, leaders speak of what should be considered as evil as being the opposite. (Note: Hitler spoke of purifying the Aryan race as his "holiest obligation.")

Elimination of the old code and adoption of the new slogan-oriented code is just the first step in the firm's devolution into business evil. Svendsen (2001) indicates four steps capable of resulting in members accepting evil:

(1) The wrong doing must be presented in such a way as originally being only a minor first step. For example, a violation of an auditing requirement might be presented as having only a minor impact on the final result, or that it would be only temporary and rectified later.

(2) The group members must be distanced from the evil decision. "People at the top decided it this way, so I am not blameworthy even thought I could speak out that this is wrong. It is not I who is committing this wrongdoing."

(3) The wrong doing is broken into a division of tasks where each member is seen as only a small cog in the wheel. Responsibility is therefore spread so that no one need feel guilty about the overall result.

(4) An escalation in acceptance of the new immoral values can then occur so that the new values are generally accepted by the firm, while each member can still rationalize themselves as decent because they had little responsibility for the result.

4. Psychological Studies of Unethical Conduct

In recent years, experimental psychology has developed theories of psychological disengagement with respect to personal devolution of moral standards. This psychological literature attempts to explain the process of first acceptance of personal immoral actions followed by rationalization and then further immoral actions. This literature powerfully reinforces the organizational evil processes of Arendt and Svendsen. Some of this relevant psychology literature is reviewed here.

Aquino and Reed (2002), Bandura (1990), And Bandura et al. (1996) show that unethical behavior elicits self-censure, which provides the principal restraint on this behavior. When ethical beliefs conflict with actual behavior, Elliot and Devine (1994) show that psychological dissonance, a stressful form of discomfort, occurs that motivates a process of attitude change. The actors in question either modify their behavior to align with their ethical values, or they modify their values. (Also see Baumeister and Heatherton (1996).)

Bandura (1990), Bandura et al (1996), and Detert, Trevino and Sweitzer (2008) offer an explanation of the process of realigning ethical beliefs with actions, namely beliefs are modified through *moral disengagement*, thereby relieving the cognitive dissonance. This disengagement process allows the unethical conduct to become personally acceptable. The disengagement takes any of four possible forms:

(1) The unethical conduct is portrayed as serving a moral purpose.

(2) The unethical conduct is betrayed as being caused by external causes.

(3) The consequences of the conduct are interpreted as being innocuous.

(4) The victims of the unethical conduct are dehumanized.

Bandura, et al (1996, 2001) show that this moral disengagement also acts as a predictor of future immoral behavior. Vollum, et al (2004), shows that disengagement predicts violence towards animals, and Aquino, et al (2007) and McAllister, et al. (2006) show that disengagement predicts support for military action.

Henkel and Mather (2007) show that people are "revisionist historians" when recalling their own personal past, that they engage in "choice supportive memory distortion" that over attributes positive features to options they actually selected, and also over attributes negative features to options they rejected. We are therefore currently motivated to selectively recall those previous motivations that supported our previous actions. Associated with this evidence of selective recall is the phenomenon that individuals are found to be routinely more critical of the ethics of others than of their own ethics. Messick, et al (1985, p. 497) shows, "We believe we are fairer than others because we think that we do fair things more often and unfair things less often than others." Epley and Dunning (2000), and Epley and Caruso (2004) show that people are more suspicious of the ethical motives of others than of themselves. Miller and Ratner (1998) and Ratner and Miller (2001) show that others are generally perceived as more self-interested and motivated by monetary rewards. Alicke (1985) Baumeister and Newman (1994), and Messick and Bazerman (1996), all show that people believe that they are personally more honest, and that they try harder to pursue ethical actions, than others.

These *moral disengagement* studies show that people are more prone to justify their own immoral actions than those of others. The disengagement and cognitive dissonance frees the individual from the guilt and stress of self sanction. This explains the individual acceptance of initial unethical steps, and of paramount importance, disengagement makes it difficult for those who do speak out to persuade others of the importance of the keeping the code of moral standards. Knowing that others are disengaged would logically lead even those who have Arendt's *noble nature*, to be reluctant to speak. Why make waves when one perceives little possibility for actual successful persuasion, but far greater possibility for humiliation?

Some of the experimental evidence does, however, show possibilities for prevention of the dissolution. The experiments of Shu, Gino and Bazerman (2009) show that the individual levels of disengagement depend upon the severity of the moral violation. They show that *moral disengagement* occurs only post personal unethical actions, and not after the actions of others. Furthermore, their research experiments support the conclusions of Gino, et al (2009) and Mazar, et al (2008) that being in a permissive environment rather than a strict environment results in greater disengagement. The "permissive environment" pertains to whether the students who were subject to possibilities of cheating were reminded of an "honor code" or not prior to the opportunity for cheating. This was interpreted as making morality more "salient" by making the improper behavior more "clear cut." Mazar, et al. (2008) found that a-priori drawing attention to ethical standards reduces dishonest behaviors.

Shu, Gino and Bazerman (2009) argue that there is a difference between active and passive acceptance of moral standards; that making a voluntary decision (actually selecting among various options) versus accepting a passive result yields greater commitment to the action. Similarly, individuals may commit more strongly to moral behavior when they actively agree to ethical standards (by signing an honor code as an example) rather than just passively reading the code. Their moral disengagement would be lower for the former action than the latter passivity. Shu, Gino and Bazerman found experimental support for these hypotheses. They also unfortunately found support for selective memory after unethical behavior. Nonetheless, it appears that active reinforcement of the code may result in a greater degree of ethical enforcement.

This experimental research and literature support notions presented above that there is a dissolution process for abandonment of ethical codes in business. Individuals are easier on themselves with respect to violations, that they suffer selective memory bias with respect to rationalizing the immoral conduct, and that the degree of moral disengagement becomes more sever the further into the process individuals move. Prevention would logically rely on early and active (rather than passive) reinforcement of the code. Also, offering objective evidence that contradicts the cognitive dissonance might be a possible palliative.

5. The Prevention

Svendsen (2001) points out that any ex-post remorse for the final result of wrong-doing follows a gradient that begins with "How could I have been so stupid?" If the group dynamic is allowed to progress, then statements such as, "Why did I not resist?" follow. If the dynamic is allowed its full development, then statements such as "What have I let myself become?" follow. The task of prevention is to not allow development of the first stage, or at least to not allow the second stage to occur.

This task is best facilitated by frequent and full active-review of the properly adopted ethical code such as presented above. This notion of "active review" is meant in the sense of Shu, Gino and Bazerman (2009), i.e., an active signing or recognition of the relevant code principles. For example, internal controls and/ or auditing principles ought to be reviewed regularly, but after this review, and after the agent answers questions about the review, a signature indicating acceptance of the code should be elicited. Furthermore, this review should emphasize Kant's *third formula for the categorical imperative*, i.e. that the proper motivation for keeping the code of moral maxims is to pursue a broader social goal and not a narrow personal goal. The agent should accept the idea that the reason for keeping the code is not just because they will be separated (fired) if they do not, but because the agent's actions serve a broader social goal.

Group members must be persuaded to believe that the ethical maxims manifested by the codes serve either society's interests, or at least the best interests of the firm. This would make psychological disengagement, as associated with code violations, more difficult. For example, agents should be brought to realize that without the accounting rules and accuracy, both society and the firm suffer and ultimately break down if violations become commonly accepted. For another example, consider that agents must be brought to realize that without general respect for fellow employees, the firm cannot function effectively.

Each of the code's moral maxims must therefore be frequently and actively reviewed, explained and accepted as being in the interests of the firm and society in general. This is necessary so as to limit moral disengagement. To further encourage engagement, and discourage disengagement, it is particularly important to emphasize respect for the thinking individual members of the group. Once the voicing of reflective thought is discouraged, once dissenters are humiliated or marginalized, then disengagement is generated, and the dynamic of code violation is not likely to stop outside of external interference via society's laws or vigorous interference from other stakeholders. Disengagement by the involved agents facilitates Svendsen's first stage. By the time that the "How could I be so stupid?" stage is reached, harm has occurred. Beyond this stage, prevention is particularly difficult. Note that the term "stupid" here means lack of reflective thought. It is this reflection that prevents moral disengagement, and hence it is to be encouraged and reinforced.

As indicated previously, however, this reflection is not sufficient to prevent this harm. The noble nature of stating "This is wrong!" publicly within the group is necessary. This also requires the voicing of a cogent argument about why it is wrong. Hence, public dissent must be *a priori* encouraged and not humiliated. This discouragement of humiliation must be part of the code itself, and its importance explained frequently. The rational dissenter must be praised so that the *evil devolution process* is prevented. This is the key step that has the potential to prevent ethical code deterioration. As reviewed in the section above, the moral disengagement process allows the unethical conduct to become personally acceptable. The purpose of the "noble nature of speaking out that *This is wrong!*" is to prevent disengagement in any of its four forms:

(1) Firmly voicing a contradiction that the code violation somehow serves a moral purpose.

(2) Firmly voicing a contradiction that the code violation is caused externally and hence forced on the actors.

(3) Firmly voicing a conviction that the consequences of the code violation are not innocuous.

(4) Firmly voicing a conviction that the ultimate victims of the unethical conduct should not be dehumanized or belittled to any extent.

Review Questions:

(1) Briefly review the various notions of evil, especially evil as a process? What is the Socratic view of evil?

(2) Where do we find business codes of ethics? How do codes of ethics interfere with reflective thought?

(3) Review the inherent tendencies of competitive markets that lead to systematic violations of society's sense of ethics?

(4) What is the role of reflective thought in preventing evil?

(5) Explain how Arendt contradicts Kant about the causes of evil?

(6) What is meant by "Socrates' midwifery?" Explain what Arendt means by "the noble nature?"

(7) Describe Svendsen's process that occurs to transform the authoritarian firm to the totalitarian firm? What is the difference between

these two types of firms, and what are the consequences of this transformation?

(8) What is "moral disengagement?" Review the process that leads to this disengagement?

How can we prevent the process that leads to evil?

Appendix: Enron as an Example

Enron presented one of the major accounting scandals of the early years of this century. Enron began as an energy company in 1985, but it largely grew to become an energy trading company, trading in futures and forward contracts. [87] By 2001, Enron was the world's largest energy trading companies through holding 25 percent of all energy contracts. It claimed $40 billion in revenue in 1998, $60 billion in 2000, and $101 billion in 2001. Its stated goal was to grow revenue by 15 percent per year.

Enron's ethical conflicts concerned five significant issues:

(1) Its use of mark-to-market accounting practices, although perhaps conforming to FASB rules, were deceptive as to its real cash revenues.

(2) It used numerous (about 3,000 transactions) off-the-book special purpose entities (SPEs) such as limited partnerships and limited liability companies, that it ostensibly only partly owned, but in fact fully controlled, to remove liabilities off its balance sheet, although it still owed these obligations. There were almost 900 of these SPEs.

(3) The SPEs were owned and controlled by officers of Enron, who personally benefitted from these subsidiaries although this involved conflicts of interest that violated Enron's stated ethics code.

(4) Enron sought to coerce its auditing company (Arthur Anderson and Co.) into not revealing its accounting manipulations.

---

[87] *Forward contracts* are merely signed commitments for future delivery or purchase. *Futures contracts* are forward contracts traded on organized exchanges. For Enron, these contracts involved energy, electric power and natural gas.

---

(5)   When questions were raised about its accounting irregularities, and the conflicts of interests of executives with the SPEs, Enron sought to publicly humiliate its dissenters.

FASB Rule 125 allowed companies to sign contracts for future delivery of some good, and at a stated price, and to book this future income as current income (mark-to-market). If the price drops between the date of signing the contract and fulfillment date, the company can book this as positive revenue even though it has yet to be actually received. According to mark-to-market, if the price increases, a loss should be booked. Enron merely entered positive revenues, and had its SPEs book its losing contracts. According to FASB 125, as long as the SPE owned at least 51 percent outside ownership, then Enron need not book this transaction on its own books. Most of these SPEs' were registered as Cayman Island companies where the other owners were executives of Enron, either Chairman Kenneth Lay, or CEO Jeffrey Skillings or CFO Andrew Fastow. With limited liability in effect, these SPEs (881 in total by 2002) involved no personal losses for these executives.

This practice, since it was so large in effect, although within the letter of the FASB code, it clearly violated the spirit of accounting practice since the performance and health of Enron was hidden. This practice was deceptive to its core. This allowed Enron to book deceptive positive revenues so that performance objectives could be consistently met. Executive bonuses depended upon meeting these performance objectives of 15 percent growth per year in revenues.

Enron's Code of Ethics addressed the issue of conflicts of interest in two sections. The first stated that, "An employee shall not conduct himself or herself in a manner which directly or indirectly would be detrimental to the best interests of the company or in a manner which would bring to the employee financial gain separately derived as a direct consequence of his or her employment with the company." The code also continued to state, " ....it follows that no full time officer or employee should : (c) Own an interest in or participate, directly or indirectly, in the profits of another entity which does business with or is a competitor of the company unless such ownership or participation has been previously disclosed in writing to the Chairman of the Board and Chief Executive Officer of Enron Corp., and such officer has determined that such interest or participation does not adversely affect the best interests of the Company." The Board waived this policy for Andrew Fastow on three occasions.

In 1999, Arthur Anderson, Enron's auditor, led by the Enron Account Executive David Duncan, initially questioned these SPE arrangements, calling them "form over substance transactions." Pressure by Enron on its auditor, however, eliminated further questions about this practice.

Several analysts who questioned the accuracy of Enron's reported accounting numbers were publicly attacked. For example, a reported for *Fortune*, Bethany McClean questioned Enron's profits given its large off-balance-sheet transactions led to Ken Lay calling her editor to ask that she be removed from the story. During an analyst interview, Jeffrey Skillings called Ms. McClean an unrepeatable derogatory name. Also, when John Olson, and analyst for Merrill Lynch questioned advised his clients to avoid Enron due to their questionable earnings, he was fired. Enron was a client of Merrill Lynch. Internal employees were given the same treatment. When Sherron Watkins, was Vice President for Corporate Development questioned the off-the-books transactions, and consequential true debt load of Enron, Mr. Fastow accused her of wanting his job. She was fired. Other employees who questioned Enron executives were also fired and humiliated.

Enron's stated policy was to eliminate underperforming employees. Of course, the executives decided the criteria for this performance. Approximately 20 percent were fired each year from 1998 through 2001. The culture of conformance was no doubt strengthened as a result.

In the end, Andrew Fastow stated in court, "Within the culture of corruption that Enron had, that valued financial reporting rather than economic value, I believed I was a hero." Perhaps we can perceive Svendsen's steps of devolution in the Enron story:

(1) No doubt the off-balance-sheet transactions were minor at first, but they grew to be $25 billion out of the $38 billion in actual debt that Enron had in 2002. Violations of the spirit of accounting codes, and its own internal Code of Ethics were accepted by all including the Board, and escalated over 1999 through 2002.

(2) Dissent was minor until the end when strong statements of regret were made. Dissenters were consistently humiliated until the end.

(3) Leaders in this devolution saw themselves as heroic.

References

Adler, N.E., E.S. Epel, G. Castellazzo,J.R. Ickovics (2000), "Relationship of Subjective and Objective Social Status with Psychological and Physiological Functioning." *Health Psychology*, 19, p. 586-592.

Alicke, M.D. (1985), "Global Self Evaluation as Determined by the Desirability and Controllability of Trait Adjectives," *Journal of Personality and Social Psychology*, 49(6), 1621-1630.

Aquino, K. and Reed, A. (2002), "The self Importance of Moral Identity," *Journal of Personality and Social Psychology*, 83(6), 1423-1440.

_____, Reed, A., Thau, S., and Freeman, D. (2007), "A Grotesque and Dark Beauty: How Moral Identity and Mechanisms of Moral Disengagement Influence Cognitive and Emotional Reactions to War," *Journal of Experimental Social Psychology*, 43, 385-392.

Arendt, Hannah (1951, 1979), *The Origins of Totalitarianism*, Harcourt, Brace and Jovanovich.

_____, (1963), *Eichmann in Jerusalem: a Report on the Banality of Evil*, Viking Press.

_____, (1971), *Thinking and Moral Considerations*, Harcourt, Brace and Jovanovich.

_____ (2003), *Responsibility and Judgment*, edited by Jerome Kohn, Schoken Books New York.

Ashby, Warren, (2005), *A Comprehensive History of Western Ethics: What Do We Believe?*, Prometheous Books.

Bandura, A. (1990), "Selective Activation and Disengagement of Moral Control," *Journal of Social Issues,* 46, 27-46.

_____, (1999), "Moral Disengagement in the Preparation of Inhumanities," *Personal and Social Psychology Review,* 3, 193-209.

_____, Barbaranelli, C., Capara, G., and Pastorelli, C. (1996), "Mechanisms of Moral Disengagement in the Exercise of Moral Agency," *Journal of Personality and Social Psychology,* 71, 364-374.

_____, Barbaranelli, C., Capara, G., Pastorelli, C. and Regalia, C. (2001), "Sociocognitive Self-Regulatory Mechanisms Governing Transgressive Behavior," *Journal of Personality and Social Psychology,* 80, 125-135.

_____, Underwood, B. and Fromson, M.E. (1975), Disinhibition of Aggression Through Diffusion of Responsibility and Dehumanization of Victims," *Journal of Research in Personality*, 9, 253-269.

Baumeister, R.F. and Heatherton, T.F. (1996), "Self Regulation Failure: An Overview," *Psychological Inquiry*, 7, 1-15.

_____, and Newman, L,S. (1994), " Self-Regulation of Cognitive Inference and Decision Processes," *Personality and Social Psychology Bulletin*, 20, 3-19.

Baynes, Kenneth (2000), "Habermas," *Routledge Encyclopedia of Philosophy*, Routledge Publishing Co., p. 328.

Baier, Kurt (1958) *The Moral Point of View*, Cornel University Press.

Bonhoeffer, Dietrich (1997), *Letters and Papers from Prison*, Trans. Reginald Fuller, Frank Clark, et. al., Simon & Shuster, New York.

Bowie, Norman E. (1999), *Business Ethics: A Kantian Perspective*, Blackwell Publishers, Malden, MA.

Brickley, James, Clifford Smith, and Jerold Zimmerman (2007), *Managerial Economics and Organizational Architecture*, McGraw-Hill, Irwin,

Brickley, James and Clifford Smith and Jerold Zimmerman (1999), "The Economics of Organizational Architecture," in *The New Corporate Finance*, edited by Donald Chew, Irwin McGraw-Hill, Second Edition.

Chambers, Donald and Nelson Lacey (1996), "Corporate Ethics and Shareholder Wealth Maximization," Financial Management, Spring/Summer, p. 93-95.

Clarkson, M.B. (2002), "Principles of Stakeholder Management," *Business Ethics Quarterly*, Vol. 12, No. 2, April, p. 257-264.

Copeland, Thomas and Fred Weston (1983), *Financial Theory and Corporate Policy*, Second Edition, Addison Wesley, p. 11.

Dancy, Jonathan (2000), "Intuitionism," *A Companion to Ethics*, edited by Peter Singer, Blackwell Companion to Philosophy Series, Blackwell Publishing Co., p 411-420.

Darwin, Charles (1859), *The Descent of Man*, reprinted by Princeton University Press, 1981.

Detert, J.R., Trevino, L.K., and Sweitzer, V.L. (2008), "Moral Disengagement in Ethical Decision Making: A Study of Antecedents and Outcomes." *Journal of Applied Psychology*, 93 (2), 374-391.

Elliot, A.J., and Devine, P.G. (1994), On the Motivational Nature of Cognitive Dissonance: Dissonance as Psychological Discomfort," *Journal of Personality and Social Psychology,* 67, 382-394.

Epley, N., and Caruso, E.M. (2004), "Egocentric Ethics," *Social Justice Research*, 17, 171-187.

_____, and Dunning, D. (2000), "Feeling "Holier than Thou": Are Self Serving Assessments Produced by Errors in Self- or Social-Prediction," *Journal of Personality and Social Psychology,* 71, 364-374.

Financial Economist Roundtable (2002), "Statement on the Crisis in Accounting, Auditing and Corporate Governance," *Journal of Applied Finance*, Vol. 12, No. 2, Fall/Winter, p. 61-66.

Frazier, Robert L. (2000), "Intuitionism In Ethics," *Routledge Encyclopedia of Philosophy*, Routledge, p. 403.

Friedman, Milton (1970), "The Social responsibility of Business is to Increase Profits." *The New York Times Magazine*, New York.

Galbraith, John Kenneth (1985), *The New Industrial State*, Houghton Mifflin.

Gino, F. Ayal, S., and Ariely, D. (2009), "Contagion and Differentiation in Unethical Behavior: The Effect of One Bad Apple on the Barrel," *Psychological Science*, 20 (3), 393-398.

_____, and Pierce, L. (2009), "The Abundance Effect: Unethical Behavior in the Presence of Wealth," *Organizational Behavior and Human Decision Processes,* (Forthcoming).

Gourevitch, Phillip (1998), *We Wish to Inform You that Tomorrow We Will Be Killed With Our Families: Stories from Rwanda,* Farrar, Strauss and Giroux, New York.

Habermas, Jurgen (1999), *Moral Consciousness and Communicative Action*, Translated by C. Lenhardt and S.W. Nicholson, The MIT Press, Cambridge.

Hare, R.M. (1981), *Moral Thinking: Its Levels, Methods and Point*, Oxford University Press.

Henkel, L.A. and Mathur, M. (2007), "Memory Attributions for Choices: How Beliefs Shape Our Memories," *Journal of Memory and Language,* 57, 163-176.

Honneth, Axel (2000), "Frankfurt School," *Routledge Encyclopedia of Philosophy*, Routledge, p. 328.

Jensen, Michael (2002), "Value Maximization, Stakeholder Theory, and the Corporate Objective Function," *Business Ethics Quarterly*, Vol. 12, No. 2, April, p. 235-256.

Kant, Immanuel (1784), *What is Enlightenment?* in *Basic Writings of Kant*, edited by Allen W. Wood, The Modern Library Classics, The Modern Library, New York.

_____, (1785), *Fundamental Principles of the Metaphysics of Morals*, in *Basic Writings of Kant*, edited by Allen W. Wood, The Modern Library Classics, The Modern Library, New York.

_____, (1781), *Critique of Pure Reason*, in *Basic Writings of Kant*, edited by Allen W. Wood, The Modern Library Classics, The Modern Library, New York.

_____, (1788), *Critique of Practical Reason*, in *Basic Writings of Kant*, edited by Allen W. Wood, The Modern Library Classics, The Modern Library, New York.

_____, (1793), *Religion Within the Limits of Reason Alone*, in *Basic Writings of Kant*, edited by Allen W. Wood, The Modern Library Classics, The Modern Library, New York.

Kerouac, Jack (1957), *On the Road*, Viking Press, New York, NY.

Kraus, M.W., P.K. Piff, D. Keltner (2011), "Social Class as Culture: The Convergence of Resources and Rank in the Social Realm," *Current Directions in Psychological Sciences*, 20, p. 246-250.

Kymlicka, Will (2000), "The Social Contract Tradition," *A Companion to Ethics*, edited by Peter Singer, Blackwell Companion to Philosophy Series, Blackwell Publishing Co., p 186-196.

MacIntyre, Alasdair (1981), *After Virtue*, University of Notre Dame Press.

Mazar, N. Amir, O., and Ariely, D. (2998), "The Dishonesty of Honest People: A Theory of Self-Concept Maintenance," *Journal of Marketing Research*, 45 (6).

McAlister, A.L. , Bandura, B. and Owen, S. (2006), oral Disengagement in Support of War: The Impact of September 11," *Journal of Clinical and Social Psychology*, February, 2006.

McCarthy, Thomas (1999), "Introduction," in *Moral Consciousness and Communicative Action*, by Jurgen Habermas, the MIT Press.

McDowell, John (1985), "Values and Secondary Qualities," *Morality and Objectivity*, edited by Ted Honderich, Routledge Publishing Co., p. 110-129.

Messick, D.M., and Bazerman, M.H. (1996), "Ethical Leadership and the Psychology of Decision Making," *Sloan Management Review,* 9-22.

_____, Bloom, S., Boldizar, J.P. and Samuelson, C.D. (1985), "Why We are Fairer than Others," *Journal of Experimental Social Psychology*, 21, 480-500.

Miller, D.T. and Ratner, R.K. (1998), "The Disparity between the Actual and Assumed Power of Self Interest," *Journal of Personality and Social Psychology,* 74(1), 53-62.

Midgely, Mary (2000), "The Origin of Ethics," *A Companion to Ethics*, edited by Peter Singer, Blackwell Companion to Philosophy Series, Blackwell Publishing Co., p. 3-13.

_____ (2000), "Kantian Ethics," *A Companion to Ethics*, edited by Peter Singer, Blackwell Companion to Philosophy Series, Blackwell Publishing Co., p. 175-185.

Nagel, Thomas (1986), *The View From Nowhere*, Oxford University Press.

O'Neill, Onora (2000), "Kantian Ethics," *Routledge Encyclopedia of Philosophy*, Routledge, p. 433.

Plato, (1999), *The Collected Dialogue Including the Letters,* edited by Edith Hamilton and Huntington Cairns, Bollingen Series LXXI, Princeton University Press.

Piff, P.K., D.M. Stancato, S. Cote, R. Mendoza-Denton, and D. Keltner, (2012), "Higher Social Class Predicts Increased Unethical Behavior," *Proceedings of the National Academy of Sciences*, January 26, p. 1-6.

Piff, P.K., M.W. Kaus, S. Cote, B. Cheng, D. Keltner (2010), "Having Less, Giving More: The Influence of Social Class on Pro-Social Behavior," Vol. 99(5), November, p. 771-784.

Porter, Michael (2000), "How to Profit From a Downturn," *Wall Street Journal*, 11/12/2001, Eastern Edition, p. A22.

Price, Richard (1948) *Review of the Principle Questions and Difficulties in Morals*, Oxford University Press.

Ratner, R.K. and Miller, D.T. (2001), "The Norm of Self Interest and its Effects on Social Action," *Journal of Personality and Social Psychology,* 81(1), 5-16.

Rawls, John (1951), "Outline Of A Decision Procedure For Ethics," *Philosophical Review*, 60, no. 2, April, p. 177-197. Reprinted in *Collected Papers–John Rawls,* Edited by Samuel Freeman, Harvard University Press, 1999.

_____(1958), "Justice As Fairness," *Philosophical Review*, 64, no. 1, January, p. 3-32. Reprinted in *Collected Papers–John Rawls,* Edited by Samuel Freeman, Harvard University Press, 1999.

_____ (1967), "Distributive Justice," *Philosophy, Politics and Society,* Edited by Laslett and Runciman, Oxford: Blackwell, 1967. Reprinted in *Collected Papers–John Rawls,* Edited by Samuel Freeman, Harvard University Press, 1999.

_____(1980), "Kantian Constructivism In Moral Theory," *Journal of Philosophy*, 77, September, p. 515-572. Reprinted in *Collected Papers–John Rawls,* Edited by Samuel Freeman, Harvard University Press, 1999.

_____ (1989), "Themes in Kant's Moral Philosophy," From Harvard University Lecture, Reprinted in *Collected Papers–John Rawls,* Edited by Samuel Freeman, Harvard University Press, 1999.

_____ (2001), *Justice as Fairness: A Restatement*, The Belknap Press of Harvard University Press.

Roberts, Julian (2000), "Lorenzen," *Routledge Encyclopedia of Philosophy*, Routledge, p. 509.

Rohatyn, Felix (2002), "An Agenda for Corporate Reform," *Wall Street Journal*, 6/29/02, Editorial Page.

Ross, William (1930), *The Right and the Good*, Clarendon Press.

Schmeitzer, M.E. and Hsee, C.K. (2002), "Stretching the Truth: Elastic Justification and Motivated Communication of Uncertain Information," *Journal of Risk and Uncertainty,* 25, 185-201.

Sidgewick, Henry (1874), *The Method of Ethics*, reprinted by Macmillan, 1907.

Smith, Adam (1776), *An Inquiry Into The Nature and Causes of the Wealth of Nations*, repreinted by Clarendon Press, 1996.

Sullivan, Roger, (1994, 1997), *An Introduction to Kant's Ethics*, Cambridge University Press.

Svendsen, Lars (2001, 2010), *A Philosophy of Evil*, Dalkey Archive Press, London, First English Translation, 2010.

Tenbrunsel, A.E. and Messick, D,M. (2004), "Ethical Fading: The Role of Self Deception in Unethical Behavior," *Social Justice Research,* 17, 223-236.

Tugendhat, E. (1982), *Traditional and Analytical Philosophy*, Cambridge University Press.

Vollum, S., Buffington-Vollum, J. and Longmire, D.R. (2004), "Moral Disengagement and Attitudes about Violence toward Nonhuman Animals," Society and Animals, 12, 2009-235.

Walzer, Michael (1995), "Social Contract," *The Oxford Companion To Philosophy*, Oxford University Press, p. 163-164.

White, Mark (2011), *Kantian Ethics and Economics*, Stanford University Press, Stanford, CA.

www.ingramcontent.com/pod-product-compliance
Lightning Source LLC
Chambersburg PA
CBHW050529190326
41458CB00045B/6759/J